Loser Take All

Of Related Interest from Continuum

American History/American Film, New Expanded Edition, John E. O'Connor and Martin A. Jackson, eds.

American History/American Television, John E. O'Connor, ed.

And the Winner Is . . . The History and Politics of the Oscar Awards, New Expanded Edition, Emanuel Levy

The Cinema of Stanley Kubrick, New Expanded Edition, Norman Kagan

Fellini the Artist, Edward Murray

Framework: A History of Screenwriting in the American Film, New Expanded Edition, Tom Stempel

The French through Their Films, Robin Buss

Hitchcock: The First Forty-Four Films, Eric Rohmer and Claude Chabrol

Italian Cinema: From Neorealism to the Present, New Expanded Edition, Peter Bondanella

Modern European Filmmakers and the Art of Adaptation, Andrew S. Horton and Joan Margretta, eds.

A Project for the Theatre, Ingmar Bergman

The Screening of America: Movies and Values from Rocky to Rain Man, Tom O'Brien

Screening Space: The American Science Fiction Film, Vivian Sobchack

Silent Magic: Rediscovering the Silent Film Era, Ivan Butler

Small-Town America in Film: The Decline and Fall of Community, Emanuel Levy

Take 22: Moviemakers on Moviemaking, Judith Crist

Teleliteracy: Taking Television Seriously, David C. Bianculli

Toms, Coons, Mulattoes, Mammies, and Bucks: An Interpretive History of Blacks · in American Films, New Expanded Edition, Donald Bogle

World Cinema since 1945, William Luhr, ed.

For more information on these and other titles on the performing arts or literature, write to:

The Continuum Publishing Company
370 Lexington Avenue
New York, NY 10017

Loser Take All

The Comic Art of Woody Allen

New Expanded Edition

Maurice Yacowar

A Frederick Ungar Book
CONTINUUM · NEW YORK

1991

The Continuum Publishing Company
370 Lexington Avenue
New York, NY 10017

Designed by Jacqueline Schuman

Printed in the United States of America

Library of Congress Cataloging-in-Publication Data

Yacowar, Maurice.
    Loser take all : the comic art of Woody Allen / Maurice Yacowar. —
— New expanded ed.
      p.   cm.
    "A Frederick Ungar book."
    Includes bibliographical references (p.   ) and index.
    Filmography: p.
    Discography: p.
    ISBN 0-8264-0551-7
    1. Allen, Woody—Criticism and interpretation.   I. Title.
PN1998.3.A45Y33   1991
791.43'092—dc20   91-15507
                                             CIP

With love and hope
to my children
Mimi and Sam

What then is the function of the critic? Precisely to interpret the audio-visual electronic image and fragmentize individual coercive response against a background of selective subjectivity. He can do this either standing up or sitting. . . .
    —Woody Allen, "Woody, the Would-Be Critic"

Contents

Part Four: Woody's Films: Guilt-Edged Cinema

Part Five: Through the Eighties

(Picture sections may be found on pages 106–13 and 218–24.)

Acknowledgments

I wish to thank Brock University for a research grant that made this study possible. My work was made a pleasure by the staffs at the Brock University Library, the Ontario Film Institute, and the Motion Picture Division of the Library of Congress in Washington, D.C. For their comments and assistance I am grateful to my colleagues, Joan Nicks and Jim Leach, Harold Mantell, Dr. Richard Gollin of the University of Rochester Film Studies Program, and my superb copy editor, Faye Zucker. I had splendid secretarial assistance from Joan Gordon, Jenny Gurski, Carole LaMothe and Debby Thorne. Most of all I must thank Stan Hochman for patience, labor, and encouragement beyond an editor's duty. (1979)

The author is grateful to Emily Carr College of Art and Design for time and resources and to Gerrie Brooks for expert editing. (1991)

Preface to the
New Expanded Edition

In hindsight, we could predict no less. But how pleasant to report
that in the decade since this book first appeared, Woody Allen has
moved from strength to strength, never repeating himself, ever
finding new forms to advance his meditations upon death, libertinism, and the pursuits of angst and art. He refuses either to rest on
his laurels or to compromise his moral concerns.

Since *Manhattan* Allen has secured his reputation as a major
filmmaker. He has been studied in French, German, and Italian
and in graduate theses. The recent biography by his friend, Eric
Lax, helps illuminate Allen's peekaboo play with autobiography.
While other American independent filmmakers have emerged in
the eighties—Albert Brooks, the Coens, Jonathan Demme, Henry
Jaglom, Jim Jarmusch, Spike Lee, David Lynch, Paul Morrissey—
Allen's canon remains distinctive for its literate density, diversity and
volume. By no one else does the prospect of a new film seem so
assuringly yet mysteriously An Event.

This second edition considers all Allen's film work from *Stardust
Memories* through *Alice* and his Broadway play, *The Floating Light
Bulb*. Because Allen has outgrown the "Jester and Outsider" image
of the 1979 wrap-up, a new conclusion reflects his current stance—
beyond persona. The filmography and bibliography have also been
updated. Major reviews are listed in the chapter notes.

Loser Take All

Introduction:
The Serious Business of Comedy

In the last fifteen years Woody Allen has grown from a cult favorite into America's foremost humorist. After an apprenticeship as
a gag writer, Allen became a stand-up comedian. His work in club
and campus shows has been preserved on three long-play records,
which have twice been reissued as two-record sets.[1] Allen received
his first international attention when he wrote and appeared in the
phenomenally successful film, *What's New, Pussycat?* (1965). His
own first two features, *What's Up, Tiger Lily?* (1966) and *Take the
Money and Run* (1969), established his coterie of fanatic followers.
He wrote two successful Broadway plays: *Don't Drink the Water*
(1966) and *Play It Again, Sam* (1969). Then came a series of increasingly ambitious films: *Bananas* (1971), *Everything You Always
Wanted To Know About Sex* * (**but were afraid to ask*) (1972),
and *Sleeper* (1973). During this period he made frequent forays
into print. His work in *Playboy* or *Esquire* involved comic pretenses to being a man-about-town. His more intellectual prose humor began to appear in *The New Yorker* and *The New Republic*.
With the release of his feature film, *Love and Death* (1975), it became clear that Allen was not "just a comedian"—as the popular
prejudice might have it—but a serious, probing artist with a consistent and distinctive vision. He happens to work in the comic
mode.

In 1977 Allen's "The Kugelmass Episode" won the O. Henry Award
as best short story of the year. In that same year, *Annie Hall*, Allen's
greatest achievement to date, won Oscars for best picture, best original screenplay, best actress (Diane Keaton), and best director (Al-

len). Allen's three personal nominations—for his coauthorship of the screenplay with Marshall Brickman, his lead performance, and his directing—had only one precedent: Orson Welles for *Citizen Kane* in 1941. *Annie Hall* was also named best film by the National Society of Film Critics and by the New York Film Critics Circle. The British Academy of Film and Television Arts cited the film as the year's best feature, with the best screenplay and best editing, and cited Allen as best director, and Ms. Keaton as best actress. When *Variety* surveyed the ten-best lists proposed by thirty-two American film reviewers, *Annie Hall* was the most frequently selected film. It was named on thirty of the thirty-two lists (compared with the twenty citations for each of the films tied for second place, Fred Zinneman's popular *Julia* and the prestigious Luis Buñuel's *That Obscure Object of Desire*). Perhaps even more impressively, *L'Avant-Scène* immediately published a French translation of Allen's screenplay, his first film so honored since *Quoi de Neuf, Pussycat?* Indeed when the National Theatre Company of New York City advertised for new stage and company manager trainees, its ad in *Variety* was headed: "This is the only thing Woody Allen is not in the running for this year." The cult comedian had become recognized as an artist to be reckoned with.

The truth is that from the very beginning, Allen's comedy has deserved thoughtful study. But artistry is not as readily recognized in comedy as in other art forms. While comedy may be the most widely appreciated art, it is also the most undervalued.

There are several explanations for this. For one thing, although comedians admit that "comedy is a serious business," one that requires painstaking care, discipline, timing, and planning, comedy must seem spontaneous. The comedian's labors to seem effortless may lead the viewer to believe that he is merely being diverted and amused. Moreover, the spirit of comedy requires that a comedian express his ideas indirectly, rather than explicitly. Thus, just by choosing to work in the comic mode, the artist is already concealing the seriousness of his purpose. In addition, audiences may share Horace's distinction between the *dulce* and the *utile* in art—as if what is enjoyable cannot also be useful, and what is instructive cannot delight. There may even be a physiological basis for our customary condescension toward comedy. When we watch a comedy our instinctive reaction is something other than thoughtful consideration: we laugh. Because this laughter provides a release from the tension set up by the work, no other response is necessary. We can laugh the work aside. Whatever the reason, our disrespect for comedy is so deeply ingrained that we use the same word, *serious*, as the antithesis of both *comic* and *trivial*. The implication is that nothing important can be conveyed by comedy.

Woody Allen has pointed out that "laughter undermines respect. The frivolity attached to laughter prevents people from respecting it and taking it seriously." [2] While admitting that "comedy is harder to do than serious stuff," Allen notes that comedy makes a lesser impact: "When comedy approaches a problem, it kids it but it doesn't resolve it. Drama works it through in a more emotionally fulfilling way." [3]

The comedian's traditional response to being taken lightly is to pretend that his work is innocent of meaning. In 1972 Allen warned against the tendency to "over-analyze" his movies for "heavy, intellectual nonsense," when "all I want people to do is laugh at the movie." [4] But the only films he had then made were the ones he later described as "trivial." He admitted that *Sleeper* had "a slight point—nothing profound, but a slight, satirical point about which way I thought society was moving." *Love and Death* also had "a slight satirical point about dying and war, and the transitory quality of love." [5] Allen's serious concerns were exposed more openly in *Annie Hall*, in his noncomic feature, *Interiors* (1978), and in *Manhattan* (1979) but he had focused on the same themes in his early comedies. For example, both *What's New, Pussycat?* and *Manhattan* explore the difficulty of reconciling one's self with a desired image, and the greater tension between the urge to assert one's individuality and the need to immerse oneself in some larger identification, whether through art, religion, or romance. This consistency between Allen's later "serious" work and his earlier comedies proves his 1974 remark that "great humor is intellectual without trying to be." [6]

In this book we will examine all Allen's available works. We begin by defining the persona or image that Allen developed in his monologues, because he has used that image as his base in almost all his work, even in the films that he has made for other directors. We will survey his plays and his prose and then proceed to his most important body of work, the feature films. In each case our intention will be to define the structure and themes of the work.

Our purpose is to determine what Allen's jokes mean, what response they prompt besides laughter. Whether in a "serious" work or in a comedy, a detail expresses its meaning in two ways. It may evoke associations beyond what it literally denotes, which is the function of metaphor, or it may derive specific meaning from its context, from its relation to other details in the work. A couple of examples from Allen's Broadway comedy, *Play It Again, Sam*, will demonstrate how the precise wording of a joke can advance the wider themes of the play.

First, when the hero recalls the infrequency of sexual intercourse in his marriage, there is a pointed metaphor in his memory of his wife: "She used to watch television during it—and change channels with a remote control switch." The "remote control" of the television becomes a metaphor for the wife. But it also relates to the hero's attempt to live up to the romantic image of Humphrey Bogart. On his dates the hero tries to switch on a Bogart image as his wife is said to have flicked on different television images. In the comic climax of the play, the hero keeps turning from his receptive date to the phantom of Bogart, who offers procedural advice from the sidelines. When he is making love, then, our hero has neither self-control nor passionate abandon, but is being operated by remote control. The gag about his wife relates to the central theme of the play: the hero's control by a romantic ideal that is remote from him. (Allen uses a similar joke in the Italian episode in the film *Everything You Always Wanted To Know About Sex*. But when that hero complains that his wife watches television when they make love, Allen omits the "remote control" metaphor, which uniquely fits *Play It Again, Sam*.) A second example is the hero's remark that he doesn't thaw his TV dinners but licks them as if they were popsicles. The wacky image sugests the childishness of a man licking a three-course popsicle, the coldness in the appetites in his life, and his impatience. Just as he will not wait to cook a dinner, so he is unable to allow a relationship with a woman to develop. The metaphor in this quip is a suggestive stroke of characterization.

We should also expect that jokes within a work will relate to each other, because in a work of art all the material is conceived under the same pressure of the imagination. The jokes are all thought of in the same breath, so to speak. By examining the metaphoric effect of Allen's jokes and their interrelationships, we should be able to define the meaning and the integrity of his work.

However funny it is, the Allen canon consistently expresses the anxieties of a modern urban sensibility, with its dreams of glory and its frustrations, its sense of isolation, and its doubts about the existence of a God and the dignity of man. Allen is especially interested in the relationship between art and life. On the one hand, art affords relief from the uncontrollable forces in reality. On the other, our self-conception is obscured by the myths and rhetoric that film and other media inflict upon us. Consequently Allen's work involves two kinds of self-consciousness. One is the self-reflexive aspect of the work—its form is part of its subject. As Alvy Singer tells Annie Hall, "the medium enters in as a condition of the art form itself." The other is human self-consciousness; Allen based his career upon the candid exposure of a sensitive, frightened, and warmly representative modern soul, the Allen image or persona.

Part One

The Public Face of Woody Allen

Each great comedian has presented a single character type, whatever his individual role. Whereas in a dramatic performance the role ends when the curtain falls, in the comic tradition the successful performer plays variations on the one character type or persona with which he has become identified. Jacques Tati is always Monsieur Hulot; Chaplin, the Little Tramp; Bob Hope, the cowardly lecher; and so on. Often a joke will depend on the associations that the actor has developed with his audience. For instance, in one of Jack Benny's most brilliant radio gags a robber demanded, "Your money or your life." An excruciatingly long silence followed, as Benny weighed the alternatives. The joke depended on the audience knowing that Benny's persona was stingy to a mythic degree.

Audiences expect a continuity between the comedian's projected image and his private self. As Woody Allen told Larry Wilde, the most difficult part of being a comedian is the pressure of having "to consistently get laughs. . . . You have to be on all the time." [1] No one expects Paul Scofield to act like Macbeth when he comes to dinner, but our comic actors are expected to be comical all the time—and in a consistent image. If a comic actor differs from his image he is abandoned, as was the case when Chaplin ventured into explicit political statement and when Fatty Arbuckle, that cuddly, overgrown "boy" of the silent screen, was implicated in a fatal orgy.

Woody Allen's audience has come to expect a precise set of characteristics in every role he plays. This persona provides the basic language by which Allen can communicate with his audience in whatever medium he works—club monologues, prose, theater, and film.

Often an Allen joke will depend upon a particular aspect of his persona. Because Allen pretends to be doubly afflicted with lust and with inadequacy, an innocent phrase may have bawdy overtones when he uses it. In one *Playboy* piece Allen pretends to a theatrical career that included the "title role" in Chekhov's *The Cherry Orchard*.[2] This claim exposes both his persona's ignorance of theater (since there is obviously no "title role" in that play) and his sexual inexperience (as associated with "cherry"). A similar sexual-literary joke occurs in *Annie Hall* (1977), when the Allen character, to cover his embarrassment at Annie's loud mention of her "sexual problem," turns the phrase into a literary title: "*My Sexual Problem.* Henry James. The sequel to *Turn of the Screw.*" This joke pivots upon the sexual possibility of the word "screw" in the authentic James title. Both jokes assume the audience's sense of the Allen persona as a failed lecher with intellectual pretensions.

Nor need such jokes be verbal. In *Bananas* (1971) a doorknob comes off in the Allen character's hand when he tries to enter an office to date a spectacular secretary. In the context of sexual address, this fumble can be read as an image of sexual inadequacy. Later, in a scene of lascivious eating à la Tony Richardson's *Tom Jones* (1963), he impales himself on his fork. Like the puns, these innocent visual gags are transformed by the persona's sexual obsession and ineptitude.

Another important association with Allen's persona is its Jewishness. Allen has made so many jokes about being Jewish that his audience will respond to the faintest Jewish inflection. For example, the hero of Allen's Broadway comedy, *Play It Again, Sam,* is so deeply rooted in the Allen persona that he seems Jewish even though he is not identified as such—and even when a non-Jewish actor plays the role. Hence this anonymous review of one production: "Bob Denver [is] a sort of young Jewish Lear, or maybe Othello—anyhow, not Romeo." [3] Similarly, in *Love and Death* (1975) Allen plays a nineteenth-century Russian lad with non-Jewish parents and with a (non-Jewish) Orthodox priest to teach him the difference between Russian Jews (with horns) and German Jews (with stripes), but the spectacled, nervous boy grows into Allen's Jewish persona nonetheless. Finally, Sidney, the unseen hero in the last episode of *Everything You Always Wanted To Know About Sex* (1972), is Jewish; that is the last-minute discovery with which his nervous sperm cell (Allen) consoles himself. But Sidney's sexual performance is temporarily sabotaged by a priest. This paradox, which assumes our familiarity with Allen's Jewish persona, suggests that sexual guilt is interdenominational. Alternatively: you don't have to be Jewish to be traumatized. But it helps.

Allen's distinctive persona is an invention based on the pretense that he is openly confessing his private fears and failures. His remarkable success may be due to the intimacy that his audiences have felt with this persona. Allen recalls that when he began as a stand-up comedian he thought he could win laughter just by reciting funny material. But his audience preferred "intimacy with the person. They want to like the person and find the person funny as a human being." Allen warns would-be comedians not to try to get by solely on the strength of their material: "That's just hiding behind jokes. It's not getting out in front of an audience and opening themselves up." [4] Rather than hide behind jokes, Allen presents a persona that expresses both true and pretended anxieties.

Of course, this frightened and frustrated *schlemiel* is not Allen himself. Woody Allen is far more agile both intellectually and physically than he allows his persona to be. Rather, it is an extrapolation from Allen's experience. But even when it does not reveal Allen's own self, his persona is true to our sense of our own insecurities and aspirations. We all have our anxieties; Allen expresses them for us. His remarkable gift to his audience is his candor in shamelessly exposing his dreads and his dreams—even though his weakness and failure are fictitious.

Allen says that he rejects even the funny and innovative scripts submitted to him because they merely imitate his work. Their authors are "working from the outside, not from inside themselves. The scripts lack a center, because they're copying my center, which can't be done, since they are not me." [5] Based only loosely upon Allen's own self and experience, his persona expresses the anxieties that his audience is itself unable or unwilling to expose. In this respect Allen's persona acts simultaneously as both a mask and a mirror. It hides what Woody is *really* like, but it shows us something of his inner life— and it reflects our common nature.

1

The Monologues:
The Wag and His Tales

As a stand-up comedian, Woody Allen's expressiveness begins with his basic physical appearance—for club performers are seen as well as heard. Allen is a five-foot-six-inch, 120-pound *nebbish* with retreating red hair and large eyeglasses astride a long nose. His appearance suggests smallness and fragility. That this is Allen's own sense of his image can be deduced from his recreation of a college concert in *Annie Hall* (1977). Alvy Singer (Allen) is shown in long-shot, dwarfed by the stage, by the curtains, even by the light that picks him out in the darkness.

This impression is confirmed by contemporary reviews of his early performances:

> On stage, he is a little less slender than the microphone, which he frequently seems to lean on for support. Sometimes he wraps his arm around his head as if to fend off drafts—or blows—and his fingers dribble nervously over his hair. . . . It seems an effort for him to hold up his glasses.[1]

The dominant impression is anxiety and vulnerability—a frightened little fellow "with closely-bitten fingernails," who "onstage or off, when he gets through talking about himself he seems two inches high." [2] As William K. Zinsser described this "born loser . . . who walks onto a stage and immediately makes his presence unfelt," he may be uncertain of what will happen next, but he knows that it will be bad.[3] Allen considered his most striking trait to be his "enormously sad face": "If you didn't know I was a comic, I would be a study in sadness. My face is naturally sad, because it's drawn and my eyes are droopy. It's easy to hate yourself." Allen suggests that his sad face places him in the tradition of such American comics as Chaplin, Hope, and Groucho: "physically amusing-looking and kind of typical—fearful, brash." [4] But Richard Schickel found Allen's appearance distinctive: "We all knew, of course, that being a stand-up comic was the loneliest job this side of the Presidency"—and this was during the *Kennedy* years—

> but the tradition was for the comedian to brazen it out, affect a sublime and aggressive self-confidence—the Henny Youngman syndrome. So just by appearing, bent like a question mark, his delivery hesitant, his eye contact with the audience nonexistent, looking as if he might bolt and run at any moment, he parodied the conventions of his art.[5]

Paradoxically, this nervous, sagging image generated enormous excitement, as Vivian Gornick recalls Allen's Bitter End cafe shows of 1964:

> Anxiety was the juice that electrified him, that set him going, and kept him running. And thousands of us drank in his anxiety like adrenalin, because it was the same for us. Half in the culture, half out, we too were anxious.

The sense of anxiety gave Allen "his persona, the deep inner reference that makes for wholeness," Gornick remembers. Moreover, "it meshed so perfectly with the deepest undercurrent of feeling in the national life that it made outsiders of us all." [6]

As the recordings confirm, Allen's manner of delivery was consistent with the vulnerability and sadness of his image. Instead of the slickness of a Bob Hope or Henny Youngman, he cultivated the halting, stammering style of a timid boy attempting intimate conversation. He seemed to grope for the right word or to pry a personal secret out of a depth of inhibitions. As a result, Allen's act seemed less a public performance than a private confession.

The two examples of opening remarks that are recorded on his double album, *Woody Allen: The Night-Club Years, 1964-1968,* demonstrate this intimacy with his audience. Side One begins with Allen remarking that in the eight months since he last appeared at that club, "a lot of significant things have occurred in my private life that I thought we could go over tonight and evaluate." On the phrase, "we could go over tonight," he seems to have to overcome a lump in his throat. No glib performance, this, but an invitation for the listeners to share the speaker's self-examination. Similarly, Side Four opens with Allen proposing to review with the audience some of the outstanding features of his private life—"then we'll have a brief question and answer period and evaluate them." By offering up his ostensibly private life for public analysis, Allen subordinates the joke to his overall effect. As he told an interviewer: "I work on funny lines but what I'm really interested in is creating an image of a warm person that people will accept as funny, apart from the joke or the gag." [7] Of course, there are different kinds of "warm," from Myron Cohen to Sammy Davis, Jr., from Mary Tyler Moore to Linda Lovelace. Allen's warmth was based on a persona of searching candor and confessional intimacy. These qualities were projected in his unprepossessing appearance, his casual dress, the shrinking nervousness of his delivery, and the material of his act, the jokes themselves.

Basically, Allen's monologues are wacky anecdotes about his presumed deficiencies. He has a line of "doctor" jokes that express his physical delicacy. For example, "My body won't tolerate drugs." He abandoned his ambition to become a spy because "spies have to swallow microfilm, and my doctor says I can't have celluloid." Allen continued this pattern in his films. In *Casino Royale* (1967) he tries to ward off a firing squad: "My doctor says I can't have bullets enter my body at any time." To avoid a duel to the death in *Love and Death* (1975), the Allen character claims he's "not allowed to do anything to the death." The persona is a cowering adult who wants to be an overprotected child.

Allen's persona is as vulnerable psychologically as it is physically. From his first monologues through *Manhattan* (1979), Allen drew on his own experience in psychoanalysis. In one monologue he reports trying to declare his analyst as a Business Deduction, but the taxman contends it is Entertainment. The compromise is to declare it a Religious Contribution. The tax-form terms establish three perspectives upon psychoanalysis. It is seen first as a vital part of Allen's profession; then from the tax-man's perspective as a diversion; and finally, as a sacred social institution. This ironic view reconciles the believer's faith and the official's skepticism.

Allen's jokes about psychoanalysis prove his readiness to use material that traditional comics would consider too personal for comedy. He treats psychoanalysis as an extension of ordinary medical treatment: he took group analysis because he "couldn't afford private." Psychosis is an extension of normalcy in the story in which he captains "the latent-paranoid softball team" that played the neurotics on Sunday mornings—"the nail-biters against the bed-wetters." This is a funhouse-mirror image of healthy, All-American, Sunday morning sports. But when Allen steals second base he feels guilty and gives it back. His consistency in language and morality is violated by the conventions of the game, for if "stealing" is wrong in everyday society, then it should be wrong in all its contests. Such rigor in logic and morality is not normally found in society; it is an affliction of the maladjusted.

The Allen persona is often befuddled by inconsistencies in custom. Thus his divorce was complicated by a "strange law" in New York State "that says you can't get a divorce unless you can prove adultery." This stipulation leaves our hero in a quandary, torn between God and Governor Rockefeller, because one of the Ten Commandments prohibits adultery but the divorce law requires it! However, "the law is a ass," as Dickens's immortal Mr. Bumble observed. Hence in a moose-hunting anecdote, Allen claims "there's a law in New York State against driving with a conscious moose on your fender Tuesdays, Thursdays, and Saturdays." That story ranges beyond this dig at society's plethora of prohibitions. What seems to be a wild fantasy turns out to be a finely tuned parable about social prejudice.

The account begins with a premise that is amusingly improbable for the Woody Allen image: "I shot a moose once." The moose is only stunned, however, and recovers consciousness on Allen's fender. Our hero decides to leave the moose at a costume party where "it won't be my responsibility." He tells the host, "You know the Solomons," and since this is not a lie, Allen has not compromised his "responsibility." "We enter. The moose mingles. Did very well. Scored." Here Allen pauses just long enough to trick us into thinking that an Allen hero (the moose) can score romantically at a party. Then we are disabused of that fond hope: "Some guy was trying to sell him insurance for an hour and a half." The "score" was tricking someone else instead of being tricked. After this taste of success, the moose suffers defeat. In the best-costume contest he places second to the Berkowitzes, a couple who came dressed as a moose. Furious, the moose locks horns with the Berkowitzes and they knock each other out. When Allen leaves, he takes along the Berkowitzes by mistake. In the morning they wake up in the forest still wearing their moose suit. "Mr. Berkowitz is shot, stuffed, and mounted in the New York Athletic Club. And the joke is on them 'cause it's Restricted."

This story is constructed as three parallel sets of jokes. In the first the incongruous image of Allen as a hunter is paralleled by that of the moose at a party; both enjoy improbable and partial success. The second parallel involves the absurd images of first the live moose and then the costumed Jews on Allen's fender. This absurdity is topped in each case by the claim that New York State has passed laws to cover that eventuality. The third parallel is between these absurd laws and the banning of Jews from the New York Athletic Club. The theme of the story is encapsulated in two jokes. In the best-costume decision the characters fail to distinguish between true and false. The fake moose beats out the real one. The second joke, the moose's success at a party, is a counterpoint to the NYAC exclusion of Jews. The rough, antlered beast becomes a shifting emblem for the banned Jewish outsider, who may be admitted as a trophy, as a "catch," but is never quite accepted for himself.

Allen commonly expresses his alienation in terms of his Jewishness. In another story he recalls being used as a kind of trophy himself, when an advertising agency hired him as their "show Jew." Because his Jewishness is not sufficient qualification, he reads memos from right to left (as Yiddish and Hebrew are read). He is eventually fired for taking off too many Jewish holidays (i.e., for living up to his image requirements). Not for Allen the easy assimilation enjoyed by other Jews in his jokes, such as the reform rabbi who officiated at his wedding: "A *very* reform rabbi. A Nazi." In this vein, too, he describes the B'nai-a-Go-Go, a synagogue converted to a disco with topless rabbis (no skullcaps).

Allen often chuckles at the religious compromises made with the secular world. His rabbi advises Allen not to compromise his integrity by doing a vodka ad in the Bahamas with Monique van Vooren—

and then does the ad himself. This rabbi was seduced into show business when he tried to ad-lib a late-night-television prayer and confused the Ten Commandments with the Seven Dwarfs.

Allen is as remote from orthodox Judaism and its security as he is from the culturally assimilated. He claims to be alienated from his Old World parents, whose "values in life are God and carpeting." These simple, religious folk can look up (to God) and down (at carpeting), but they are not at ease in the changing world around them. Thus they are shaken when, during a Sunday-night-dinner visit, Allen announces his divorce. In a scene of absurd normalcy, Father is watching the Indiana Home for the Criminally Insane Glee Club perform on the Ed Sullivan Show, while Mother knits a chicken. Told of the divorce, Mother steps into the furnace (a morbid image for the Jewish mother's martyrdom). In this sketch Allen's attempt to live his own life brings him into conflict with his Old World parents. Their Sunday night diversions admit lunacy on the one hand and domestic inanimacy on the other, but they cannot deal with the changing emotional and social climate without feeling martyred.

In these examples, Allen's persona is so alienated in its Jewishness that he can relate neither to his orthodox parents nor to the assimilated swingers. He is so Jewish that he is even alienated from Jews and victimized by Jews. In another story Allen confronts a bully, Guy de Maupassant Rabinowitz, whose Christian (!) name reveals his parents' attempt to deny their Jewishness. In the 1944 Roosevelt-Dewey election they voted for Hitler. When Allen places second in a music contest, his prize is "two weeks at an interfaith camp, where I was sadistically beaten by boys of all races and creeds."

On the recordings, immediately after the Rabinowitz anecdote comes another parable of Jewish alienation, this one cast as a science fiction plot. The earth's entire population is turned into tailors one afternoon. A fleet of pantless extraterrestrials land on earth and demand pants right away for a wedding. When they return for their pants, they leave their dirty laundry. As in Allen's moose story, the conclusion provides a consoling but unlikely twist: "They're foiled, because they travel 117,000,000 light years to pick [their laundry] up and they forget their ticket." This story puts all mankind into the subservient position of the Jews. But after mankind experiences the Jews' oppression, it is rewarded with the satisfaction of a punch line that gives it the last word. The story expresses the oppressed's delight at a small triumph, a small reversal against a powerful oppressor. By clinging to the letter of the law, the Jewish laundrymen can thwart even the power from outer space.

These stories satirize the varieties of social exclusion. The science fiction story allows the non-Jewish audience to experience both the oppression and the comic relief familiar in Jewish life. Allen often treats religion as an obstacle. For example, he recalls a great love affair that did not lead to marriage because of the principals' religious differences: he was an agnostic and she an atheist, so "we didn't know what religion not to bring up the children in." That is to say, even an abandoned religion remains an influence and an intimidation.

Religious differences also figure in the story of Allen's double date with Peter O'Toole, whose sexy girl friend brings along a sister for Woody—Sister Maria Therese. His prospect of sensual delight dwindles into a philosophical rapport of dubious utility: "We agreed that He was extremely well adjusted for an only child." The nun and the lascivious Jew agree about the human aspect of Christ, but as they remain separated by their religious differences, our hero's romantic hopes are dashed.

Some of Allen's most characteristic jokes suggest the uselessness of intellectual activity. Indeed, the intellectual quip that deflates intellectuality is even more characteristic of Allen than are his Jewish and sex jokes. In this vein he describes his college courses in Truth, Beauty, Advanced Truth and Beauty, and Intermediate Truth, as if education consists of arbitrary claims to a universal verity. Typical of his satire of intellectual pretense, he imagines a swinging bachelorhood, with his pad hung with "Picassos by Van Gogh"—the artist is reduced to a generic term for merchandising of an image. So too the commune in which hippies play records of the mime Marcel Marceau and try to make opium out of paper Veterans' Day poppies. Here one would-be artist tries to cut off his ear with an electric razor, a modern inconvenience not available to Van Gogh, while Allen's girl friend studies to be a female male nurse. These jokes satirize the characters' confusion between the real and the ersatz.

A more important concern to Allen than ineffectual or pretentious intellectual activity, however, is intellectual and artistic activity as corrupted by coarser elements. Art is violated by crime when a ballet performance of *The Dying Swan* is enlivened by rumors that out-of-town bookies have fixed the performance so that the swan will live. The comedy here derives from the idea that the underworld could take a practical interest in a ballet. In another monologue Allen develops a crime-film parody in which his house is besieged by officers from the New York Public Library. Allen comes out, hands high, kicking the overdue book in front of him. In a story about his being kidnapped, the FBI lacks tear gas and so two policemen induce a parallel effect in the kidnappers by performing the death scene from *Camille*. In all three examples, art and life are continuous, but implausibly related. They satirize the exaggerated claims for the uses of art and education in meeting the problems of everyday life.

Indeed Allen suggests that man can find security neither in art nor in intellect. Though Jewish tradition values education for the security it may bring, Allen chronicles its futility or devises unbelievable cases of its usefulness. In one routine Allen reports how badly his college classmates have fared in life. One hip girl using the rhythm method of birth control cannot keep the beat. The boy-most-likely-to-succeed is a junkie. Against this whirligig of hope and disappointment, the Allen persona clings to the small orders of language (the junkie is married to a "junkette") and of manners (as a wedding present, Allen gives the junkies a sixteen-piece starter set of silverware, all spoons). But for none of his characters has education proved a help for life. Indeed his wife's study of philosophy only enabled her to prove that he did not exist.

In Allen's humor, the intellect fails most significantly when pitted against the brutish violence of the world. Allen continually demonstrates the helplessness of brain against brawn. The earnest little student is forever beaten by bullies, as in the assault on him at the interfaith camp. In order to escape mugging, the adult Allen moved to a doormanned apartment house; two weeks later he was attacked by the doorman. In a related story, Allen is attacked by Floyd, a brute with "vegetable mentality." Allen contrasts his student wisdom with the ways of the street; his "I was one of the kids that took" refers to violin lessons. When Allen boldly confronts the bully, the predictable outcome is reported with civilized decorum: "I spent that winter in a wheelchair. A team of doctors labored to remove a violin." Civilization is weak.

In a similar story, Allen uses a trick fountain pen to fend off a Neanderthal mugger. It is supposed to squirt tear gas but merely stains him with ink. Again, the defenses and strategies of civilization are futile. The pen is weaker (and messier) than the sword. Equally futile are the various cliches by which the hero tries to mollify the bully—sympathetic references to his broken home, a promise to send him to camp, and so on—as if a beast could be controlled by the formulae of a social worker's idealism. In these stories Allen dramatizes not just his own physical vulnerability but the weakness of civilization and culture in the face of a brutish and violent reality. The accoutrements of modern culture and the sophisticated intellect having failed him, the civilized man is forced to fall back upon "the old Navajo Indian trick of screaming and begging."

Allen's persona suffers at the hands of intellectuals as well as brutes. In his "Reminiscences" of blissful days with Hemingway and Gertrude Stein he is habitually punched in the mouth by both. Violence has infiltrated art and culture itself. Not for Allen the simple confidence that man is a creature saved from animalism by his spiritual and intellectual awareness. The vegetable, beastly, and intellectual brutes who assault Allen suggest that a reconsideration of what constitutes humanity is in order. Man approaches vegetable insentience at one extreme and animal brutishness at the other. Hence the character named Leo, who is part Mexican and part nonfat dried milk.

Even more striking than Allen's alienation from strangers is his alienation from his own family. Allen reverses conventions of family sentiment when he says that his parents put a live teddy bear in his crib with him and that they bronzed his baby shoes while he was still wearing them. Elsewhere, he depicts a family life that is as vicious and competitive as the worst of the business world. In one story, as a tax dodge Allen incorporates himself and makes his family his board of directors. Immediately a majority block tries to squeeze him out; he and an uncle retaliate by having his grandmother jailed. In another story, Allen works as a delivery boy for his father's grocery store. The son unionizes the other workers, goes on strike, and drives his father out of business. It's a dog-eat-dog world, or vice versa.

Nor is there either community or comfort in the persona's married life. Allen has a solid file of wife jokes in the ignoble tradition of Henny Youngman's "Take my wife, please" (and Phyllis Diller's revenge through her husband, Fang). Allen's marriage jokes are inflected toward his characteristic anxieties, so even his most conventional material carries his personal tone. One joke has his wife making such Nazi recipes as Chicken Himmler. In his marriage jokes Allen also continues his own self-criticism. He has his wife rowing furiously so that he can water ski. He admits that he put his wife "underneath a pedestal." Nor does he himself emerge unscathed when he charges that she was so immature that she sank his toy boats while he bathed in the tub.

Perhaps the liveliest story in which Allen uses the family to express his alienation deals with a favored cousin. Even Allen's parents preferred this cousin to their own son. The cousin is married to "a very thin girl from the neighborhood who had her nose lifted by a golf pro." This wording implies the girl's restructuring of her Jewish nose, her acceptance into the world of golf clubs, and her consequent snobbishness (the lifted nose) toward the unaccepted, such as Allen. The final dimension of Allen's intimidation by the cousin and his wife is sexual. A mutual fund salesman, the cousin has provided for his wife through every kind of insurance, including "orgasmic insurance": "If her husband fails to satisfy her sexually, Mutual of Omaha has to pay her every month." (The choice of Mutual of Omaha to insure mutual orgasm is typical of Allen's genius for detail.) The wife is the cousin's most glamorous advantage over the deprived Allen. Her thinness, her social assurance, her sexual insurance, her raised nose, and her raised consciousness are all representative of a dream come true: assimilated Jewishness and ascendant womanhood. But this ideal only widens Allen's sense of inadequacy.

The Allen persona has as much difficulty with the physical world as he does with the human. Indeed, he encounters machinery that is as malevolent as man. Allen cannot work with any mechanical objects, because "anything I can't reason with or kiss or fondle I don't get along with." Of course, this proscription would include most of his human contacts, but his immediate reference is to a clock that runs counterclockwise, a tape recorder that keeps saying, "I know, I know," a sunlamp that rains on him, and a sonic elevator whose diction is superior to his own. Moved by a doomed idealism, he calls a con-ference of all his antipathetic appliances. This story does not just satirize uncontrollable gadgetry; it postulates a world in which the mechanics of "things" oppose peace, harmony, generosity, and rea-son between both individuals and nations. It amplifies Allen's ad-mission that he has "always been at two with nature."

Despite all these failures, however, it should not be concluded that the Allen persona is always a loser. Sometimes he lies. Indeed, there are two kinds of happy endings in the Allen monologues. One in-volves such an extravagant pretense to adequacy as to be mock he-roic. The other is the pure and simple fantasy.

In the eighteenth century, John Dryden described the mock-heroic style by summoning up the image of a little man wearing a suit of armor that was ludicrously too large for him. In Woody Allen's time, nobody wears armor when he sallies forth to confront the dan-gers of the day. Instead the Allen mock-heroic hero is "armored" in an implausible pretense to adequacy. Because this pretense does not fit him, there is a comic discrepancy between the hero's smallness and the image that he tries to project. His poor fit exaggerates his smallness. For example, Allen gives a mock-heroic account of how he prepared for the role of God in Paddy Chayefsky's play *Gideon*:

> I put on a blue suit. Took taxi cabs all over New York. I tipped big 'cause He would have. Got into a fight with a guy and I forgave him. It's true. Some guy hit my fender and I said unto him, I said: "Be fruitful and multiply." But not in those words.

In that discreet euphemism for an obvious vulgarity, Allen emulates the spiritual detachment of God, but his conception is limited to strictly secular terms (the blue suit, the big tipping, etc.). When Allen says he was "typecast" as God, his pretension is mock heroic; it only emphasizes the persona's arrogance, pettiness, and vulgarity.

Allen's mock heroism more often involves his pretending to be a man-about-town. He deflates himself almost immediately—the horse he bets on has training wheels. More commonly, what is normal life for other people is impossible for Allen. His attempt simply to enjoy normal life becomes a mock-heroic undertaking. This is ob-vious in his story about his pet dog, a routine that begins and ends with a sense that his family tradition is one of inadequacy and smallness. At the beginning we hear of Allen's father, a caddy in a minia-ture-golf course; the menial job is reduced even further by its small-scale setting. At the end we hear of Allen's grandfather, who was such "an insignificant man, at his funeral his hearse followed the other cars." Allen lives down to this family tradition. His desire for a pet is gratified when a neighborhood pet shop offers for sale such cut-rate, damaged pets as a bent cat, a straight camel, or—Allen's gift—a stuttering dog that goes "b-b-b-bow-wow" when teased by cats. As this dog is an image of his master's sense of inferiority, we readily accept the next twist in this fantasy. Allen gets his dog's draft card by mistake and is inducted into the K-9 Corps, where he learns to heel and is bullied by his sergeant, a Mexican hairless. The entire story is conceived as a Lilliputian fable, but the Allen hero is even deprived of the hollow vanities of Gulliver's advantages. This story is followed by a variation in which his parents give him an ant that they insist is a dog. He wistfully names it Spot, but the facts catch up with him as he is walking home late one night: "Sheldon Finkelstein tried to bully me. Spot was with me. I said 'Kill!' And Sheldon stepped on my dog." The terse sentences suggest a manly pretense to authority and power. Allen's dignity depends on his delusion that his ant is a dog, but the bully shatters the dream of a normal boy-dog relationship. The entire routine, involving the father, the grand-father, and two pet "dogs," posits a loser whose every attempt to enjoy normalcy is a mock-heroic pretense.

The Allen persona's most frequent pretense to adequacy in-volves his sexual activity. When he is not admitting his sexual failure, he pretends to be a stud. Of course, these contrary claims are con-sistent with mock-heroic comedy, for the extravagance of his lover's pose implies that he is concealing his inadequacy. In both stances Allen satirizes man's sexual vanity. In his admissions of failure there is a corrective, rare candor; his mock-heroic fantasies reflect the more familiar human trait of sexual vanity.

In reporting his first divorce Allen claims that he "volunteered" to commit the legally-required adultery because he's "basically a stud." He pauses to allow the audience to laugh at the disparity between this claim and his frail, fumbling image. In another routine he rises in indignation when the audience laughs at his sexual pretensions; why, on his honeymoon night his wife stopped the proceedings to give him a "standing ovation." Of course, this ostensible compliment reveals his partner's uninvolvement. The persona's narcissism is confirmed by a subsequent story in which he picks up a beautiful girl, takes her to his hotel room, suavely removes his glasses, and then mistakenly shifts his ardor to his own reflection in the mirror. "I was the best I ever had," he concludes. His confusion began with the innocent vanity of removing his glasses, but there is a deeper vanity in his shattering act of self-love.

Another sexual encounter ends with a similar pursuit of a fantasy. Two minor motifs are established by gags in the introductory part of the story. One is the quantification of sexual experience: "I believe sex is a beautiful thing between two people. Between five it's fantastic"; the host of one party supposedly had six sex-change operations trying to find something he liked. The second motif is the attempt to escape physical limits through the power of the imagination. Allen tells of a policeman's horse which after being fed a sugar cube containing LSD appeared at a protest rally in Georgia—liberated and politicized by his experience. Allen recalls that after puffing a joint he "broke two teeth trying to give a hickey to the Statue of Liberty." Unlike the horse, the Allen persona is clearly unable to conquer the intransigence of physical reality.

These themes converge in the climax of the story. Allen picks up a beautiful girl and proceeds to make love to her. To prolong his lovemaking he imagines a baseball game and becomes so involved in his fantasy that he loses the reality of his situation. His confusion of fantasy and reality is conveyed in the language, where baseball terms assume sexual significance from the context: "the Giants are up," "Alou pops out," and "I didn't know whether to squeeze or steal." When he finally notices that the girl has gone to the showers early, physical reality is shaded by a second meaning from the dominating baseball fantasy. But at the end, the hero is happier for having won the ball game in his imagination than for having had sex with the beautiful, real woman. Moreover, having been so candid in his sexual description, he retreats to a false modesty when he declines to describe exactly how he won the ball game: "This is too personal." In this brilliant anecdote Allen details the danger of macho vanity, especially in athletics and sex, and the danger of losing one's sense of ʾality to the seductive powers of the imagination.

The baseball story typifies Allen's satire of competitiveness and self-consciousness in sexual engagement. It seems to be one of Allen's favorite themes because he often plays variations upon it. In *Play It Again, Sam* (1969) the Allen character admits he was thinking about Willie Mays. "Yeah," replies his girl, "I couldn't figure out why you kept yelling 'Slide!'" Allen reverses the baseball-sex routine in a prose piece, "Fine Times: An Oral Memoir," in which Babe Ruth is reported to have been smitten with a woman. Because this woman hates sports Babe Ruth pretends that he teaches a course in Wittgenstein's philosophy. Later his concentration shifts so that he ends up with four hits and two stolen bases, "but this is January and there are no games scheduled. I did it in my hotel room." [8] Babe Ruth, the ideal of swaggering manhood and burly prowess, is converted into a pseudointellectual who daydreams athletic success. In effect, Babe Ruth turns into Woody Allen.

In these examples, Allen's sex comedy dramatizes the tensions between man's normal capacity and the ludicrous ways by which he tries to exceed it. In defending himself against Vivian Gornick's charges of sexism he noted:

> "I don't think of it as girl-chasing," he said with dignity. "People are lonely, they have difficulties with women, sex is a great area of human concern. I'm trying to show a guy caught up in all that." [9]

Allen does not deal with sex per se so much as with human needs, delusions, and fantasies.

The mock-heroic pose occasionally allows Allen a happy ending. At other times a story may end with a success so improbable that the whole thing is clearly a fantasy. In the best example of this, Allen is on his way to a costume party in a Deep South town. Since he is going as a ghost, he wears a white sheet, and thus it happens that he is picked up by a car of Ku Klux Klansmen, also in sheets, en route to a Klan rally. When Allen eventually realizes his predicament he strives to fit in. He says "You-all" and "grits" but eventually betrays himself. When the Klansmen make their donations to the cause, Allen reverts to the tradition of Jewish fundraising rallies by making a pledge. The Klansmen, realizing that he is Jewish, prepare to lynch him. As he awaits death, his life passes before his eyes. He is a kid in Kansas, "swimmin' in the swimmin' hole, fishin' and fryin' up a mess o' catfish." Suddenly he realizes that this is not his life. He is to be hanged in two minutes and the wrong life is passing before his eyes. He snaps out of his reverie and makes so impassioned a plea for brotherly love that the Klansmen not only release him but buy "$2,000 worth of Israel bonds." On that last phrase, Allen's voice rises slightly, as if there were more to follow. But there isn't. Instead he says a simple, "Good night." The impossibility of *that* ending to *that* story expresses a despairing view of man's hope for brotherhood; Allen uses an impossibly exaggerated happy ending to emphasize his pessimism.

In this comic saga of alienation, the Jewish urban misfit has an idyllic vision of Middle-American innocence and community. But it's not his life. Trapped by the alien Klan, he cannot even find refuge in his own memory; instead he reverts to the alien fantasy of Mickey Rooney movies. In Allen's story, pockets of animosity and resentment—the New York Jews, the Klan, etc.—pretend to a common culture, a shared image of innocence, as represented by the conventions of Hollywood's Kansas. But this dream misrepresents the experience of America's victims of isolation. When the Klansmen buy Israeli bonds, Allen's outrageously improbable ending confirms the larger disillusionment that the story expresses: American ideals of innocence and brotherhood are mythical.

Richard Schickel did not overstate his case when he described Allen as "a walking compendium of a generation's concerns, comically stated," that leaves us feeling "that our own interior monologues have been tapped and are being broadcast." [10] By amplifying personal anxieties Allen developed a persona in which his audience could see their own secret fears exposed and expressed. That Allen's persona reflected general social and psychological concerns is clear from the way in which Allen was used in films made by other directors.

2

The Actor as Hired Image

In his monologues Allen had complete control over his material, but when he began to work in films he found that the actor was just a prop, not the primary force. The authority lay with the director or the producer, though the fact that Allen was the writer of his first film as well as a performer in it gave him more of an influence on the project than he would otherwise have enjoyed as an unknown actor. Though Allen the writer could not protect his original intentions against changes by the director, he could at least help to shape the basic premise. In this chapter we shall define the Allen influence on three films that he made for other directors: *What's New, Pussycat?* (1965), *Casino Royale* (1967) and *The Front* (1976). The film of *Play It Again, Sam* (1972) will be discussed in the chapter on Allen's plays, because it began as a Broadway comedy. In all four films, however, the different directors deployed the Allen persona in a consistent way.

What's New, Pussycat?

Producer Charles K. Feldman was so impressed with Allen's club work that he hired him to rework a sex comedy planned for Warren Beatty. (The title, *What's New, Pussycat?* comes from a catch-phrase Beatty used when he phoned his ladies.) Beatty's crowded professional schedule forced his replacement by Peter O'Toole. Directed by Britain's Clive Donner, this fast, all-out bawdy romp became what was then the biggest grossing comedy in film history.

Few critics were as appreciative as the audiences. Adelaide Comerford attacked the film for assuming "sexual amorality to be the contemporary norm" and for sending its "two-dimensional character-burlesques into unrelated and often inappropriate sight gags," with dialogue "sophomorically blue, and occasionally perverted." [1] This was the typical American reviewer's reaction. Andrew Sarris of the *Village Voice* stood virtually alone in favor of the film, first recommending it in a capsule review, then returning with a full-column defense against its critics. Sarris applauded the film's taste in treating its characters with dignity, in honestly confronting the sexual obsessions of our age, and in allowing its characters the therapeutic freedom to express their desires without dissembling or hypocrisy. He reported that after four viewings he still found "new nuances in the direction, the writing, the playing, and, above all, the music." [2] Later Raymond Durgnat praised the film as "Lubitsch on roller skates" and itemized its blend of Neo-Marxism, Spasmodicism, Social Atomicism, Molecularism (or "more precisely 'Introverted disintegrationism' "), Hyperessentialism, Dadaism, Mack Sennettism, Fauvism, and Bouduism—Durgnat had the advantage of critical hindsight.[3] In France, the film was awarded the Jean George Auriol-Paul Gilson Prix and its screenplay was featured in a special issue of *L'Avant-Scène* on the new British cinema.[4] Of course, it was from the box office and not the critics that Woody Allen gained the clout he needed to make his own first feature.

Set in Paris, *What's New, Pussycat?* details the sexual problems of three men. Peter O'Toole plays Michael James, an obviously English editor of a fashion magazine, *Chic*. Luscious ladies fall in love with him at first sight for, as the characters often remark, when the light falls upon him in a certain way he appears almost handsome. The other two male leads devoutly desire such transformation.

Peter Sellers plays Dr. Fritz Fassbender, an infantile psychoanalyst who is married to a huge Valkyrie but lusts after one of his patients, Miss Lefebvre (Capucine). Miss Lefebvre conceals the fact that she is married to a murderously jealous man and is having an affair with an anarchist; she falls in love with Michael James.

Woody Allen plays Victor Shakapopolis, a starving painter who takes a job helping strippers dress between numbers for twenty francs a week. "Not much money," Michael observes. "It's all I can afford," replies Victor. He must pay for the delights that accrue to Michael's job and the frustrations that accrue to Fassbender's. Victor especially loves Carol Werner (Romy Schneider), but she loves Michael James.

While Victor and Fassbender are tormented by their sexual failures, Michael is tormented by his sexual success. He truly loves Carol but continually succumbs to the temptations of other lovelies, who include Paula Prentiss as stripper Liz Bien, a suicidal American in Paris on a bongo scholarship, and Ursula Andress as a skyjumper.

Something of Allen's intention in his screenplay may be deciphered from his 1965 article for *Playboy*:

> My initial story described the search of a psychotic gynecologist and a Lithuanian jockey for stable values in a world threatened by the influx of bad singing groups—with Romy Schneider, Capucine, Paula Prentiss and Ursula Andress cast as the 1936 Notre Dame backfield.[5]

Indeed the first two characters mentioned can be taken as a funhouse distortion of the Sellers and Allen roles, with the ladies (or the Four Horsemen, as the 1924 Notre Dame backfield was known) the object of their quest for a happy stable. The film does deal with modern man's search for stable values and harmony in a world of kinkiness and cacophony. This interpretation is supported by the poem recited by the Paula Prentiss character. Her "Ode to a Pacifist Junkie" seems to deal with sex (not unlike the movie) but, as she explains, is really "a plea for better housing."

All seven central characters crave "better housing," either physical or psychological. Fassbender flees his Gothic castle and wife for the svelter lines of the disco. Carol and Liz crave a man and a home so much that each claims to be Michael's fiancée; in one scene, Miss Lefebvre pretends to be his maid in order to avert Carol's suspicions. All three women play at domesticity, but Miss Lefebvre flees what Carol and Liz desire. When Ursula Andress, dressed only in a snakeskin jumpsuit, parachutes into Michael's open car, she represents both the modern, free woman and the open life that Michael enjoys but yearns to be sheltered from. Michael initially avoids having Carol move in with him, but he finally espouses and spouts a piece of traditional wisdom—

> Human fulfillment does not come from short, physical, random adventures but from a deep relationship which is quite often right under one's very nose.

—that is attended by a flashing, gaudy sign: "Author's Message." Without exception, however, the sheltered creatures in the film crave freedom and the free ones crave shelter. That is the predicament of these permissive times. As Michael tells Fassbender, eroticism is the disease of our age, but we prefer the disease to the cure.

The theme of shelter lends significance to the decors provided the characters. For example, in keeping with his infantile fixations and his life of archaic frustration, Fassbender is associated with a very old style of home, a cold stone castle. In the other men's more modern homes, the room divisions are thin and ineffective. In one scene we hear Victor's scream of agony when he hurts himself and retreats into his bathroom to preserve his stoic image. In another scene, Michael has only a thin curtain separating his fiancée in the living room from Miss Lefebvre in the bedroom. Both scenes show the futility of trying to compartmentalize one's love life. This is also the point in a witty transition from Miss Lefebvre's claim that she can only give herself to a man in a romantic environment, to her making love to Michael in a stuck elevator. Because the setting is subordinate to the characters' wills, a permanent, secure shelter is impossible for characters with wandering desires.

The film reaches its climax in a setting that summarizes the film's concern for "better housing." The Chateau Chantel is a quiet family hotel during the regular season, but in the off-season it is a hotbed for erotic irregularities. There all the freedoms and frustrations of the permissive age converge in glorious chaos. The gamut of sexual misconduct is suggested by the various rooms named after notorious lovers. When one man asks room service for "twelve loaves of bread and a boy scout's uniform" to be delivered to the Marquis de Sade Room, Michael properly observes that "the joint is jumping." The hotel symbolizes romantic shelter because between its seasons of conventional family bliss, it needs the uninhibited release of private fantasies. The jumping joint reflects man's need for both stable housing and sexual experiment.

The libertinism of the Chateau Chantel eventually pours out into the countryside as the characters flee the police in a wild (but un-funny) chase. The implication seems to be that periods of unin-hibited license must be brought under control.

However, the film rejects marriage as a compromise between erotic passion and social decorum. When Michael weds Carol at the end of the film, their bliss—and with it the conventional morality of the "Author's Message"—is undercut in two ways. First, across the beautiful young couple falls the shadow of the Fassbenders' mar-riage. When Fassbender hands Michael his own wife's wedding ring ("These are perilous times"), we recall Fassbender's early remark to his wife: "I hate you. I hate you. I've hated you from the moment we were first married." The second omen is Michael's inability to stop flirting. When the new bridegroom tells the attractive clerk (Françoise Hardy) his name for the marriage license, he appends the "Pussycat" by which he has been courting the ladies all along. The film ends with Carol sending Michael on the honeymoon alone and Fassbender pursuing the clerk. As Andrew Sarris concludes, "the prevailing mood is sad, because sex is ultimately sad." [6]

Allen was dissatisfied by the film for several reasons. He found it "overfancy," with everything "big and jazzy. They couldn't do any-thing small." [7] In addition, he found the humor broadened: "They couldn't get the humor with the analyst and the patient dressed like normal people and had to dress Sellers up with a Beatle wig." [8] Moreover, Allen's role was diminished by the reassignment of choice scenes to O'Toole or Sellers, who were then bigger star attractions. For instance, O'Toole replaced Allen in the barroom drinking scene with Sellers, and Sellers replaced him in the Cyrano scene outside Lefebvre's bedroom. The effect of both substitutions was to coarsen the kind of comedy. As modest Victor became less important, the psychiatrist became both more prominent and physically more out-landish. "I could have made it twice as funny and half as successful," Allen concludes. [9]

Even more important losses from Allen's script can be spotted if we compare the film to Marvin H. Albert's novelization of *What's New, Pussycat?* "based on an original screenplay by Woody Allen." For one thing, the film simplifies the relationship between Victor and Michael, omitting several of their scenes together, most importantly the one in which Michael in blissful innocence survives Victor's attempts to murder his rival for Carol's love. Gone too is a delightful sequence in which Victor's every attempt to kiss Carol is rebuffed by her "Please, Victor—not here!" This happens in the Bois de Boulogne, at a shooting gallery, and even in the Tunnel of Love!

Another regrettable omission is this scene in Victor's favorite romantic haunt, the sewers of Paris:

> "Look, this has gone far enough. It's time you chose—it's either Michael or me. We can't go on undecided like this any more! Make up your mind, *now*. If it's Michael, I won't see you any more. If it's me, give him up forever. But I want to know your decision *here and now and for good!*"
>
> "I can't decide!" Carol wailed.
>
> Victor's determination evaporated, leaving him a tired, empty shell. "Okay, listen—I'm hungry. You wanna eat?"
>
> They climbed out of the sewer. . . .[10]

Eliminating this extremely funny scene simplifies Victor's character by omitting his heroic resolution, his immediate compromise, his morbid romanticism, and the wild chance that Carol actually might choose the Woody Allen character over the Peter O'Toole one.

A more serious omission was the suggestion that the marriage of Carol's parents has survived only because they are oblivious to each other. When Michael, Carol, and her parents set out for a night on the town, Allen evidently had Mr. Werner enthuse:

> "I adore this city. It's magnificent. I wish your mother were alive to see this moment!"
>
> "But I *am* alive," Mrs. Werner snapped. "I'm right here."
>
> "Ah, so you are, *Liebchen*. Sorry . . . I got carried away." [11]

In the same vein, in the last chapter of the novelized version both Werners, quite oblivious to what the couple is telling them, persist in inflicting unnecessary advice upon Carol and Michael. To her mother's "Why don't you two make up and name the date and . . ." Carol can only sigh, "Mother, we *have* named the date." This insensitivity in the established marriage validates Michael's earlier dread that "marriage is forever. It's like cement."

Nevertheless, the film's felicities keep it still fresh some twenty years later, its lustful characters forever panting and forever young. The dash and exuberance of the technical devices—the Richard Williams titles, the processing tricks, the Burt Bacharach score—express the very spirit of freedom that the film develops in its characters. Because Donner's film continually overflows the borders of conventional film narrative, we are continually reminded that we are watching a film. For example, when the fully clothed Michael joins Carol in her shower, she asks, "Shall I get dressed or is this foreign movie time?" Later Mrs. Fassbender is furious at having been "foiled by a cheap cinematic illusion." A patient slavers over a sexual dream from Alfred Hitchcock's *North by Northwest* (1959) (a train entering a tunnel). The characters' lives seem to have been shaped by their sense of film (an important Allen concern in his own first features, as we shall see).

In a similar vein, the film often cites the performers' existence outside their present roles. When Fassbender introduces the Ursula Andress character as "a personal friend of James Bond," he is referring to the actress's earlier film, *Dr. No* (1962). In a crowded nightclub, O'Toole is approached by the uncredited Richard Burton, his friend and costar from *Beckett* (1964). Even Paris seems to be pointing to its past when Lautrec joins Zola, Gauguin, and Van Gogh (a fresh bandage over one ear) at a sidewalk cafe. Implicit in all these gags is the sense of characters playing roles, of a drama between images rather than between people.

The most important example of a character carrying the sense of its actor is Victor, whose role draws upon Allen's persona. He is a wide-eyed, bespectacled, weak, and boyish innocent adrift amid worldliness. He must overcome his discreet cowardice to fight a Nazi-type in the public library(!). A menorah beside his bed bears silent witness to the fact that Victor is Jewish. And though lecherous, he is sexually inexperienced. When he fumblingly tries to help one stripper put on her veil, he nervously apologizes that "there were all boys in my family." He faints during a game of strip chess.

Moreover, Allen makes his character the one most accessible to viewer identification. This is due partly to our warm familiarity with his persona, and partly to Victor's relative normalcy. Michael with his manic eyes and incredible sexual success is one extreme; Fassbender with his fixations and weird mien is the other. Victor is the human norm by default.

The fact that Victor is played by the author of the screenplay gives the film an added dimension, allowing it to be taken as a projection by the Allen persona. If Michael's job is, as he claims, "a lecher's dream," then Allen is the lecher who dreamed it. Furthermore, O'Toole's role as a lover who wishes he were a writer is a reversal of Allen's persona—the writer who wishes he were a lover. This connection is confirmed in the most explicit film allusion in *What's New, Pussycat?*: Michael has a dream that is clearly a parody of Marcello Mastroianni's dream in Fellini's *8½* (1963). In it he is assailed by his past loves and must whip them back to their places. O'Toole may relate to Allen as Mastroianni did to Fellini—as a suave and potent surrogate. That Michael functions as a wishful extension of Allen's Victor may explain why the handsome WASP played by O'Toole should refer to the prayer shawl beside his bed; he trails a tinge of Allen's Jewishness. The difference is that Michael is a fully matured man, in contrast to the boyish Victor. Hence the flashbacks that chronicle Michael's precocious sexual maturation; neither Victor nor Fassbender were blessed with equivalent predicaments.

If Michael is Allen's ideal projection, then Fassbender is the antithesis, the monstrous embodiment of the Allen persona's dread of animalism. Among the statues in this therapist's office is a King Kong threatening a fair damsel. "Control your animal needs or I will have them shaved within the half hour," Fassbender warns one patient. And to Michael's plea that he has dire needs, Fassbender replies, "So have I. What do you think I am? Human?" Once we recognize Allen's persona in Victor, then the two other male leads can be seen as alternative fantasies by which the boyish Victor defines the range of his own possible sexual development. Michael is the figure that the emerging man would like to become, Fassbender the embodiment of frightening energies and frustrations. Michael represents the Allen persona's dream, Fassbender his dread.

This relationship is confirmed by Allen's and Sellers's facial similarity—their long-nosed, spectacled, and worried faces suggest popular notions of intellectuality and physical inadequacy—and by a telling quai-side scene between them. Victor has come to celebrate his birthday with a solitary but formal dinner. Fassbender has come to kill himself. After some confusion, they agree to conduct the suicide first and then to celebrate Victor's birthday together. This drunken fuddle suggests a fraternal continuity between the animal Fassbender and the timorous Victor; one's death can be followed with the celebration of the other's life, without loss.

What's New, Pussycat? is a film of shifting perspectives. Characters who seem different from each other reveal points of identity when we draw back and view them in a fuller context. Similarly, what seems to be freedom turns out to be compulsion in the wider view. What seems to be innocence can turn out to be extremely kinky (as the therapy group discovers cricket to be, for example). Indeed Donner has developed a pattern in which a widened perspective significantly alters the meaning of the shot. For example, in one flashback the young Michael James repeatedly asks, "What did I do?" Gradually the camera draws back to reveal the seemingly innocent lass in the foreground to be obviously pregnant. The widened perspective has mutely explained what Michael did. Another close-up shows Victor nonchalantly driving the red sportscar that Fassbender prescribed to bolster his virility. The original sense of the image is undercut when the camera draws back: Victor is driving on the sidewalks. There is a similar instance at the Chateau Chantel, where Victor is on a bed, appearing to sing opera to the lovely lady beside him. But the camera retreats to reveal a phonograph playing in the foreground; Victor has only been miming. In all these cases the widened perspective undercuts the narrow view. The device conforms to the characters' ambivalent quest for stable shelters, and to Allen figuring both as a character within the plot and as the author fantasizing it.

At one point Carol asks Victor, "Why does everyone have so much trouble in love?" The film provides several answers. One is the inescapable solitude of the human heart and its libidinous quest for connection. Thus the pathetic union between Fassbender and Victor —who meet as lonely individuals and hop off as comrades, wrapped together in a flag—is contrasted to the Werners' dull marriage and to the hopeful union of Carol and Michael. By intercutting the two scenes, Donner suggests that the marriage institution represented by the Werners is a response to the solitude in the Fassbender-Victor scene. Another answer is the mutual encumbrance of love and sex. Liz Bien's point is that the soul needs "better housing" than the body, which is subject to vagrant needs and unsteady devotions. Nothing is really new, Pussycat. We have always been tormented by the opposing appeals of protective shelter and uninhibited freedom.

Casino Royale

In the commercial film industry imitation is the sincerest form of greed. *Casino Royale* (1967) is a case in point, for its original impetus was unrelated to the expressive possibilities of film art.

To begin with there was the desire to exploit the remarkable success of the James Bond film series. Having procured the rights to the first of Ian Fleming's novels about the elegant spy, the producers were undeterred by the fact that it was the coarsest and shallowest of the series, that it presented the weakest image of Bond, and that Sean Connery was unavailable to play the lead role.

The second intention was to repeat the success of *What's New, Pussycat?*. To this end the producers signed Woody Allen, Peter Sellers, and Ursula Andress, commissioned Burt Bacharach to write the score, and Richard Williams to devise another set of effulgent titles. They also tried to get a script that had Allen's tumble of bawdiness and absurdity. Two precise references to *What's New, Pussycat?* acknowledge this embarrassing paternity: Bacharach's earlier score emanates from a manhole in West Berlin, and Peter O'Toole makes a cameo appearance reminiscent of his encounter with Richard Burton in the earlier film.

A project more than a film, made purely and simply as an investment, *Casino Royale* is, as Allen has said, "an unredeemingly moronic enterprise from beginning to end." [12] The entire film is misshapen, partly because it was finally reduced from its original three-hour length to a release print of 131 minutes, and partly because there seems to have been no single controlling intelligence. No fewer than five directors are credited. John Huston directed the first twenty-five minutes, Robert Parrish the Baccarat games, Joseph McGrath the scenes of extravagant comedy—particularly those involving Peter Sellers—and Kenneth Hughes and Val Guest the rest. The same confusion of contributors can be found in the credits for the screenplay—Wolf Mankowitz, John Law, and Michael Sayers, as "suggested by the novel *Casino Royale* by Ian Fleming." Too many cooks. . . .

The plot assumes that the Sean Connery Bond is an imposter who was assigned Bond's name and number (007, as the cultural historian may recall) in order to promote the bureau's image abroad. The real James Bond is portrayed here by David Niven as a suave, unflappable, and completely capable gentleman. Like Moses, this Bond has a stammer but this flaw disappears when the going gets tough. The film follows Bond's heroic attempts to preserve his celibate honor from various seductresses employed by the nefarious SMERSH. At the same time, Baccarat expert Evelyn Tremble (Sellers) is also assigned the use of Bond's name when he is deployed to best the villainous SMERSH front man Le Chiffre (Orson Welles). Their duel at cards is virtually the only element of the novel that survives in the film. At the end of the movie it is revealed that the SMERSH mastermind, Dr. Noah, is actually James Bond's jealous and incompetent nephew, little Jimmy Bond (Woody Allen).

Allen appears only at the beginning and end of the film, but his role is of strategic prominence In the first scene he is a spy about to be executed in South America. Resolving to escape, he leaps over a stone wall—only to find himself facing another firing squad. At the end he confronts his Uncle James and is finally able to overcome his chronic speechlessness in Bond's presence. The effect of these two scenes is to shift the attention away from the James Bond heroics to a familiar Allen theme: the loser's dream of glory. The Allen frame makes *Casino Royale* not a Bond adventure but an ironic reflection upon the Bond phenomenon. In this respect *Casino Royale* seems to follow in the footprints of *Pussycat*. Earlier Allen and Sellers had played pretenders to the romantic prowess of Peter O'Toole; here they assume the name and power of James Bond. This may be what Allen meant when during the project's early stages he described it in an interview:

> If it works out, it should really put an end to the Bond stories. . . . I wrote the last part of the script, my part, and at first they said it went in a different direction from the rest of the script. Then months later, they wrote and asked me if I had the carbon of the pages I sent them because now they were heading in my direction and would reshape the whole script to fit it.[13]

Clearly the adjustment was not complete, for the result is a vulgar and flabby film from which a mock-heroic satire is crying to get out.

Like Allen's screenplay for *What's New, Pussycat?*, *Casino Royale* offers a range of masculine potency. The ideal is the thoroughly expert and self-controlled James Bond. As Niven plays him, he is untroubled by the Connery-Bond's heroic weakness for the ladies, though he does have the sexual appeal and the skill. At the opposite end of the spectrum is our familiar Allen figure, who openly displays the inadequacies and aspirations of the ordinary man. Little Jimmy Bond plans to unleash a bacillus that will make all women beautiful and destroy all men taller than four-foot-six (that is, all men who are not one foot shorter than Woody Allen). Although Jimmy has replaced important world figures with robot look-alikes subject to his commands, he cannot control an old player piano and a mechanical horse. "All this trouble to make up for your feelings of sexual inferiority," Uncle James sagely observes, "I'm beginning to think you may be a little bit neurotic." Jimmy's captive (Daliah Lavi) puts the case more firmly when she calls him "a wretched, grotesque, ridiculous, insignificant little monster." In any case, Jimmy Bond plans Woody Allen's Utopia, "a world where all men are created equal, where a man no matter how short can score with a top broad." At the end he has swallowed an atomic pill that gives him a supernatural case of hiccups; the punishment has been trimmed to fit the mite in myth's clothing. With the Allen persona and not James Bond providing the mainspring of the plot, the film implies that the Bond mythology supplies vicarious dreams and delights by which an audience can overcome its own sense of inferiority—especially in matters of sex.

The film's function as masculine wish fulfillment may account for the curious number of jokes about genitals. For example, Niven's Bond sneers at the naive gadgetry of Charles Boyer's poison-capsule fly-buttons. Later the gadget makers refer to Bond's crotch as a poison-capsule compartment, indicating the agency's view of sex as solely a means of espionage. Early in the film, one agent in a pissoir turns full-front to another agent when he is asked to show his "credentials." These jokes may relate to the sexual anxiety in the novel, in which Bond undergoes an anxious recuperation after being flogged on the testicles, but more generally, they seem consistent with the view that the Bond sagas have been so successful because they address sexual tensions. Finally, the bureau's exploitation of sex and the Niven-Bond's power over but aloofness from fleshly interests show Allen restoring a sense of proportion to a popular culture dominated by unrealistic sexual ambitions. This would relate *Casino Royale* to the Allen heroes in *What's New, Pussycat?* and *Play It Again, Sam*, and to the mock-heroic sexual pretenses in his monologues.

There is a pertinent joke in Allen's *Playboy* promotion piece for the film. His explanation of one photograph—"I have Detainer Daliah [Lavi] strapped down with shiny aluminum bonds and am searching desperately for a reflection." [14]—not only supports the persona's boyish narcissism even in the presence of a nude beauty, but in Lavi's "bonds" suggests an emblem of the James Bond fad. When Allen peers into her bonds for a flattering and distorting reflection of himself, we have a miniature of how the James Bond phenomenon works. An anxious sexual failure peers into the shimmering Bond for a heroic image of himself.

The Allen persona brings the one element of sense and coherence to the film of *Casino Royale*. Regrettably, the material between the Allen scenes is so witless and uncontrolled that sitting through it becomes something of an endurance test.

The Front

In the nine years between *Casino Royale* (1967) and *The Front* (1976) Allen established himself as an important filmmaker in his own right. His appearance in Martin Ritt's *The Front* was heralded as a new direction because it was a straight dramatic role. Allen played Howard Prince, a seedy cafe cashier and bookie, who serves as a front for a television-writer friend blacklisted during the McCarthy period in the 1950s. The part remains consistent with Allen's persona, however, for Prince is a wisecracking, slightly neurotic loser who by a con seems to become a success.

Actually, the film contrasts two well-known comic personae. Allen is balanced by Zero Mostel, who in what was to be his last film plays Hecky Brown, a Catskills mugger who commits suicide when the blacklist ruins his career. The interplay of these personae adds a variety of resonances to the script.

For one thing, Allen has a contemporary image; Mostel's is older, more traditional, and tied in with resort and vaudeville associations. Allen suggests the pressing needs of the immediate, while Mostel expresses the past and its continuing echoes in the present. The younger character is a con man who lives by satisfying short-range needs and convenience; the older one is honest and aware of historical responsibilities. The contrast between the second-generation-American Mostel and the third-generation Allen suggests some attenuation of the immigrant's absorption into the melting-pot society.

The two actors also present an important physical contrast: Allen, small and tight; Mostel, large and open. In addition, Mostel's rubbery exuberance and energy emphasize the passivity and self-centeredness of the Allen character, who for a long time is content to be a profiteering channel for the work of others. The fact that both characters are played by such familiar actors helps to root the story in historical reality. The plot is validated by our knowledge of both actors beyond these roles. Finally, although Howard Prince is not a moral, open character, the candor of the Allen persona prepares us for Prince's reform.

As usual, Allen's jokes do more than just sustain his persona. For example, here a quip expresses his character's intellectual pretensions —"I figure that if you're going to write about human beings, then you may as well make them people"—but it also establishes the distinction between being merely human and being humane. This is the point that distinguishes the right and left political factions in the film.

Prince's quips tend to be evasive. For instance, when the sponsor of a television program remarks that "some of the actors are pretty pink," Howard replies that it's "just the make-up," but he lacks the courage to make a direct defense. Later, to the McCarthyist committee's implicating question, "Do you know Alfred Miller?" Prince's reply draws upon a familiar Allen joke: "How do you mean? . . . In the Biblical sense?" As his wisecracks become more aggressive, Prince is learning what his friend Miller (Michael Murphy) tried to teach him: "You always think there's a middle you can dance around in, Howard. I'm telling you, this time there is no middle."

The metaphor of a middle-man suits Prince well, for that is what he has been as a cashier, bookie, and front, and that is originally the extent of his moral commitment—to try to find a secure and profitable midpoint between opposing camps. When his girl friend describes her upperclass family background, where "the biggest sin was to raise one's voice," Prince responds, "In my family the biggest sin was to buy retail." In addition to Howard's Jewishness and aggressiveness, the quip expresses his dealings as a middleman. He later tries to justify his evasiveness in terms of being an insider: "You want to do something, you got to be where it counts. On the inside. . . . You're out—and you're a nobody." Before he can grow as a human being, Prince has to overcome this desire to be inside, to be accepted by all groups regardless of the moral compromises necessary.

Prince's success is kept within the limits of development that the Allen persona can accommodate. After all, our hero is a seedy bookie. Prince bears the weight of the Allen persona in smaller ways. Thus, to his girl friend's reminder that "there are other aspects to our relationship than sex," Prince replies: "I know there are. Like what?"

At one point there is a conflict between her wish to attend a controversial Paul Robeson concert and his to go to a basketball game. Though both alternatives involve going to watch something, attending the Robeson concert was also an act of political assertion. As one often finds, the Allen character is a watcher and his lady is a doer. This moment in Walter Bernstein's script may derive from Allen's own experience, for Allen has recalled that he was originally unaware of the implications of McCarthyism. When his neighbors in Flatbush went to a Robeson concert, a mob stoned them and smashed their car. "When I heard about that, I considered it for a minute and then I turned on the ball game." [15] Allen's own experience, as well as his persona, have been fed into this film.

Nevertheless, *The Front* remains a typical Martin Ritt work that anatomizes an attractive character who has a significant though subtle moral deficiency. Ritt tends to cast popular stars—for example, Paul Newman as Hud—in these central roles as a kind of test in which the audience's habitual approval of the actor must be modified by its recognition of his character's flaw. Ritt admits the shock value of his use of Allen: "Audiences go in expecting a Woody Allen comedy, and come out shattered." [16]

The film has its faults. For one thing, it might have been less self-righteous had this Hollywood film exposed the moral cowardice in the film community instead of focusing on its traditional enemy, television. For another, the Mostel and Allen personae were not an unmixed blessing since the film's indignation tends to be softened by Mostel's sentiment and Allen's plucky wit. Allen's presence in particular deflects the audience's response away from uncomfortable thoughts associated with McCarthyism toward safer and more familiar considerations and themes: The Nebbish Who Came into the Cold. Reviewer George Trow contends that Allen was miscast because his persona tends to be guilty of selfishness but not cowardice and because while the Allen persona can be probed and examined it does not admit of character development.[17] It is unnecessary to accept all Trow's points in order to agree that the Allen persona may have weakened some vital lines of character and concern in the film. But thanks to its star-casting *The Front* played on many more screens and to many more viewers than did, say, David Helpern's documentary about the blacklist, *Hollywood on Trial* (1976). With Allen, Ritt was able to reach audiences unaware of this tragically symptomatic period in America's recent history.

The differences between *What's New, Pussycat?*, *Casino Royale*, and *The Front* far outweigh their similarities. Nevertheless, all three films are based on the consistent traits, anxieties, and values associated with the Woody Allen persona. In all three, the Allen image is used for mock-heroic comedy. Allen plays a loser whose pretensions to glory—or even adequacy—only diminish him further.

Part Two

Woody in the Theater

Even when Woody Allen was doing monologues he aspired to be a playwright. His drama was a logical extension of his club act, where his persona related vignettes to a live audience.

While he was working on *Casino Royale* (1967), Allen wrote his first Broadway play, *Don't Drink the Water*. When it opened at the Morosco Theater on November 17, 1966, produced by David Merrick and directed by Stanley Prager, it was a huge success. His second Broadway hit was *Play It Again, Sam*, produced by Merrick and directed by Joseph Hardy, which opened at the Broadhurst on February 12, 1969. *Don't Drink the Water* is currently the fifth most frequently performed play in American amateur theater and *Play It Again, Sam* the eleventh.[1] The surprising preference for *Water* over *Sam* is presumably due to the dwindling supply of Bogart impersonators.

Allen's one-act dramas, *Death Knocks, Death, God,* and *The Query,* suggest that Allen has not lost interest in theater in the ten years since his last full-length play. Indeed, in 1979 Allen joined the eight-member artistic directorate planning to reopen the Lincoln Center's Vivian Beaumont Theater. We can look forward to Allen's further work in the theater, both as a director and as a playwright.

3

Don't Drink the Water (1966)

Woody Allen's first full-length play involves a Newark caterer, Walter Hollander (played by Lou Jacobi in the original production), who is vacationing with his wife (Kay Medford) and daughter Susan (Anita Gillette) in an unnamed Iron Curtain country. After Hollander is caught innocently taking photographs in a restricted area, the family is forced to take refuge in the American embassy. In the absence of the ambassador, the embassy is temporarily under the control of his incompetent son, Axel Magee (Tony Roberts). It already harbors a refugee, Father Drobney (Dick Libertini), a priest who spends his time doing magic tricks. Eventually, the Hollanders and Drobney escape, and Susan and Axel are married.

Given Allen's reliance on his persona in his monologues and early film work, it may be surprising that there is no Allen character in his first play, especially since he was to write himself the central role in *Play It Again, Sam* (1969). The Allen persona, however, is represented in *Don't Drink the Water* by three characters, each of whom expresses a different aspect of the familiar image.

One is Father Drobney, who as the opening narrator is something of an author-substitute. More important, he is an extension of Allen's image as a religious outsider. Like the familiar Allen persona, the priest is besieged and isolated because of his religion. Drobney recalls his choice six years earlier, when he was surrounded by four million Communists determined to kill him: he could remain in the embassy or "go outside and attempt the biggest mass conversion in history." [1] He chose discretion over valor. By making a Catholic his figure of isolation, Allen achieves the same effect as in his "science fiction" monologue about all the inhabitants of earth being turned into Jewish tailors: he broadens the Jew's sense of alienation into a universal state of being.

Allen's identification with Father Drobney is confirmed by their common passion for magic. In the play, this hobby is an indication of the priest's lapse from his calling, a bathetic reduction of the religious service. Betraying a serious disproportion in his values, he swears at a misfired trick: "Damn it! Sorry. (*Crosses himself, looking upward*)." Moreover, since magicians pretend to supernatural powers, we suspect that Drobney's magic fulfills some of his previous needs. Thus he is now as eager to have an audience as he had once been to have a congregation: "I have dreamed of this moment for years. What miracle shall I start with?" Mrs. Hollander's reply points up the incongruity of a priest doing magic: "I don't know—can you walk on water? . . Isn't it wonderful, Walter—a tricky priest." And again: "I think it's marvelous a man of the cloth has a hobby besides just God." Drobney's every entrance diminishes his religious aspect, especially when we see him futilely struggling to extricate himself from a straitjacket. Drobney's religion has isolated him from the surrounding community, and his devotion to magic suggests he is also alienated from his proper faith. The priest's faith in magic is a kind of comical despair.

The second expression of Allen's persona is the fumbling Axel Magee, who manages to survive both his incompetence and his impolitic honesty to win the girl. Like the Allen persona, Axel is a comically awkward lover. Attempts to kiss Susan end with him falling through an open doorway and over the sofa. His words are no smoother than his actions: he proposes they go skiing, because "It's very romantic. I broke my pelvis once." Axel's opposite is Donald, Susan's fiancé, a man "so confident and totally controlled" that Susan wants to escape marrying him. Her taste runs to off-beat men, "the type that would turn my father's hair gray. A manic-depressive jazz musician—a draft dodger, and a defrocked priest." Susan rejects Donald because he is "the answer to a father's prayer." But Axel is just right for her, because he is a disappointment both to her father and his own.

Axel is introduced as "the only man in the history of the foreign service to accidentally wrap his lunch in a peace treaty." After two weeks in Brazil he had that country importing coffee. In Panama he was hung in effigy—by his own embassy! Here again we have the Allen failure, a small figure diminished all the more by being cast in a role too large for him. Axel's failures are aggravated by the fact that his father is so successful: "My mother used to hit me with a copy of *Time* magazine with my father's picture on the cover." Susan and Axel's marriage will enable both of them to defy and escape their domineering fathers.

In the tradition of New Comedy, the young lovers are opposed by an older generation that is a cold, unsympathetic emblem of stultifying order. Part of Walter Hollander's function in the play is to represent the authority that Susan must escape. "I just want her to do the right thing, that's all," he says, but "what I tell her is the right thing." Hollander's unromantic view of marriage—"When you get married you give up happiness."—seems influenced by his career in catering:

> We were the first to make bridegrooms out of potato salad. . . . We did the bride's body in Jell-o—her head in a nice clam dip—with fruit punch spouting out of her throat. It was a class affair.

Hollander shows himself insensitive not only to language's metaphoric power—the quivering jelly of a bride, her nausea of fruit punch—but to marriage's potential vitality and passion. He is doubly defeated during the course of the play. Not only does his daughter marry the loser, but Hollander continually hears that his partner is mismanaging their company. As both defeats represent the triumph of chaos over order, the comic-romantic spirit is asserted over cold control.

Despite this negative characterization, Walter Hollander is the third representative of Allen's persona. For one thing, he expresses Allen's sense of the vulnerability of the flesh. The very title of the play refers to the touristic tradition of digestive upset abroad. As Hollander complains, "No, we had to go to Europe. Thirty-five-hundred dollars for three weeks of uninterrupted diarrhea." Fastidious about food, he refuses to eat anything European, new or exotic: "I will not eat oysters. They're alive when you eat them. I want my

food dead—not sick, not wounded—dead." His digestive squeamishness may relate to his sense of his own dissipating flesh:

> I'm an old man with orthopedic shoes.

> Did you ever see a man with a hernia running from a tank?

> I will not sleep on a cot. I'm a dignified human being with a
> hernia.

Just as Axel struggles for self-respect in the face of a career of
unrelenting failure, so Hollander asserts the dignity of man in the face
of physical decay. These jokes relate to a well-established tradition
of hypochondria in Jewish humor, one that has been traced to the
chronic precariousness of Jewish life in Europe.[2]

Hollander's anxieties about food can also be seen as expressing
Allen's dread of new experience. As the title emphasizes, this play
posits a world that is constitutionally threatening. It is a frightened
recluse's view of globe-trots, so to speak. Hollander's defensive bel-
ligerence and fear reflect the timidity of Allen's persona. To the
brave, exploring new terrain is expanding, but to Hollander: "I
needed this like a growth." In the Jewish-comic lexicon of paranoia,
a growth will inevitably prove to be malignant.

Hollander also expresses the Allen persona's sense of being under
constant siege. As he alternately swaggers and cringes in the embassy island on a hostile Communist sea, he recalls our Allen figure,
besieged by the FBI, or the public library, or an intimidating uncle,
cousin, date, or Nazi-type rival. The play expresses the xenophobia
of a Newark Outsider. The paradox is that here the helpless Outsider is not Allen's usual loser figure but a member of the secure,
affluent, upper middle class. By plunking him down in an antagonistic
country, Allen forces this complacent Insider to recognize his own
vulnerability and, however briefly, to identify with the oppressed and
isolated losers of the world. There is a metaphoric resonance to
Hollander's remark that his partner cannot run the firm because
"he's the inside man. I'm the outside man. It requires personality."
Hollander's "outside" personality, which consists of glib extroversion
and aggressiveness, may make him an Insider back home, but abroad
it makes him an abrasive Outsider. Similarly, Hollander claims that

he doesn't "escape from places. That's not my field. I enter and I stay!"

Several minor comic patterns in the play reinforce the playwright's major concerns. For example, the Hollanders are satirized for their rigidity in thinking. Hollander's habitual thought patterns impede their escape plot:

> MAGEE: The night after tomorrow there's going to be a reception here—
> WALTER: Who's catering it?

Nor can Mrs. Hollander adjust to the seriousness of their new situation: "It'll give you a chance to wear your dark blue mohair." When the planned exchange of the Hollanders for a captured spy named Gray Fox falls through, she remarks: "What do you expect from a Gray Fox. Is that a name for a grown person?" She discourages broaching the escape plans to Walter because "You know how he hates to take me anyplace." These jokes dramatize her complacent incomprehension.

Allen also satirizes international politics. The first gag in the play is the speeding-up of the "very martial and pompous and official" national anthem until it "sounds rickey-tick." Although Father Drobney introduces the ambassador as a diplomat of "clarity and wisdom," the ambassador's first words modify that impression: "Jesus, look at all those Communists!" Too truthful to be a success in diplomacy, Axel displays a disqualifying candor when he confronts his enemy:

> Look—you spy on us—we spy on you—everybody knows it. Why do we suddenly pretend it's so unusual? . . . It's no secret. Espionage goes on between our countries every day. Why be so hypocritical about it?

Axel's impolitic tendency to say what he sees, without guile, relates to Allen's sense that society communicates through codes of esoteric signs and conventions. Only the naive Axel would take a surface impression as the truth: "They're American tourists—didn't you see the shirt that guy was wearing?" For Axel, a caterer's notebook is only a caterer's notebook, but the politically experienced police agent Krojack is convinced that it is a manual detailing the deployment of enemy forces. (Perhaps not, after all, an entirely inapt description of a Hollander wedding!)

Much of the comedy here involves the misinterpretation of signs. For example, Hollander's predicament stems from his failure to have interpreted correctly the guards, dogs, and barbed wire around the security station. As his wife asks, "What did you think it was—a place that sold guards and dogs and barbed wire?" Unable to adhere to any code but his own, Hollander rejects the passwords by which he is to contact underground aid: "he might as well wear a neon sign saying, 'I am a spy.'" Outside his own small secure world Hollander is confused and helpless before strange codes and conventions. Only the insider understands the languages of his land. To the outsider the language is a meaningless babble. This is the "insanity" in Hollander's rejection of Axel's escape plan: "Magee—you're crazy. Do you know you're crazy? Years of insanity have made you crazy." Allen's innocents cannot understand the alien codes in which they have become entangled. Even the notorious spy Gray Fox is caught when he pretends to be a Berkeley student. Is that a disguise for a subversive?

The Hollanders and the chaos that they cause conquer all, even the unflappable Kilroy, the efficient embassy clerk who seems likely to succeed the ambassador. First felled by Mrs. Hollander's waxed floors, then by Walter's marksmanship, then by a rioter's brick, Kilroy becomes convinced that he is the Wright Brothers (and perhaps the Smothers Brothers as well) and dissolves into a dialogue with himself:

> Come quickly, Wilbur. I'm coming, Orville. I'm telling you, Wilbur, we can do it. Do what? Get those machines to fly. Orville, you're crazy. But so are you. . . . Orville, you always were Mother's favorite.

The character whom we "read" as sobriety personified is found to possess a fragile, easily disintegrated personality, fraught with delusions, anxieties, and jealousies. In Allen's comic vision, there is no security, only figures of chaos decked in pretenses to control—but basically ineffective.

Allen rejects this early dramatic effort as "a really terrible play," just a series of funny jokes strung together.[3] He says he modeled it after George S. Kaufman's *You Can't Take It With You* (1936), "based on the premise of a whole family living together and getting on each other's nerves," and that he structured it along the lines of John Patrick's *Teahouse of the August Moon* (1955).[4] Today these models are not as obvious as Allen's own concerns.

Howard Morris directed a film adaptation of *Don't Drink the Water* in 1969. Although Allen's agent Charles Joffe produced the film, Allen did not participate in the project.

The film seems generally true to the play but there are some striking infelicities. For example, where the play opened with the embassy and then brought in the implosion of Hollanders, the film begins with a precredit sequence in which the family prepares for its holiday. The play established a quiet "inside" that was turned into chaos and siege with the entrance of the Hollanders (who are innocent of spying but guilty of just about everything else). The film follows this family from safety into danger. The play's balance of sympathies is disrupted by this reversal and by the consequent sentimentalizing of the Hollanders. There are also moments of unpardonable excess, such as the stripper music that accompanies Father Drobney's attempt to escape his straitjacket (as if the original image were not funny enough) and the ingratiating slow burn and heavenward eyeroll that delimit Jackie Gleason's performance as Hollander. Allen is too fine an artist for his work to be tampered with so crudely.

4

Play It Again, Sam (1969)

Woody Allen wrote his second full-length play as a vehicle for himself. In it he played Allan Felix (translation: Allan the Happy!), a young film critic who is struggling to revive his sex life and self-respect—necessarily in that order—after his wife, Nancy (Sheila Sullivan), has left him. In the first of a series of memories or fantasies, Felix recalls her explanation for leaving him:

> I can't stand the marriage. I don't find you fun. I feel you suffocate me. I don't feel any rapport with you, and I don't dig you physically. For God's sake don't take it personal! [1]

For advice and for a model to emulate, Felix turns to the spirit of his screen idol, Humphrey Bogart (Jerry Lacy). Felix has several dates arranged for him by his best friends, Dick Christie (Tony Roberts) and his wife, Linda (Diane Keaton). But each time, Felix's attempt to project a suave Bogart image disintegrates into ludicrous bumbling.

As Felix and Linda hunt for a girl for him, they drift into an intimacy that leads to love—and even to one night of lovemaking when Dick is away on business. Now Felix changes from being miserable about his failure to being miserable about his success; he flays himself for having stolen his best friend's wife. Linda, however, decides to stay with her husband. Felix gallantly consolidates his friends' marriage by paraphrasing Bogart's famous renunciation of Ingrid Bergman in *Casablanca* (1942). Then he banishes his ex-wife from his memories. At this point Bogart leaves him because "You don't need me anymore. There's nothing I could show you that you don't already know." The play ends with Felix meeting a beautiful girl who has just moved into the apartment upstairs. Not only does she share his passion for film, but she is a fan of his writing. She is his dream come true—a point heightened by the fact that in the original stage production she was played by Barbara Brownell, who had appeared earlier in the play as his lurid fantasy of an impending date, Sharon.

In its structure and fantasy sequences, *Play It Again, Sam* seems to have been modeled after the George Axelrod success, *The Seven Year Itch* (1952). But Allen's is the more resonant and complex play.

For one thing, Allen's own performance in the play gave it a significant inflection. Allen performed in a drama based on his own persona and even perhaps on his own divorce from actress Louise Lasser. In other words, he was doing on Broadway the kind of intimate self-exposure that he had done earlier in the closer confines of a coffeehouse or club. This candor is especially important here, because one of the lessons that Allan Felix learns in the play is that a man must accept himself. As Felix tells Bogart, "The secret's not being you, it's being me. True, you're not too tall and kinda ugly. But I'm short enough and ugly enough to succeed by myself." Woody Allen playing Allan Felix is an ironic alternative to Felix playing Bogart. Allen playing Allan involves an element of self-acceptance that is lost when another actor plays the role—and his character learns not to play a role. The Felix character is so rooted in Allen's image that when the talented Dudley Moore played the part in the London production the respectful reviews noted that he did not quite catch Allen's "personification of neurotic, failure-haunted, urban Jewish-American manhood gone to seed." [2] Allan Felix is steeped in Woody Allen.

The play also explores the ambivalent effects of film upon our self-conception. The Bogart model is a trap for Felix; it represents his failure to be himself, and it restricts his possiblities for action. At times Felix seems paralyzed by his imagination. His former wife was right to complain that Felix is a watcher, not a doer. Whether he is recalling failures or fantasizing implausible successes, his tendency to live out imaginary scenes is an impediment to normal life. When he is imagining Dick's possible responses to the loss of Linda, Felix's cinematically-inspired fantasies keep him from directly confronting his dilemma about whether to continue the affair. Similarly, Felix is impeded in his attempt to seduce Linda when he continually turns to the Bogart image for advice. In both cases, instead of dealing directly with his own emotions, he retreats into film-based fantasies.

Fortunately, Felix outgrows this evasive use of film images so that his closing quotation from *Casablanca* is an advance upon his earlier dependence on film. For one thing, he ceases to distort his sense of reality to cohere with film conventions; instead he begins to use film language to express his sense of what the situation is. His use of film language at the airport is a kind of action, where his earlier fantasies were an evasion of action. Now Felix uses *Casablanca* as a means of acting in the best interests of all three—his friends and himself. (The fact that Linda has already decided to stay with Dick diminishes neither the integrity of Felix's decision nor the fact that the watcher has become a doer.) For all its seductive dangers, then, the film-based fantasy also has its rewards. Through emulating Bogart, Felix discovers both a language for his feelings and the basis for his proper self-acceptance. He learns from Bogart that one thrives by being oneself. Ultimately Bogart does not represent a mythic ideal, but the fact that one can transcend physical limitations without sacrificing integrity and without denying one's nature.

In this regard, it should be noted that the central film allusion in the play, its title, is itself mythical. No one in *Casablanca* ever says "Play it again, Sam," although there is a Sam who is told to play *it* ("As Time Goes By") again. Ironically, a supposed quotation from a myth is itself mythical. Life consists of varieties of reality that include fantasy, fictions, and even fictions about fictions. *Play It Again, Sam* is a complex fiction with some basis in Allen's personal reality (his separation from Lasser), some basis in Allen's "public" reality (his persona in the starring role), some basis in social reality (the pressures common in post-divorce situations), but its liveliest base is in the phenomenon of fiction, as dramatized in the hero's relationship with the Bogart myth.

Allen confirms these points in a *Life* cover story about the play: "I know he [Bogart] never actually said 'Play it again, Sam,' but I said it enough for both of us." [3] Pretending to an even lowlier self-conception and ambition than his Allan Felix, Allen claims to have identified immediately with Peter Lorre in *The Maltese Falcon* (1941): "The impulse to be a sniveling, effeminate, greasy little weasel appealed to me enormously." Moreover, he says, his father identified with Mischa Auer, his mother with Lon Chaney, and his psychiatrist with Sidney Greenstreet. His girl friend may have been free from the models of the silver screen, but she could not resist the lure of afterimage: she ran off with the drummer of a rock group called the Concluding Unscientific Postscript. Our identification with star images is a kind of unscientific afterthought. Allen's use of a mythical title from a mythic film starring a mythic hero encapsulates his sense of the range of realities that shape our awareness. For both short and unattractive heroes, Felix and Bogart, *Play It Again, Sam* demonstrates the triumph of myth over matter.

Most of the comedy in the play derives from the discrepancy between Allen's image and Bogart's, playing up Felix's folly in projecting an untrue image of himself. The theme permeates the play's metaphors both in language and in gesture. For example, Felix's confession that he cannot live up to Bogart's hard drinking involves a false image: "I have one thimbleful of bourbon, I run out and get tattooed." "You don't need an image," Linda assures him, when he is worrying which books and records he should leave "casually" lying about. Felix ironically confirms this when he pretends that his apartment was professionally designed: "The key to decorating is to avoid looking like you used a decorator."

Felix pretends that he is not pretending, but when he tries to be nonchalant, he only reveals how tense he is. In one scene he pretends to be casual as he takes his date's coat; he becomes so casual that he drops it. He recovers it and swirls it around elegantly, spilling a variety of tinkly things in the room. When he affects a low, Bogart-like voice, Felix emits nothing but an ambiguous growl. By the scene's end, his living room has been virtually destroyed by his pretense to being comfortable.

Yet Linda is able to fall in love with this embarrassing wreck because he is so concerned with projecting a false image for *other* girls that he is himself with her. By the time he realizes that he is in love with her, their relationship has reached the stage where she can intuit what he feels despite what he may say or do. When Linda, after fleeing Felix's first embrace, returns and asks "Did you say you loved me?" she has sensed a truth that was unspoken in Felix's fumble and fluster.

Linda and Felix are essentially kindred spirits. As Dick observes: "You're like him. The two of you can get emotionally wrapped up in a weather report." An easy intimacy develops between them because they share their vulnerability even at its most unromantic. Thus Linda reports seeing Dick off to Cleveland: "I got up, helped him pack, drove him to the airport, and threw up in the United Airlines terminal." Felix understands: "That's a good terminal. I've thrown up there."

Similarly, after their night of love Felix opens the third act with glowing reminiscence: "We couldn't fight it any longer, I took you in my arms and we made love. Then we each got upset stomachs. The main thing is that we're honest." Here Allen deflates romantic rhetoric by pointing up the embarrassing vulnerability of the flesh— nerves, nausea, indigestion. Freed from the conventional unrealities of romance and from the idealizing of false images, their love is based on their common human weakness. Linda's part in Felix's life is the antithesis of Bogart's, which is based on romantic posing.

Linda's emotional estrangement from her husband helps her to fall in love with Felix. In some ways Dick Christie is a positive alternative to Felix—tall, handsome, confident, bustling young executive, whose very surname (Christie) suggests a social belonging that is denied Allen's Jewish persona. But Dick's air of efficiency is as false as Felix's affectation of Bogart. One running gag has Dick constantly phoning his office to leave a trail of phone numbers through which he might be reached; he is never called. The implication is that the confident executive may be as insecure and as neurotic as Felix. Moreover, Dick's business deals backfire: Florida land bought for a golf course turns out to be quicksand, and fifty building lots in Tennessee are radioactive. All in all, Dick Christie seems more like the incompetent Axel Magee—also played by Tony Roberts in Allen's first play—than the competent executive he pretends to be. Vainly pursuing an elusive image of success, Dick becomes so preoccupied that he fails to assure Linda of her importance to him. He almost loses her to Felix.

Even the minor characters embody Allen's themes of uncertain identity and false images. One of Felix's blind dates, Vanessa, speaks of her "endless stream" of lovers and her view of sex as "something wonderful and open—to be enjoyed as fully and frequently as possible." But to Felix's primed embrace she responds with an indignant "Aaaaagh! What do you take me for?" Another date, Sharon, appeared in an underground movie, *Gang Bang*: "They have the raunchiest titles, but it wasn't a bit sexy." An industry based on the projection of false images of eroticism projects a false image of itself. At one point Sharon notes that Felix sounds "like the back of a record jacket." Later she catches him out when he plagiarizes a suave phrase from a photography ad that she has just read aloud. The underground movie, the record flackery, the photography reference, and the fact that Sharon is one of several models vainly pursued by Felix all suggest a proliferation of prefabricated romantic and erotic ideals impossible for ordinary mortals to achieve. They all impede Felix's attempts to come to terms with the modest reality of his physical nature.

When *Play It Again, Sam* was filmed in 1972, Allen wrote the screenplay and repeated his starring role as Felix, along with Keaton, Roberts, and Lacy from the original cast. The direction was assigned to the more experienced Herbert Ross, and the result was a deeply satisfying adaptation.

The most obvious change was caused by a film technicians' strike in New York—the setting is switched to San Francisco. Given the Allen persona's roots in New York and his familiar disdain for California, this might have damaged the adaptation. But, as Harry Wasserman has pointed out, Ross exploited the San Francisco locale expertly. He contrasted Felix's blue funk with the gorgeous colors of the countryside and, in three consecutive scenes involving Felix's affair with Linda, used the San Francisco hills as emblems of the rise and fall of Felix's hopes.[4]

Allen's screenplay also adds a few quips that show Felix responding with morbid gloom to the beauty of the seaside:

> This is a terrific beach-house. Let's burn it down and collect the insurance.

> Look, you can see the seagulls flying over the cesspool.

> I don't tan. I stroke.

And Allen has remarked on the paradox of this splendid city's having the highest suicide rate in the United States.[5] In one scene, when Felix sidles up to a beautiful girl in an art gallery, she recites a litany of gloom about "the hideous, lonely emptiness of existence" in this "useless, bleak straitjacket in a black absurd cosmos." The exterior shots in the film show Felix similarly "at two" with his setting: he staggers choking out of a cab previously occupied by grass-smoking hippies, he is attacked by a lapdog, and when he amiably slaps a man's shoulder, he knocks him into the Bay. Everything about romantic and free San Francisco emphasizes Felix's personal failure.

The very act of filming the play, however, involved a radical change in Allen's original conception. Allen's play concerned a man obsessed with a film image, in a film-related profession, and with a habit of seeing his life in terms of film scenes. The film of the play assumes an additional element of self-reflection because a film about film is an experience different from that of a play about film, even if the text were exactly the same.

This point is acknowledged in the opening shot. The first thing we see is the airport scene at the end of *Casablanca*. The camera draws back to reveal the screen frame around the image, then the cinema audience, then Felix's back as he watches the film. In effect we and Felix are in the same relationship to the *Casablanca* quotation, except that we watch him watch it; he remains immersed in the film even when he swaggers out of the cinema. In the airport scene at the end, Felix is in the same position—on the right hand side of the screen with his back to us—as at the beginning. The image of the watcher watched establishes the tension between total immersion in viewing and self-consciousness. Furthermore, we are reminded that a film image can come between ourselves and our experience, as Felix here mediates between us and the airport scenes. In this spirit, Ross interrupts the first passionate kiss between Linda and Felix with his own obtrusive rhetoric of a revolving camera, and then with intercut footage of a kiss from *Casablanca*. The implication is that the characters' experience of the kiss may be both heightened and rendered remote by their recalling a film scene at that moment. Similarly, when Linda and Felix are seen in bed together, the lovers are dwarfed by a large poster of Bogart's *Across the Pacific* (1942), a title that suggests the gulf of fantasy between them. Bogart came between them in the earlier scene of fumbling courtship; now his poster diminishes their intimacy.

Felix's first fantasy of Nancy, his former wife, is introduced with a subtle visual gag. As he soliloquizes, Felix takes a spatula and scrapes two fried eggs from his plate back into his frying pan. He seems to be living backwards. Indeed he is, inasmuch as he regresses into fantasies and attempts to model his life after art, instead of taking art as an illumination of life.

Perhaps it was to suggest that, for Felix, a work of art establishes a pattern that he tries to achieve in his life that Ross expanded the function of *Casablanca* for the film. The play opened with Felix watching television and hearing Bogart reject Mary Astor at the end of *The Maltese Falcon*. Ross's opening with *Casablanca* has several effects. We get the full impact of the movie screen image instead of just the sound of the small television. As will be true in the scene with the bedroom poster, Felix is shown dwarfed by his Bogart image-world. Moreover, Felix's life is given the specific parallel with *Casablanca* instead of with the general Bogart image; he is given a specific plot into which he will fit his life. As Felix matures and learns Bogart's self-acceptance, he will fulfill the pattern established by the *Casablanca* opening. Felix's watching of the film in the first scene and his silent mouthing of Bogart's lines are in effect a rehearsal for his later surrendering his love. The expanded *Casablanca* reference suggests that a film image can be a coherent, pervasive model (for better or worse).

Ross leaves Felix all alone at the end of the movie. This differs from the play, where Felix has the responsive new girl friend, and it differs from *Casablanca*, where Bogart walks off into the haze with Claude Rains. The director emphasizes what he calls Felix's virtue of "renunciation. About doing it well, about behaving well under stress. Grace under pressure." [6] Of course, he found this theme in the play, where Bogart admires Felix for deciding to return Linda to Dick: "You're passing up a real tomato because you don't want to hurt a guy. If I did that there wouldn't be a dry eye in the house." To emphasize Felix's growth, Ross leaves him without any happy substitute for Linda. He is freed not just from his fantasies about the past, but also from any images that promise success.

Some of Ross's sensitive use of detail is tellingly comic. In Felix's bakery fantasy, for example, he wields a phallic piece of limp dough against the jealous Dick's knife. Some is ironic, as when Felix, shopping for romantic candles for his date with Linda, by mistake buys the *yahrzeit* candles used by Jews to memorialize their dead. He is corrected by the gentile Bogart: "They're for a Jewish holiday."

Ross is especially effective in tracing the development of Linda's love for Felix. When they plan their eventful evening they sit alone in a park before an empty bandstand. The setting suggests that the relationship is developing in the context of a public performance, but there is no performance, no performer, no audience—just two timid souls together. Similarly, Ross presents two scenes in which Linda relates to Felix while her husband sleeps beside her. In one she fondles the toy skunk that Felix gave her as a birthday present; in the other she talks to him on the phone. Both shots express the characters' connection despite their separation by distance and by her marriage.

Finally, Ross adds short scenes in which Linda ambivalently considers Felix's prospective dates and each one's unsuitability for him. We sense her honest appreciation of a man whose self-respect is undermined by mythic ideals. This sensitive, adventurous adaptation is true to the original play even when it departs from it.

5

The One-Act Plays

Woody Allen's work in the one-act play is a small but impressive achievement. He seems to have considered the form amenable to philosophic statement because it is free of the commercial considerations that affect a full-length play. Of the four examples discussed here, the first three can be taken as a trilogy about man's mortality, and the fourth an exploration of the functions of comedy.

Death Knocks

The comedy in *Death Knocks* derives from the domestication of Death. Allen plays a mock-heroic variation on the Christian allegorical tradition in which Death is a dark-garbed figure who engages a mortal in a game of intelligence (usually chess, as in Ingmar Bergman's 1956 film, *The Seventh Seal*). In Allen's version, Death's antagonist is a paunchy, fifty-seven-year-old dress manufacturer, Nat Ackerman; their game is gin rummy.

An image of human fallibility with a Jewish accent, Allen's Death is not the awesome power traditionally portrayed. When he first appears, he puffs loudly, trips over the windowsill, and falls into the room. He's "shaking like a leaf," so he wants a drink: "Now can I get a glass of water—or a Fresca?" [1] He had climbed into Ackerman's room with some difficulty, he says: "I get my heel caught on some vines, the drainpipe breaks, and I'm hanging by a thread." Death "hanging by a thread" is a reversal of the familiar image: man hanging by a thread to delay inexorable Death. At the end of the play Ackerman beats Death at gin. Because Death does not have enough money for his return fare, he must drift around until the following evening, waiting for a chance to recoup his losses from the indomitable Ackerman. As Ackerman tells a friend over the phone: "But, Moe, he's such a *shlep!*" (Yiddish for "a shabby good-for-nothing"). Of course, this Death looks like Ackerman: "Who should I look like? I'm your death." In *Death Knocks* Allen dramatizes a simple, complacent man's confrontation with his own death.

Ackerman survives the meeting because he too is a simple *shlep*. He has not contemplated the universal significance of death, nor is he prepared to go along with his own death—he gives as his reason a contract recently signed with Modiste Originals! Ackerman's simplicity may make him seem foolish. Although he is playing for his life, Ackerman proposes that they "play a tenth of a cent a point to make it interesting." But it is this very simplicity that allows him to triumph. In this spirit too, such phrases as "Death knocks," "deal," "playing for time"—all potentially menacing in their macabre associations—are rendered harmless by the context of rummy. Ackerman is not even fazed when Death admires his taste in art: "I love those kids with the big eyes." To us this reference to a particularly sentimental fashion in popular art is chilling, because the love of children is different when man expresses it and when Death does. Because Ackerman does not recognize the power of Death, Death has no power over him. Allen may well envy this hero, whose very simplicity prevents his domination by death.

Death

In *Death* another simple salesman is roused from his peace to confront his mortality. This time the hero is Kleinman (Yiddish for "little man"), who is awakened to join a vigilante hunt for a murderer. Kleinman spends the play trying either to find safety or to determine what his function in the hunt is. At one point, he is accused of being the murderer, but his lynching is interrupted when word arrives that the killer has been caught elsewhere. When Kleinman meets the killer, he finds he is Death. Again Death resembles the hero. Mortally stabbed by Death, Kleinman urges his society to "co-operate . . . God is the only enemy." [2] But the others take this to be delirium and continue their wild hunt for Death.

Death is a companion piece to *Death Knocks*. For one thing, since Kleinman is a more complicated character than Ackerman, his Death raises more complex issues. Whereas Ackerman was content with his simple ignorance, Kleinman is baffled and continually asking questions: "What's going on?" "What are you talking about?" "What killer?" "Which maniac? Which strangler?" "When did it start? I don't know why I wasn't told anything." His bewilderment about his role in the vigilantes' plan represents man's isolation in the absurd cosmos. As his friend, Al, notes: "Each of us only knows one small fraction of the overall plan at any given moment—his own assignment—and no one is allowed to disclose his function to another." But Allen's hero, as usual an outsider ignorant of the codes used around him, is never told his part in the plan.

Moreover, though Ackerman has never contemplated death, Kleinman has. But Kleinman has tried to assure himself that his death will be "comfortable," and will not come before he is "through the long journey of life." Just as he has tried to distance himself from thoughts of death, Kleinman has also attempted to avoid the unsettling doubts raised by philosophic speculation. This is demonstrated in his conversation with the prostitute, Gina, whose every searching idea Kleinman tries to evade. To her reminder that we are all creatures on a globe floating in space—"You can't tell which way is up"—Kleinman replies: "You think that's good? I'm a man who likes to know which way is up and which way is down and where's the bathroom." When she asks if he is implying that the universe is finite, he retreats: "I'm not saying anything. I don't want to get involved." Informed that light travels 186,000 miles per second, he replies: "That's too fast if you ask me. I like to enjoy a thing. There's no leisure any more." The evasive Kleinman is exposed to challenges from which Ackerman's simple life and mind have protected him.

Kleinman is also caught up in a more pressing social reality than Ackerman. Hence the variety of characters with whom Kleinman must deal during the play—his unsympathetic wife, a doctor, the disturbing prostitute, a policeman, a man who has recovered from death, and the factions of plotters and counterplotters. At one point Kleinman is caught between them, in an atmosphere of madness and paranoia: "Choose, you worm," one citizen commands, "I've got a good mind to cut your throat, the way you shilly-shally." Kleinman's dying instruction that we "co-operate" has a social context missing from the insular world of Ackerman.

In his every distinction from Ackerman, Kleinman is closer to the Allen persona. As *klein*man, he has Allen's shortness. Instead of Ackerman's aggressiveness in business or at cards, he has the persona's defensiveness. Thus he offers to "pledge a few dollars" or to "write letters and complain," rather than join the vigilantes. He has Allen's "great fear of death! I'd rather do almost anything else than die!"—indeed in that quiet "almost" he seems careful lest there be something not yet encountered that he might fear more than death. Kleinman admits to the persona's "extreme nausea" and his difficulty with women. After he kisses Gina, she promptly bills him, and Kleinman dissolves into guilt: "I didn't mean to act like an animal—I'm really one of the nicest people I know!" Kleinman also has the Allen persona's dread of liberty. He tells Gina that he prefers to be in bed at night because it's "weird" when the stores are closed and there's no one to stop you if you want to jaywalk or run naked down the streets: "It's a funny feeling. There's no civilization." Finally, Kleinman has the persona's sense of doom. Even the good-luck charm with which his wife sends him off into the dangers of the night suggests that there is little hope. This "charm that wards off evil" was supplied by "a crippled beggar."

While Ackerman embodies a naïveté that Allen might envy, Kleinman has a cowering awareness that is no doubt closer to Allen's own. If Death is a loser in *Death Knocks*, in this play he is a "screwball," a maniac, who doesn't kill because he likes to—he just does it. If he could see how ridiculous it all is, he tells Kleinman, he'd "be sane." Here death is the final absurdity in man's absurd existence.

The thrust of these two plays is precisely the point Allen made in an interview when he explained why his film comedies were dealing more and more with death. "Any man over thirty-five with whom death is not the main consideration is a fool," Allen said, as if describing his insouciant Ackerman. He went on to give what amounts to a summary of *Death*: "The enemy is God and nature and the universe—that's what's killing us. The enemy is not the Chinese or the guy next door to you, the enemy is out there." [3]

God

God is Allen's most complex and sophisticated one-act play, in part because of its vital theatricality. Although the first two plays read as well as they would work on stage, the meaning and the power of *God* inhere in its staging. Allen explores man's uncertainty about the existence of God through the metaphor of life as a stage on which man plays a perplexing variety of roles, with an uncertain script and no confidence that there is an audience out there.

The play opens in 500 B.C. Athens. "Two distraught Greeks in the center of an enormous empty amphitheatre" represent the alienation both of actors and of man.[4] Allen's central characters exist on several levels. They are first introduced by their functions—a Writer and an Actor prepare for a theatrical production in ancient Greece. They are later identified by name. That is, they are assigned personalities apart from their professional functions. But their names, Hepatitis and Diabetes respectively, suggest that their individuality is an affliction, like a disease. The performance of the Writer's play, *The Slave*, within Allen's play allows several of the characters a third level of identity in the roles they play. For example, the Actor, Diabetes, appears as the slave, Phidipides.

These levels of identity frequently overlap. At one point the Actor reminds the Writer that they don't really exist in real life: "You are aware that we're characters in a play right now in some Broadway theater? Don't get mad at me, I didn't write it." Later, the Writer says to the audience, "You follow him? He's an actor. Eats at Sardi's" —and then names the actor playing the Actor.

Consistent with this overlap of roles within the characters onstage is the technique by which members of the audience are embroiled in the action of both the outer play and *The Slave*. One is a Brooklyn College co-ed, Doris Levine, who is summoned onstage to answer the question, "Is freedom chaos?" Later a lusty sport named Lorenzo Miller rises in the audience and claims to be the writer who created that very audience in which he is sitting. He persuasively rebuts first a woman's claim that she is real, not fictional, then that of an indignant man, who (proving either Miller's control or his foreknowledge) rushes out and kills himself in the theater lobby.

Though this man, Miller, and Doris Levine are "plants" in the audience, a real member of the audience is interviewed earlier.

The play also draws on figures from other drama. Blanche du Bois wanders in from *A Streetcar Named Desire*, and is chased off by Groucho Marx. At this point another man in the audience rises and declares his freedom: "If anything's possible, I'm going home to Forest Hills! I'm tired of working on Wall Street. I'm sick of the Long Island Expressway!" As if inspired by Groucho's libertinism and by Hepatitis's exhiliration—"There is no more reality! Absolutely none"—he grabs a woman in the audience, rips off her blouse, and chases her up the aisle.

The play is an exercise in chaos. Its liberty from theatrical convention signifies release from social convention as well. This is the point of Lorenzo Miller's claim that he created the theater audience; they think they are free to do as they please, "but they always do what's expected of them." Life is represented as a layering of roles within roles, of fictions within fictions, with no fixed, clear, and single reality to be determined.

Consistent with the play's sense of fictions within fictions, there is a plethora of figures who can be taken as Creator or God. Author Woody Allen is himself an unseen character in the outer play. The Actor phones him for help, Allen is heard referring to his *Play It Again, Sam*, and Doris Levine rejects a chance to meet Allen, whose work she finds "pretentious." Just as Allen figures in the action as the creator of the present play, so we also have the Writer who wrote *The Slave* and Lorenzo Miller, who claims to have created the audience. Finally, in *The Slave* we have the Greek god Zeus. This confusion of creators suggests man's frantic effort to fill the gap caused by his sense that there is no one Creator (the eponymous hero of the play, *God*).

The classical Greek setting recalls a time when theater and religion were a unified experience and when man was held to be a slave to fate, with an omnipotent divinity above him. The surplus of creators and the various violations of dramatic convention in *God* underline a contrast between the certainty of pagan faith and the existential uncertainties of modern man. As the play intermingles classical characters and events with modern references and anxieties, its basic technique is anachronism. This is also its basic statement: traditional religious faith and the theater of religious faith are anachronisms. Allen's anachronism both in technique and in content points to one of his most characteristic effects—his sense of being detached from his material, of being a dislocated outsider.

By dissolving the usual distinctions between fictions and reality, creator and creation, man and role, audience reality and stage reality, Allen demonstrates both the chaos in which man lives without a sense of a god, and the consolations he imagines in order to fill that void. Indeed one pattern of jokes parodies the idea that man invented God in order to have faith in something. This pattern is simple: the character projects a conclusion and then works backward from it.

In the first instance, the Actor, dissatisfied with the ending of *The Slave*, advises the Writer to "start at the ending when you write a play. Get a good strong ending and then write backwards." This is precisely what Allen does in *God*; he begins with the modern sense of a godless, meaningless universe and then works back to the religious theater of ancient Greece. But the Writer does not have Allen's success. When he tried this technique, he "got a play with no beginning."

The Actor's mind characteristically works in this fashion. He projects a conclusion and then works backward from it. Here the Writer has reminded the Actor of his generosity in allowing this "starving, out-of-work actor" an opportunity for a comeback:

> ACTOR: Starving, yes . . . Out of work, perhaps . . . Hoping for a comeback, maybe—but a drunkard?
> WRITER: I never said you were a drunkard.
> ACTOR: Yes, but I'm also a drunkard.

The Actor projects a charge, then denies it, and then admits its truth.

A final example involves the Actor in his role of Phidipides in *The Slave*. He is to bring to the king a message, which is simply, "Yes." But as he does not know what the question is, he is uncertain whether he is bringing bad news (for which he would be punished) or good. Phidipides assumes that an affirmative answer must be good, until another character suggests, "What if the question is, Does the queen have the clap?" When the king appears, Phidipides drops to his knees and pleads for mercy:

> I'm a lowly messenger, I don't create the message. I merely transmit it. It's like her majesty's clap.

The character adopts a projected possibility (the queen's clap) as if it were a certainty. As it happens, the king's original question was "Is there a God?" The mechanism of the joke in these three examples is a parody of the idea that man created God in his own image, for the consolation (or torment) of having a Creator.

The Actor is the first to break free from the conventions of social and dramatic decorum. As soon as the Writer has referred to the identity of the actor playing the Actor, the Actor exults in his new freedom. The Writer remains restricted by conventions: "As long as man is a rational animal, as a playwright, I cannot have a character do anything on stage he wouldn't do in real life." But the Actor rejects the convention of rational limitations on man's life. In his world, the Actor exults, play characters could choose their own roles: "I wouldn't have to be the slave just because you wrote it that way. I could choose to become a hero." This breakdown of convention horrifies the Writer because it is a challenge to his creative authority: "Diabetes, what you're suggesting is chaos!" "Is freedom chaos?" the Actor asks; from the audience comes Doris Levine to answer.

This is a crucial moment. As it marks the first intrusion of audience-reality into stage-reality (and vice versa), it is the most striking violation of theatrical decorum. Moreover, this violation answers the question. Yes, freedom is chaos if that is an actual member of the audience coming down to join the fiction. But no—if that is part of the creator's (Allen's) plan, then behind this pretense to chaos is an underlying order and control. As in the three examples of jokes that involve working backward from a conclusion, our interpretation of "Doris Levine" will depend on which conclusion we project and work backward from: whether or not we recognize that she is playing a role written by a maker.

The Levine character is significant in other respects. As a gym major with a minor in philosophy, her program parallels the play's concern with the relationship between man's physical and mental lives. And we are continually led to wonder (as the Actor does) whether she is "an actress or a girl playing an actress." When she describes her job making "deceptively shallow serving dishes for Chinese restaurants," we are reminded of her uncertain identity; the job is another example of the confusion between self and role, depth and shallowness, reality and image.

Although by leaving the audience and joining the cast Doris Levine represents the chaos of freedom, in her own character she exemplifies repression. For one thing, after some discreet hedging she admits that she has never had an orgasm. For another, at two points she resists sexual advances by retreating to the claim that she is a fictional character, someone with an assigned role to play. She rejects the Writer's advances but cannot explain why: "I don't know. That's my line." And later: "Please. I'm a virgin. Is that my line?" However, when the Actor declares that there is no controlling hand over her life, Doris feels first fear, then exuberant license:

> But without God, the universe is meaningless. Life is meaningless. We're meaningless. (*Deadly pause*) I have a sudden and overpowering urge to get laid.

Since the other characters on stage are terrified by this outburst, she turns to the audience to find a lover. At this point the man (or playwright or god) who defined her role as a virgin is replaced by Lorenzo Miller, who becomes a maker in all three common senses of the word: literary, godly, and sexual. At the end of the play Allen tries to reassert his control over Doris Levine. By Western Union telegraph he allows her a modern blessing (and miracle): "Doris Levine can definitely have an orgasm. Stop. If she wants to. Stop." All in all, Doris Levine personifies the same uncertainties about her own identity and liberties as the Actor does, but her tensions involve a member of the modern audience and not a classical actor.

For his part, the Actor rebels against his role in *The Slave* just as he objected to the Writer's assumptions earlier. The slave grabs the king's sword and threatens to kill him with it. But it's a play sword, so it only tickles the king. In this assault by tickling, the Greek tragedy turns into Yiddish comedy:

> CHORUS: What are you doing, Phidipides? The king should kill *you*.
>
> DIABETES: Says who? Where is it written? No—I choose to kill the king.

The rhetorical question "where is it written?" is a Yiddish idiom. Before the character can assert the independence that the Actor has already claimed, he must be freed from any fear of a god. For at every level of identity in this play, the characters are governed by the conclusions that they themselves projected.

The slave Phidipides is freed when the Writer's ending backfires. The Writer's play ends in a Woody Allen variant of the traditional *deus ex machina*—the human dilemma is resolved by the spectacular appearance of a god, Zeus, who brings "salvation to a grateful but impotent group of mortals." This ending was proposed by Trichinosis (whose name refers to the one ailment from which orthodox Jews are safe!). But the machinery jams and Bursitis, the actor playing Zeus, is strangled to death. The human projection of the god thus arrives dead; even alive, the name "Bursitis" would have made the god a sign of human strain and incapacity. Allen's telegram to his characters at the end of the play pronounces man liberated from all sense of divine limitation: "God is dead. Stop. You're on your own."

After Allen's dissection of man's processes and reasons for inventing gods to dominate him, two paradoxes remain. First, whether God made man or man made God, the characters in *God* are created in the image of Woody Allen, and there is a playful anthropomorphy in the way they are imbued with the familiar traits of the Allen persona. Thus the Writer has the persona's defeatist lechery when he proposes to Doris: "Can we lower the curtain here? Just for five minutes . . . It'll be a quickie." The Actor has the persona's fastidiousness. His character, Phidipides, "longed for one thing . . . To be taller," and at the prospect of "personal freedom" he grows "nauseous." Even Doris Levine shows the very pretentiousness of which she accuses Allen, in her remark that "so often people think they grasp reality when what they're really responding to is 'fake-ositude.' "

The second paradox is that the play does not end in the liberty that the characters have achieved. Rather, it ends as it began, with mortals looking for an ending to a play. Diabetes and Hepatitis recoil from their newly won freedom and settle back into their familiar uncertainties about how their play will end. Although Allen has liberated his characters, they fear the meaninglessness of an unscripted life. If God is dead, man will invent another.

The Query

Allen's analysis of the functions of comedy centers on an anecdote involving Abraham Lincoln.[5] In the first scene Lincoln asks his press secretary (!) to plant a question at his next press conference: "How long do you think a man's legs should be?" This will allow Lincoln to make the same witty reply—"Long enough to reach the ground" —that he made when a farmer named Will Haines urgently interrupted the President's conversation with his cabinet to ask that question.

In the second scene Lincoln paces around his bedroom in remorse at having handled the question so flippantly. As he recalls the farmer's imploring eyes, Lincoln regrets that he "didn't respond to the human being. I was too preoccupied with getting the quick laugh." True to tradition, Mary Todd Lincoln is less than understanding. Indeed, she even mistakes her husband's punch line: "Your answer was clever. Long enough to reach his torso."

The difference between the two versions is instructive. Mary Lincoln's version involves the idea of climbing or aspiration (legs rising to a torso); Lincoln's wording affirms the virtues of steadfastness (both feet on the ground). Although Lincoln's joke was made in a flippant spirit, it expresses his gravity. Indeed, it is because the values implicit in the joke are important to Lincoln that he regrets having made it. Lincoln is here the comic artist, for he naturally expresses his vision and his values through comedy. As he is also a man of serious purpose, however, he doubts the appropriateness of his comic art.

This scene between the Lincolns is parallelled by the third scene, between Will Haines and his wife. We learn that Haines had ridden to beg Lincoln to pardon their son, Andrew, who was sentenced to death for falling asleep while on guard duty. Haines himself wonders why his compelling purpose was deflected into a silly riddle. He blames it on his nervousness. But his wife suggests a harsher motivation, that he did not want the pardon because he is jealous of his son, who is stronger and a better farmer. The son has "a feel for the soil like no man I've seen," but the father is "a lousy farmer," she avows. Haines admits this is true:

> I hate farming! The seeds all look alike to me! And the soil!
> I can never tell it apart from dirt! . . . I plant turnips and corn
> comes up! You think that doesn't hurt a man?

Haines was doubly served by his comic riddle. It allowed him to evade direct expression of an uncomfortable truth and then, by expressing the truth indirectly, the riddle enabled him eventually to confront it.

The play concludes with Lincoln arriving to ask Haines to explain his riddle. When the truth is revealed, both men weep and admit that the incident has caused them to reevaluate their lives. Moreover, the joke prepared Lincoln to grant Haines's request. For if a man's legs should be long enough to reach the ground, then a man should not be hanged for falling asleep. In Lincoln's flippant reply lay the spirit in which he would ultimately pardon the boy. Haines's seemingly irrelevant riddle contained a general proposition of which his son's case was a specific example.

In *The Query* Allen dramatizes the several functions of comedy. It can discover a truth or an emotion of which the speaker is unaware. This the riddle did for Haines, and the reply did for Lincoln. Comedy can release a tension caused by social or personal inhibitions. Furthermore, there is a spirit of community in comedy. The joke brings President Lincoln and Farmer Haines together. In a lower key, Lincoln planned to use the joke to impress the journalists because he had earlier found that it softened his antagonistic cabinet. Moreover, the joke prepares for the pardon. Thus Allen views the comedian the way Shelley regarded the poet—as the unacknowledged legislator of mankind. Comedy confronts the deepest tensions, it prepares the spirit for sympathy and understanding, and it is the compulsive activity of those who feel things the most intensely.

Lincoln closes the play with another joke—"Do you guys have anything to eat? A man travels so many miles, at least offer him something"—that draws more on Allen's modern Jewish character than on the Illinois backwoodsman or president. Here an iconic president and a *schlemiel* both find the comic form their natural mode of perception, expression, and understanding.

Part Three

Woody the Writer

Even if Woody Allen had not written his plays and made his movies, his short prose works would entitle him to consideration as a major American humorist. He writes occasionally for *Playboy*, *Esquire*, and the *New York Times*, but his most ambitious prose humor has appeared in *The New Yorker* and *The New Republic*. The two collections of these works, *Getting Even* (1971) and *Without Feathers* (1974), were bestsellers.

6

The Pose behind the Prose

Although in his writing Allen cannot exploit the consistent effect of his face and voice, one can sense his persona behind the prose. Allen still projects the image of a short, paranoid loser, with sexual and intellectual pretensions, a man who exists on the fringe of an unsympathetic and absurd world, and who is both teased and satisfied by improbable dreams. Therefore the forms of parody and mock-heroic satire are as common in Allen's prose as in his monologues, plays, and films.

The characters in Allen's prose are often short and suffer from feelings of inferiority and sexual inadequacy. The hero of "No Kaddish for Weinstein" is typical.[1] He feels inadequate because he stands only five-foot-four in his stocking feet ("although in someone else's stocking feet he could be as tall as five-six"), and he becomes impotent with women who finished college with a B average or who can type more than sixty words a minute. In another piece, one of dramatist Jorgen Lovborg's characters wrathfully informs her husband of a secret that only she and his mother know: he is a forty-eight-inch dwarf, whose house and furnishings have been built to scale.[2] This character embodies the male dread that his adequacy and self-respect are insecurely based on the women with whom he is most intimate.

The motif relates to Allen's wider anxiety. In "My Philosophy" he cites a book titled "Critique of Pure Dread"; the "Dread" seems a proper substitute for the "Reason" in the title of Immanuel Kant's famous *Critique*.[3] In "Conversations with Helmholtz," the Freudian psychoanalyst who "proved that death is an acquired trait" has a disciple named Fears Hoffnung.[4] This name combines the opposites, fear (Fears) and hope (Hoffnung). Hope is the family name, the native condition; fear is the personal individuation, the acquired trait.

The very titles of Allen's two anthologies express his persona's paranoia. *Getting Even* implies the underdog's revenge on a world of abusive superiors. The biography on the wrapper reports that Allen's "one regret in life is that he is not someone else"—a rather basic dissatisfaction. *Without Feathers* derives from a poem by Emily Dickinson: "Hope is the thing with feathers." The implication is that man is a hopeless creature, without feathers.

But in the first piece Allen refutes the quotation:

> How wrong Emily Dickinson was! Hope is not "the thing with feathers." The thing with feathers has turned out to be my nephew. I must take him to a specialist in Zurich.

This image of a feathered humanity, winged for a flight of the spirit, relates to a variety of bird and animal jokes in "Selections from the Allen Notebooks." [5] For example, one man finds his parrot has been made Secretary of Agriculture. Allen's father predicts that the only writing he will do is "in collaboration with an owl" (whodunits perhaps?). In these fantasies, animals transcend their limitations but man cannot. The odd human with hope (feathers) must be taken to Zurich to be cured!

In Allen's prose fantasies, man usually experiences only defeat and humiliation. Thus Allen wonders how he can believe in God "when just last week I got my tongue caught in the roller of an electric typewriter"—so much for the writer's attempt to transcend his mortal limits through art. By contrast, "some beavers take over Carnegie Hall and perform *Wozzeck*." Allen's fantasies of animal success remind us of human failure. Lacking the animals' power of metamorphosis, man's only hope is self-reliance: "A man awakens in the morning and finds himself transformed into his own arch-supports." Unable to escape his own nature, man is his own arch support—or enemy.

The comic metamorphoses in *Without Feathers* show man hopelessly rooted in his own nature. For instance, in "A Guide to Some of the Lesser Ballets," Sigmund falls in love with the leader of a pack of swans.[6] Because she is "part swan and part woman—unfortunately, divided lengthwise," Sigmund plans instead to wed the beautiful Justine, who "has no major drawbacks like feathers or a beak." The swan-woman runs headlong into a brick wall, because only death can lift the spell on her. As Sigmund watches her return to beautiful but dead womanhood, he "realizes how bittersweet life can be, particularly for fowl." Resolving to join her in death, he does a delicate dance of mourning, then swallows a barbell. Unable to acquire feathers and soar, Sigmund ingests weight and sinks.

In the book's last selection, "Slang Origins," Allen's etymology for the phrase "take it on the lam" explicitly relates feathered metamorphosis to human transcendence:

> Gradually any game with feathers was called "lamming" and feathers became "lams." To "take it on the lam" meant to put on feathers and later, to escape, although the transition is unclear.[7]

Allen's jokes about metamorphosis are fantasy equivalents to these games in which man puts on feathers to escape his hopelessness (i.e., takes it on the lam). In this vein, one character in "Lovborg's Women Considered" is bored by her husband's "habit of wearing feathers to dinner" and sickened by his middle-class mentality. The husband's name is Moltvick (the molting?). Another of Lovborg's characters, who calls his wife "nightingale! Yes, and sometimes thrush! And hippo!" must be warned that "he can never fly by flapping his arms."

Although these collected pieces were written and published separately, Allen's antic imagery has a personal consistency: man's hopelessness is reflected in his lack of feathers. Bird he never was, so he can only be a blithe spirit if he deludes himself with mad fantasy or flights of metaphor.

The Allen persona's familiar despair is also expressed in the spectacular defeats his characters suffer. In "Count Dracula," the vampire's dinner appointment happens to occur on the day of an eclipse of the sun.[8] Thus Dracula mistakenly emerges seven hours early and dissolves into a pile of white ash; his simple, hearty hosts survive in their innocence, unknowingly protected by the cosmos.

When an Allen character does enjoy success, it is either freakish or hallucinatory. For example, in "Reminiscences" a list of failures culminates in an improbable success—Juan, "a simple pig farmer who could not write his name but somehow managed to defraud I.T.T. out of six million dollars." [9] So bleak is Allen's world view that any success must be this implausible. Also in "Reminiscences," a genre normally characterized by nostalgic delights becomes a chronicle of absurd surprises: a stifling Brooklyn summer's day receives a massive snowfall; a pretzel seller is chased up a tree by vicious dogs—only to find more dogs at the top of the tree. Allen's prose establishes a world of instability and disorder.

Allen's fullest assertion of social disorder is "Confessions of a Burglar." [10] Here Allen posits a criminal world as ritualized and normative as legitimate society. As the burglar describes his early career,

> Where I grew up, you had to steal to eat. Then you had to steal to tip. Lots of guys stole fifteen per cent, but I always stole twenty, which made me a big favorite among the waiters.

The first joke depends on a shift from one sense of "to eat"—survival nourishment—to another—the luxury of restaurant dining, which in the gangster film signifies success. Further, stealing is presented as a social convention, like tipping. In the same vein, the hero's father was a bank robber until he reached the age of mandatory retirement. He "spent his last few years in mail fraud, but the postal rates went up and he lost everything." The norms of social behavior apply even among outlaws. Moreover, legal institutions are based on a profit impulse that eventually overwhelms attempts at individual fraud.

In the climax of "Confessions," the reader is advised that if he catches a burglar, he should "seize the initiative" and rob the burglar: "Then he can get into your bed while you make your getaway." Our hero reports that once when he was "trapped by this defense," he spent six years in Des Moines with another man's wife and children, until he was "fortunate enough to surprise another burglar," who took his place. This passage suggests that normal citizens crave escape into crime; that is why they read such "Confessions." Therefore Allen's burglar opens with sentimental memories of his own family and concludes with the dubious delights of a six-year sentence to Des Moines normalcy:

> The six years I lived with that family were very happy ones, and I often look back upon them with affection, although there is also much to be said for working on a chain gang.

The insider's normal family life and the outsider's crime and punishment are both ambivalent mixes of community and isolation.

True to form, Allen's burglar is such an outsider, even among the outlaws, that he is not at ease with the argot. One joke pattern involves his taking an underworld colloquialism literally. As a result, his "you had to steal to eat" quite naturally led to "you had to steal to tip." Similarly, his sister "married money. Not an actual human being—it was a pile of singles." When our hero works with "jelly," it is not the expected explosive; he transplants jelly from stale doughnuts to fresh ones. Finally, he cannot follow Raffles's example and become a cat burglar because the whiskers make him sneeze. The jokes suggest not only that Allen's burglar lacks the expertise to which he pretends—he uses familiar underworld language without knowing its specialized meaning—but that he remains an outsider even among outsiders. Here as elsewhere Allen asserts his image of a frail loser pretending to heroism but failing to achieve even adequacy.

As in the example of the burglar's "Confession," Allen's prose parody often assumes a writing style or genre, then undermines it. There is usually a satiric intention. In "Confessions" Allen satirizes the normal citizen's fascination with crime. In "Spring Bulletin" Allen parodies a college catalogue of "extension courses." [11] When he declares himself an "unextended adult" and then refers to "a catalogue of Hong Kong honeymoon accessories," the suggestion is that the courses and the erotic devices are equivalent means of "extending" oneself artificially for seductive purposes.

The piece satirizes the false pretenses often found in higher education. Much of this education is innocent of content. Thus the rapid reading course ultimately eliminates the entire text from the reader's vision. The musicology course teaches the student to play Yankee Doodle Dandy, then the Brandenburg Concertos, and then Yankee Doodle Dandy again, implying that this course is a circular business that leads nowhere. So, too, the social work course teaches "how to organize street gangs into basketball teams, and vice-versa."

In other pieces Allen parodies specific kinds of scholarship. In "But Soft . . . Real Soft," an exercise in choplogic is made plausible by its base in oddities of literary history.[12] For instance, categories are constantly changing. Thus "We all realize Shakespeare (Marlowe) borrowed his plots from the ancients (moderns)." There is a body of argument that attributes Shakespeare's writings to other hands, including Christopher Marlowe's. (For a sample, the reader might read 'Shakespeare' Identified, by the happily named J. Thomas Looney [New York, 1920].) Then, too, the "moderns" in one age are the "ancients" to another. This confusion in titles leads to a series of confusions in names:

> Ben Jonson is not to be confused with Samuel Johnson. He was Samuel Johnson. Samuel Johnson was not. Samuel Johnson was Samuel Pepys. . . . This all becomes clearer when we realize that George Eliot was a woman.

—and she was! Allen shows how easily oddities of fact can be adduced to prove ludicrous arguments. This is also the point in his tortuous explanations of "Slang Origins," where the simple "fiddlesticks" is traced back to something abstruse: "Whenever a man in the banking profession announced his marriage to a circus pinhead, it was the custom for friends to present him with a bellows and a three-year supply of wax fruit." Here common sense is abandoned for fantastical pedantry.

Often Allen parodies kinds of fiction. His "No Kaddish for Weinstein" parodies the self-analytical monologues of a below-Bellow intellectual, who "suffered untold injustices and persecutions because of his religic , mostly from his parents." Even though they are Jewish, "they could never accept the fact that their son was Jewish." Allen reverses the familiar themes of alienation, assimilation, and parental pressures in contemporary Jewish-American fiction.

"The Condemned" burlesques the entire range of existentialist concerns.[13] Although it begins as a murderer's rumination, in the manner of Albert Camus's *The Stranger*, its philosophy soon gives way to practical considerations:

> He's dreaming, Cloquet thought, as he stood over him, re-volver in hand. *He's* dreaming, and I exist in reality. Cloquet

> hated reality but realized it was still the only place to get a good steak.

Even the hero's ineffable will to live is undercut:

> Always, from some inner region, we hear the command, "Keep Living!" Cloquet recognized the voice; it was his insurance salesman. Naturally, he thought—Fishbein doesn't want to pay off.

From Camus, Allen veers into Sartre when his hero is overwhelmed by "an existential nausea, caused by his intense awareness of the contingency of life." This nausea requires "an Existential Alka-Seltzer," sold in Left Bank drugstores, "an enormous pill, the size of an automobile hubcap." From Sartre, the tone shifts into Marx Brothers when Cloquet's trial is compared to a circus ("although there was some difficulty in getting the elephants into the courtroom") and when his appeal for clemency is rejected because his lawyer "filed it while wearing a cardboard mustache." This scene evokes the trial in *Duck Soup* (1933), with Groucho's false mustache and Chico's confusion between the "relevance" of a courtroom and the "whole lotter elephants in the circus."

In "Reminiscences" Allen satirizes literary memoirs of insignificant trivia. After a plethora of surreal memories comes a splatter of name droppings; then the author recalls his first novel, tellingly titled *Proud Emetic*. He claims that "Willie" (Somerset Maugham) confessed intimate details about his own creative processes:

> I wrote "The Razor's Edge" while wearing a paper hat. In the first draft of "Rain," Sadie Thompson was a parrot. We grope. We take risks.

The supposed Maugham's closing advice—that the effectiveness of an interrogatory sentence can be increased by the use of a question mark—suggests that all in all a writer's "reminiscences" are of dubious value. Memoirs should be questioned.

"A Twenties Memory" is a memoir by someone who hobnobbed with the great artists but had no understanding of their work or language.[14] The writer betrays his literary pretensions by misusing terms. For example, he was "working on what I felt was a major American novel but the print was too small and I couldn't get through it." In the same vein, Juan Gris "began to break [Alice Toklas's] face and body down into its basic geometrical forms until the police came and pulled him off." Salvador Dali's "one-man show" proved "a huge success, as one man showed up." And Picasso "had a funny way of walking by putting one foot in front of the other until he would take what he called a 'step'." Memoirs attend to irrelevant trivia about the artists, but do not illuminate their art.

This point is also made here: "Matisse was commissioned to paint an allegory, but with his wife's illness, it remained unpainted and was finally wallpapered instead." The first joke is that the pretentious writer uses "paint" as redecoration, not art. The second derives from Allen's specifying "allegory." As it is the nature of allegory to express itself indirectly—it conceals its subject—it is fitting for an allegory to be wallpapered. The form involves a kind of overlay. Though the joke suggests the fugitive relationship between art and reality, the narrator's literal use of literary and artistic terms reveals his inability to cope with his subject matter. Thus the narrator of "A Twenties Memory" imposes his ignorance on his material in the same way that the harum-scarum analysis in "Slang Origins" can be traced to that narrator's admission that time did not allow him to research the subject properly—so his etymologies are based on "information from friends" and his own "common sense"—which proves to be uncommon nonsense.

A similar point is made in "A Little Louder, Please." [15] The narrator, whose pretentious dabbling, insensitivity, and hyperactive imagination render him incapable of understanding mime, babbles arrant nonsense:

> Finally, the mime began blowing glass. Either blowing glass or tattooing the student body of Northwestern University. It seemed like the student body of Northwestern University, but it could have been the men's choir—or a diathermy machine—or any large, extinct quadruped, often amphibious and usually herbivorous, the fossilized remains of which have been found as far north as the Arctic.

What begins as a response to an artistic endeavor quickly degenerates into irrelevant pedantry. The first line of the piece establishes the character's conflicting energies and enthusiasms:

> Understand you are dealing with a man who knocked off
> *Finnegans Wake* on the roller coaster at Coney Island, penetrat-
> ing the abstruse Joycean arcana with ease, despite enough
> violent lurching to shake loose my silver fillings.

Allen's target is the zippy dilettante unable to appreciate or concen-
trate on what is basic in art. He is a variation on the now familiar
outsider, unable to understand the language of the group he yearns
to join. But this time the satire is specifically directed against those
who impose their uncontrolled associations on the art to which they
should submit themselves. It is a sobering warning to anyone pre-
sumptuous enough to write a critical analysis of Woody Allen's
comedy.

In "Fabrizio's: Criticism and Response," Allen parodies a restaurant review and the ensuing letters from readers.[16] The piece is
Allen's rebuttal to the critics of his first noncomic film, *Interiors*
(1978). The reviewer complains about Fabrizio's surprising green
fettucine:

> Why? It all seems so gratuitous. As customers, we are not
> prepared for the change. Hence, the green noodle does not
> amuse us. It's disconcerting in a way unintended by the chef.

Roughly the same objections were raised against the new direction in
Allen's work. Here the different letter writers represent different
biases against the work in question; none is prepared to accept the
work on its own terms. Overall there is a pretentiousness and earnest-
ness that threaten to smother all enjoyment of the food and that
trivialize the political, philosophical, and aesthetic contexts to which
the food can be referred.

In "The Metterling Lists" Allen satirizes the biographer's predatory invasion of an author's private life.[17] When Allen has the (in-
structively named) Venal and Sons publish the first volume of *The
Collected Laundry Lists of Hans Metterling*, he satirizes the pseudo-
scholarship of approaching an artist through the domestic minutiae
of his day-to-day life. He may have had the "scholarly" Kafka industry in mind, but many artists have suffered the public laundering
of their private lives. Allen's article on "The Metterling Lists" is a
parody book review of this supposedly insightful research text. One
finds in it the usual tone of uncritical adoration, the usual dollop of

quotation, and even the traditional hint of gossip. Throughout the review Allen mingles inventions with allusions to real figures and works. For example, it is plausible that in the process of reworking Biblical myths Thomas Mann might have written a play called *The Hosiery of Moses* (it might have had a run on Broadway). He also refers to Metterling's associations with well-known psychoanalysts. For example, after we learn that Metterling "believed that he was either being followed or was following somebody," we are informed that Sigmund Freud "would never let Metterling get behind him."

Allen was quick to pounce on the fad that followed Eric Von Daniken's speculations about visitors from outer space. In "The UFO Menace" Allen demonstrates how idle speculation can be paraded as fact.[18] He claims to quote from Leviticus: "And an great and silver ball appeared over the Assyrian Armies, and in all of Babylonia there was wailing and gnashing of teeth, till the Prophets bade the multitudes get a grip on themselves and shape up." Allen pretends to historicity with a grammatical error—"*an* great and silver ball"—but the archaic language dwindles into modernity. In "The Scrolls," the archaeologists' dating of the material as 4,000 B.C. falls into "great doubt" when the word "Oldsmobile" is found several times in the text.[19]

In "The Schmeed Memoirs" Allen parodied the spate of Nazi reminiscences, especially the autobiography of Albert Speer.[20] Schmeed makes the usual Nazi rationalizations: A simple barber, he pleads ignorance about what was going on at the time. He did not know Hitler was a Nazi; he thought he worked for the phone company. Then there is the argument of personal needs—when our hero found out what Hitler was, "it was too late to do anything, as I had made a down payment on some furniture." At one point he had considered such subversive activities as "loosening the Fuhrer's neck-napkin and allowing some tiny hairs to get down his back," but at the last minute his nerve failed him.

Schmeed's claim that he was an insignificant cog in the monstrous Nazi mechanism is undermined by his pretense to historical importance. He expresses delusions of military grandeur: "Bormann wanted a shave, and I promised him I would get to work on some blueprints." Hitler is reported obsessed with the fear that Churchill might grow sideburns more quickly than he, so he somewhat perversely threatens a blockade to cut off England's supply of hot towels and has Speer "triple our output of shaving cream by the fall."

The satire here cuts several ways. In his barber's-eye view, Allen parodies the muddle of vanity and false humility in most Nazi memoirs. He also deflates the pretense of offering new insights into the military strategy. Finally, he specifically undermines Speer's attempt to reconcile his considerable contribution to the Nazi cause with his supposed detachment from its brutal aspects. Brilliantly capturing the mixture of the monstrous and the petty that characterizes memoirs of that time, Allen provides a comic version of the horrible banality of evil. His barber is a bracing antidote to the sentimentality of Chaplin's barber in *The Great Dictator* (1940).

As parody is Allen's characteristic prose form, bathos is his characteristic tone. The two are related kinds of ironic undercutting. Parody is a comic version of a serious work or stance; bathos is the plunge from a lofty tone to a trivial one.

Bathos is the basic rhetorical device in "The UFO Menace," as these samples demonstrate:

> Professor Leon Specimen postulates a civilization in outer space that is more advanced than ours by approximately fifteen minutes. This, he feels, gives them a great advantage over us since they needn't rush to get to appointments.

> Travelers moving at close to the speed of light would require many millions of years to get here, . . . and judging from the shows on Broadway, the trip would hardly be worth it.

What begins as consideration of a far-reaching concept is immediately reduced to matters of trivial concern. Allen points the difficulty most of us experience in integrating abstract concepts that have no immediate relationship to our everyday lives. In this spirit he involves his lecherous persona here:

> [The universe] is expanding and will one day break apart and disappear. That is why if the girl in the office down the hall has some good points but perhaps not all the qualities you require it's best to compromise.

An abstract threat is reduced to an immediate concern. Similarly, the visitors from outer space described at the end of the article are plausible projections of the strange people who claim to have seen them. "The UFO Menace" deals less with the possibility of visits from outer space than with our own anxieties and pressing needs.

Whenever Allen's characters speculate about metaphysical topics, they are brought back down to the rub of their physical existence. Thus in "The Condemned" Cloquet recognizes the difference between Being and Being-in-the-World but concludes that "no matter which group he belonged to, the other was having more fun." In "Remembering Needleman" the eulogized philosopher based his ethics on the theory that "good and just behavior is not only more moral but could be done by phone." [21] In "By Destiny Denied" Allen is "struck by an almost existential feeling of purposelessness—particularly since the massage parlors closed." [22] Allen progresses from a sweeping abstract to a petty particular.

However curious Allen's character may be about the world beyond, he is limited to his own experience and needs. In "Examining Psychic Phenomena": "There is no question that there is an unseen world. The problem is, how far is it from midtown and how late is it open?" [23] In "My Philosophy," a series of philosophical observations, each ends on a note of bathos or anticlimax:

> The universe is merely a fleeting idea in God's mind—a pretty uncomfortable thought, particularly if you've just made a down payment on a house.

> Can we actually "know" the universe? My God, it's hard enough finding your way around in Chinatown.

Allen deflates every venture into philosophy, making material and practical considerations the inescapable weight on every thought. Thus his economic theory course in "Spring Bulletin" turns from the usual academic concerns to a rare practicality: "Inflation and Depression—how to dress for each. Loans, interest, welching."

Allen's reflexive bathos crops up even in incidental phrases and situations: a magician sending his charges to the four corners of the earth advises that they go in the off-season "as three of the corners are usually booked." [24] Here the language of fable dwindles to that of a travel brochure. Bathetic collisions between discordant contexts can be found in: "Notes from the Overfed"—which a subheading informs us resulted from "reading Dostoevski and the new *Weight*

Watchers magazine on the same plane trip"; [25] If the Impressionists Had Been Dentists"; [26] and Allen's passing reference to *"Sight and Stream,* a cerebral quarterly dedicated to advanced concepts in cinema and fresh-water fishing." [27]

Consistent with Allen's parody and ironic undercutting is the tendency of his prose to center around extremely unheroic figures that assume heroic stances. Obvious examples include Schmeed, the pretentious Nazi barber, and the Camusian hero Cloquet, who "teaches Psychology of Fowl at the Sorbonne." On a larger scale, in "Viva Vargas!" Allen develops a mock-heroic imitation of the Castro revolutionaries.[28] In Allen's revolution every action ends in disaster, for, after all, the Vargas brothers, two ardent debaters and strategists, "were only last week a couple of men's room attendants at the local Hilton." As he watches the army's continual failures, the diarist valiantly tries to convert human flaws into heroic virtues. Thus "we decided to switch tactics and see if grovelling would work." Later the rebels reevaluated their position, determined "to panic and bolted in all directions." The piece is quintessential Allen: a band of losers pretend to be revolutionary heroes, despite their staggering failures. Their heroism survives only in their language.

Allen's most complex mock-heroic article is "Yes, But Can the Steam Engine Do This?" [29] The piece begins as if it were to concern itself with the writer's Kafkaesque hound, a beagle named Joseph K., but it becomes a parody of historical biography. Allen tells the heroic saga of how the Earl of Sandwich invented the sandwich. Allen's prose suggests a magnificent, laborious undertaking, and the Earl is portrayed as a true artist struggling through various obstacles to a heroic breakthrough.

The Earl is shown as obsessed with food. His graduating thesis deals with "The Analysis and Attendant Phenomena of Snacks" and at Cambridge he is charged with stealing loaves of bread for use in "unnatural experiments." These details parody familiar elements in the Hollywood films about questing (and mad) scientists. Hard upon his commitment to "the juxtaposition of foodstuffs"—a mock-heroic term for making a sandwich—our hero meets the suggestively named greengrocer's daughter, Nell Smallbore, who "is to teach him all he will ever know about lettuce."

Because the Earl is an Allen hero, his discovery of the sandwich follows a tortuous route. His first attempt is "a slice of bread, a slice of bread on top of that, and a slice of turkey on top of both." Then he tries two slices of turkey around one of bread. Truer to the heroic genre than to logic, "he works day and night, often skimping on meals to save money for food." This artist even arouses "scandal" when he introduces an open, hot, roast-beef sandwich on which the steaming meat is nakedly exposed.

Elevating the sandwich to the complexity of a scientific find and a work of art, Allen's mock-heroic form presents a commonplace act as a heroic quest, the stages of which are presented in ludicrous detail. That is to say, the act is amplified and then shrunk by the diminutive details.

At the end the narrator admits that his heroic saga may be an illusion. Not only is his grasp of history "a bit shaky," but his "capacity for romanticizing easily dwarfs that of the average acidhead." This confession explains the seemingly irrelevant title ("Yes, But Can the Steam Engine Do This?") and the equally unrelated introduction involving the narrator's beagle. The title suggests that human creativity is superior to mechanical performance, however laborious and inefficient man's effort may be. The exaggerated saga of the sandwich is not history, but a frank "romanticizing" that extols the virtue of the human effort over the mechanical. Without the solace of such myths, man might sink to the miseries of Joseph K., the beagle who visits a Jungian veterinarian in order to be assured "that jowls are not a social drawback." Heroic myths are vital consolations for people who might otherwise feel down-at-the-mouth about the human condition. Unlike machines, man needs—and can create—myths that magnify human achievement.

7

Woody's Wide, Wild World

Woody Allen's prose humor deals with a wide range of topics in politics, philosophy, religion, fantasy, and culture, both the high and the low. In ranging so widely for his material, Allen acknowledges the influence of Mort Sahl, the "original genius who revolutionized the medium," who brought "genuine insights" to his stand-up comedy, and who "made the country receptive to a kind of comedy that it wasn't used to hearing." [1]

But Allen was never as openly political as Sahl. Indeed a *Time* reporter found the monologuist Allen "not only an interesting new comedian but a rare one as well: he never mentions John F. Kennedy." [2] In his prose Allen occasionally raises political issues, especially in his work for *The New Republic*. In "Nefarious Times We Live In" (as one may or may not infer from the title) he zeroes in on American paranoia following Watergate.[3] The hero is Willard Pogrebin, who is programmed to assassinate President Ford but bungles the attempt. At first the president is not identified by name so the story develops as a general fantasy. The paranoia is given a local habitation by the naming of Patty (Hearst) and (Jimmy) Hoffa. This prepares for the climax: "President Gerald Ford shook my hand and asked if I would follow him around the country and take a shot at him now and then, being careful to miss." This, Ford explains, would enable him to act bravely and distract the nation's attention "from genuine issues, which he felt unequipped to deal with."

American political lunacy had caught up with Allen's wild fantasy and made it plausible that his accident-prone loser could join forces with America's accident-prone president.

Pogrebin is a victim of 1970s social phenomena rather than of his own inadequacies. He suffers medical abuse and force-feedings first in the U.S. army and then in a Manson-type commune. The parallel continues: the army discharges Pogrebin when he "could no longer tell the difference between [his] brother Morris and two soft-boiled eggs"; at the end of his commune experience he is arrested for trying to marry an oyster. The establishment (the army) and the anti-establishment (the commune) have both obscured human nature. Even liberation by psychological therapy is presented as a fascist oppression when Pogrebin is trapped in a concentration camp run by a macabre therapist named Perlemutter, "a doctor of the mind." As 1970s America sees the Allen persona's paranoid fears become actualities, no matter where Pogrebin turns, attempts are made to doctor his brain, which is washed until it shrinks beyond repair.

Pogrebin began as a modest artist "with no pronounced political convictions," but his saga demonstrates that it is impossible for an artist to remain remote from politics. The political abuse of Pogrebin is attended by telling allusions to art: a poisoned dart makes him look like Salvador Dali; he survives a Sumo assault by believing himself to be Igor Stravinsky; and after he is the victim of crossed electro-shock wires, he costars with several chimpanzees in a performance of *The Cherry Orchard*. Though the first two references may locate the artist in nonpolitical revolutions, the familiar "cherry" pun in the play title suggests his violated innocence. The horror of Pogrebin's saga is the passive citizen's (and uncommitted artist's) discovery that he has been manipulated and abused by violent forces along the entire spectrum of political activity.

Such topicality is rare in Allen's political works. More often he deals with processes of political argument. For example, in "Remembering Needleman" a mock eulogy turns into an ironic demonstration of how a horrifying, inhuman, and irresponsible philosophy can be rationalized. Though Needleman was obviously a moronic Nazi, the speaker nevertheless claims heroic virtues for him.

Needleman managed to offend everyone. Harvard dismissed him for his Communist sympathies, but then he alienated the left by testifying for the House Un-American Activities Committee. He justified this compromise by arguing that "political actions have no moral consequences but exist outside of the realm of true Being."

An irresponsible academic, Needleman dabbled in politics without principle, integrity, or self-knowledge. Allen makes it clear that academic study cannot be detached from real political consequences, nor political theory from its real effects. Denying responsibility for the consequences of his theories, Needleman goes so far as to rationalize away existence itself:

> After much reflection, Needleman's intellectual integrity convinced him that he didn't exist, his friends didn't exist, and the only thing that was real was his I.O.U. to the bank for six million marks.

The precise sum of Needleman's debt, the six million marks, is the Nazi toll of Jewish lives. Thus Allen recalls the real consequences of Nazi politics in the very phrase by which Needleman tries to absolve himself of responsibility. Attracted to the Brownshirts because the color set off his eyes, Needleman represents the vanity of espousing a policy without accepting responsibility for its effects. Refusing to relate cause and effect, he turns an error into a pattern of behavior. "Too proud to admit it was a mistake," when he once fell out of his box at an opera, "he attended the opera every night for a month and repeated it each time." These rationalizations and self-destructive illusions are cited by the eulogist as examples of academic brilliance.

Allen has said that he is not interested in politics because he is "preoccupied with basic questions, like why are we here, where did we come from and where do we go later." He follows politics "just enough to kid around about it," but he considers it "an aimless shuffling of group leaders" that does not deal with "the really major issues." [4] Differences in party politics diminish in the face of Allen's philosophical concerns—death, the existence of God, and the dubious validity of man's logical processes.

Allen's obsession with death is everywhere apparent. In "A Guide to Some of the Lesser Ballets," *The Sacrifice* begins as follows: "A melodic prelude recounts man's relation to the earth and why he always seems to wind up in it." This statement expresses not only Allen's fatalistic vision of life, but the essential dynamic of his prose style. His bathetic undertow expresses the downward thrust of life. When Allen observes in "My Philosophy" that "it is impossible to experience one's own death objectively and still carry a tune" the singer carries the burden of song against the pull of death.

While there is a rare cheeriness in Allen's description of a New Orleans funeral in "Reminiscences," the funeral is one without death. Amid the parade and dancing someone realizes that the man who was buried was not dead. Or even sick: "he was yodelling at the time." While the band plays on, each onlooker is buried in turn "on the theory that the deceased will go down the smoothest." When it finally becomes apparent that no one has died, "it is too late to get a body, because of the holiday rush." The joy here is possible only because the celebrants are not dealing with death as the terminal fact of the human experience.

One common armament against death is the belief in an afterlife. Although Allen often considers the idea, he usually presents it as unlikely. However, in "Conversations with Helmholtz" he leaves some doubt when he reports that Freud's death "was the event that caused the final break between Helmholtz and Freud, and the two rarely spoke afterwards." "Rarely," that is, not "never." Any afterlife that Allen imagines is dominated by the everyday concerns of this life. "I keep wondering if there is an afterlife, and if there is will they be able to break a twenty?" And again:

> What *is* it about death that bothers me so much? Probably the hours. Melnick says the soul is immortal and lives on after the body drops away, but if my soul exists without my body I am convinced all my clothes will be loose-fitting.[5]

Allen's uncertainty about the prospect of an afterlife relates to his wider doubts about the existence of God. God is made in the image of man when Allen modifies familiar Bible stories in "The Scrolls." His Job corrects God's spelling (" 'tabernacle' has only one *l*") and prays to Him: "Thine is the kingdom and the power and glory. Thou hast a good job. Don't blow it." In another story, God gives a man practical advice on how to make his shirts more salable ("Put an alligator over the pocket"). So human a God suggests the writer's uncertainty rather than his faith. This tentative belief becomes the basis of the hero's gluttony in "Notes from the Overfed." The hero is struck by his uncle's question: "Do you believe in God? . . . And if so, what do you think he weighs?" On the principle that God is everywhere, including in food, the protagonist eats everything in sight. He tries to escape his sense of his own physical nature by consuming godhead: "I last saw my feet one Thursday morning in Vitebsk."

Allen's fullest treatment of this uncertainty is in his private-eye parody, "Mr. Big." [6] Kaiser Lupowitz, Allen's hard-boiled, Bogartian detective, is hired by a sexy woman to find God. True to the genre, the woman turns out to be untrustworthy. She claims to be a nude model with the cheeky name of Heather Butkiss, but she is later identified as a Vassar philosophy major named Claire Rosenzweig, then as a Radcliffe teacher, and finally as Ellen Shepherd, a Bryn Mawr physics professor. Her identities as libertine, academic, and scientist represent three different concerns about God's existence. As Lupowitz eventually discovers, this woman gained access to God by posing as a pantheist, then killed Him at a party populated with characters from *The Maltese Falcon*. As the character seeking God is His killer, the very search, the act of doubt, may constitute the murder.

Before Lupowitz can solve the case he must confront the usual suspects, witnesses, and authorities. One is a rabbi who has rather material grounds for his faith in God's existence:

> "How do I know? What kind of question is that? Could I get a suit like this for fourteen dollars if there was no one up there? Here, feel a gabardine—how can you doubt?"

Then there is Chicago Phil, whose Italian connection relates him to Catholicism: "There's no Mr. Big. It's a syndicate. Mostly Sicilian. It's international. But there is no actual head. Except maybe the Pope." Next comes the obligatory homicide detective, Reed, who deduces that God was murdered by an existentialist in a crime of passion. (The detective's name may be an allusion to Pascal's *Pensée*: "Man is but a reed, the weakest in nature, but he is a thinking reed" [II, 10]. Of all the characters interviewed, only Reed practices logical deduction, and his conclusion blames the antithesis to his logic: passion.)

These characters, together with the setting, the language, and the other formal elements of the detective story, provide a worldly context for Allen's search for God. The very form of the private-eye allegory is part of Allen's meaning. For as soon as the private eye is assigned his quest we know that God is dead; there has to be a murder victim in a whodunit. Moreover, by treating God as Mr. Big, Allen locates the theological concerns—problems of doubt, faith, and moral authority—in the mean streets of the modern urban consciousness. With his starting point the material reality of the crime genre, Allen sends his hero out to find God in that world.

In this respect, the parody in "Mr. Big" is the reverse of Allen's usual method. As a rule, Allen treats a small subject in a narrative style that is too lofty for it. Here he applies a low literary form, the private-eye story, to a lofty subject, the mystery of God. The low form of Allen's story embodies man's material base, which prompts him to postulate the existence of a higher reality and yet prevents his total faith in it.

Often Allen satirizes aspects of institutional religion. In one of his monologues Allen describes the Dial-a-Prayer telephone service. Announcing that he believes—in the telephone company—he explains: "If you're an atheist you don't hear a voice on the other end, and if you're an agnostic you're not sure whether you heard a voice or not." This satirizes the something-for-everyone commercialization of religion—and even of religious doubts. Similarly, in "The Condemned" the atheist Cloquet asks Father Bernard if there is still time for him to convert before his execution. The priest shakes his head sadly: "This time of year, I think most of your major faiths are filled." If he can get a passport-sized photo, however, the priest thinks he might be able to get Cloquet "into something Hindu." In keeping with the general commercialization of religion, the priest is seen as a travel agent.

Most of Allen's religious jokes derive from his own identity as a Jew; perhaps only a Jew could get away with presenting so many risible rabbis. For instance, in "A Look at Organized Crime" we meet Gaetano Santucci, "also known as Little Tony, or Rabbi Henry Sharpstein." [7] It may be due to this "rabbi's" Sabbath tastes that the list of Cosa Nostra crimes includes "the transportation of a large white-fish across the state line for immoral purposes." In "The Scrolls" Allen refers to "the massacre of the Israelites by their benefactors." His rabbis often recall the Jew's historically precarious position in an inimical world. Thus in "Mr. Big" Kaiser Lupowitz visits "Rabbi Itzhak Wiseman, a local cleric who owed me a favor for finding out who was rubbing pork on his hat." In "Hasidic Tales" wild nomads find Rabbi Yekel in the Urals: "when they learned he was a Jew, they forced him to alter all their sports jackets and take in their trousers." [8] Allen also satirizes the tradition of teaching lessons for life through traditional stories. In "Hasidic Tales" he points to their dubious contemporary value by providing arbitrary moral interpretations to a series of violent, absurd tales. "It was reasoning like this that led Rabbi Yitshok Ben Levi, the great Jewish mystic, to hit the double at Aqueduct fifty-two days running and still wind up on relief."

Allen's rabbis provide a microcosm of Jewish history, especially as it involves the perpetual tension between the Jew's fidelity to his tradition and the pressures of assimilation. The rabbis all seem variants of his Rabbi Ben Kaddish (the name means "son of the prayer for the dead"), who comes from Chelm. The Yiddish version of Gotham, in Jewish folklore Chelm is a hotbed of idiocy, the fount of all Polish and Newfie jokes, regardless of race, religion, color, or creed.

Rabbi Ben Kaddish is followed by a Polish-joke rabbi, "who was said to have inspired many pogroms with his sense of humor." After Rabbi Shimmel (mold) comes the most modern rabbi, Rabbi Zwi Chaim Yisroel. He seems the closest to Allen's persona, being the "man who developed whining to an art unheard of in the West." The most assimilated of the rabbis, when asked why Jews are not supposed to eat pork Rabbi Yisroel replies: "We're *not*? Uh-oh." In this catholic spirit, the commentator explains that "some scholars believe that the Torah merely suggested not eating pork at certain restaurants."

In a more weighty deviation from scripture, Allen gives a disenchanted reversal of the famous Yom Kippur prayer. *Kol Nidrei* actually pleads for God's forgiveness for the supplicant's failure to fulfil all his oaths over the past year. But in Allen's commentary, Yom Kippur is "the sacred Jewish holiday commemorating God's reneging on every promise." Here the form of faith is used to express despair and disillusionment. By detailing the flawed humanity of Jewish savants, the "Hasidic Tales" demonstrate the difficulty of sustaining a traditional identity in an unsympathetic society—and a traditional faith in the face of apparent abandonment by one's God.

Given the alienated existence of Allen's hapless characters, it is not surprising to find them frequently seeking refuge in fantasy, whether outright dreams or echoes of films. Allen's absurd dreams tend to be extensions of his characters' reality, itself a crazy-mirror reflection of what the rest of us know. Thus Metterling's dream is a continuation of his waking anxieties: "I am at a dinner party with some friends when suddenly a man walks in with a bowl of soup on a leash. He accuses my underwear of treason." [9] This is a recognizable variation on Kafkaesque guilt and the paranoia afflicting Metterling's daytime life. Similarly, Kugelmass dreams of skipping through a meadow carrying a basket marked "Options"—but his basket has a hole in it.[10] Despite a magical interlude of bliss, Kugelmass is also to watch his options run out in both his fantasy and his real life.

The dreams may also express the characters' subconscious. In "The Condemned," for example, Brisseau has an obviously Oedipal dream in which his gray-haired mother turns into two scoops of vanilla ice cream as the hero runs to hug her on a fatally sun-drenched beach. This association of women with food has a telling parallel when Cloquet muses that after his death, "Madame Plotnick, whose face looks like something on the menu in a seafood restaurant, will still be around." Though one is a dream and the other a conscious thought, there remains the suggestion that the dream reflects a psychological reality. Allen makes this point explicit in the Emperor Ho Sin's confusions of dream and reality in "Fabulous Tales and Mythical Beasts," the dreamlike flow of irrational memories in "Reminiscences," and the hero's dreamlike stupor in "Nefarious Times We Live In." Dreams provide absurd and threatening experiences that prepare us for our waking life.

Sometimes Allen's prose fantasies are conveyed in terms of film rhetoric. For instance, the Earl of Sandwich's saga reads like the kind of Hollywood biography that used to star Paul Muni. Or in "Reminiscences," the memory of a summer street scene modulates into a parodic summary of crime films:

> Benny! Benny! A mother is calling her son. Benny is sixteen
> but already has a police record. When he is twenty-six, he will
> go to the electric chair. At thirty-six, he will be hanged. At fifty,
> he will own his own dry-cleaning store.

The film allusions suggest Allen's sense that America is a nation that has been shaped by its experience of films. That is why the peak of Professor Needleman's success is when his "classic work on linguistic philosophy, *Semantic Modes of Non-Essential Functioning* . . . was made into the hit movie, *They Flew By Night.*" Needleman's film experience is obviously at the root of his eloquent argument that "true evil was only possible if its perpetrator was named Blackie or Pete" and, despite Max Planck's explanations of animation, his insistence on making "a person-to-person call to Minnie Mouse."

Film experience has also had an important effect on Allen's language. For example, Groucho Marx's voice and speech rhythms can be heard in the title, "Yes, But Can the Steam Engine Do This?" and in the following passage:

> These modern analysts! They charge so much. In my day,
> for five marks Freud himself would treat you. For ten marks,
> he would treat you and press your pants. For fifteen marks,
> Freud would let *you* treat *him* and that included a choice of two
> vegetables.[11]

Another of the points that Allen's comedy shares with Groucho's is the puncturing of cultural pretensions. In his prose as in his performances, Allen often has his character pretend to more knowledge and culture than he possesses. In one *Esquire* piece he reports on Rome: "Of course the ruins are nice, too. New ones go up every day." [12] The Forum is "where a lot of funny things happened on the way to" and the Campidoglio "a square designed by Charlton Heston (played by Michelangelo in a recent flick)." All his *Esquire* and *Playboy* writings tend to be based on a pretense to *savoir faire*. In his *New Republic* and *New Yorker* pieces, Allen's critique of culture is more complex.

He often associates intellectualism with criminality. In "Confessions of a Burglar," for example, the hero's brother falls in with a gang of plagiarists—a refinement of forgery—and is arrested for signing his name to "The Waste Land." In "A Look at Organized Crime" we meet such hoodlums as Giuseppi Vitale (real name Quincy Baedeker) and Albert (The Logical Positivist) Corillo. Behind this curious pattern linking crime and intellectualism lurks one aspect of Allen's persona: the frightened, bespectacled little Jewish boy whose scholastic performance is the key to his parents' approval. For the second-generation American Jew, scholastic ineptitude carries with it the parentally instilled threat of juvenile delinquency. The uneducated adult remarks in "Spring Bulletin" that he was expelled from college, "the victim of unproved accusations not unlike those once attached to Yellow Kid Weil."

When Allen's intellectuals are not criminal they tend to be lunatic, like Metterling—known as the "Prague weirdo"—or like Professor Needleman, who considered speech such a "flawed method of communication" that he "preferred to hold even his most intimate conversations with signal flags." Especially lunatic are Allen's psychiatrists. When Dr. Helmholtz hears of the writer's aversion to "Lobstermato" (a tomato stuffed with lobster), he declares it "a particularly asinine word and wished he could scratch the face of the man who conceived it." In a word, higher education can leave us as foolish, lunatic, malicious, and vulnerable as ever.

In "The Gossage-Vardebedian Papers" Allen dramatizes the inadequacy of culture and education.[13] Here he presents the correspondence between two long-distance chess players. Their pretense to detached cerebral activity is demolished by the savagery of their lust to win and their obstinate egotism. The players' violence is suggested even in the diction of the first and still decorous letter:

> You will find that it is *your* king that lies close to mate, exposed and undefended, an immobile target for my predatory bishops. Ironic, the vicissitudes of war.

Chess is often declared a sublimation of man's primitive competitiveness, but Allen presents it as the pathetic last recourse by which impotent antagonists flail at one another from a safe distance.

Instead of being united in their game, the players seem to be playing two games, with different setups altogether. Vardebedian contends that he has been playing according to the correspondence, but that Gossage has played "in keeping with the world as you would have it, rather than with any rational system of order." The game—a microcosm of society—breaks down because of the players' inability to adhere to agreed upon conventions and rules and because of their unwillingness to share a common vision.

As the players' pretense to friendly competition is exposed as barely disguised savagery, their language strains to remain civil. Vardebedian charges that his opponent's "freewheeling, Marx Brothers approach to the game . . . hardly speaks well for [his] assimilation of *Nimzowitch on Chess*," which he allegedly stole. The last pretense to civility drops:

> Your queen is gone. Kiss it off. So are both your rooks. Forget about one bishop altogether, because I took it. The other is so impotently placed away from the main action of the game that don't count on it or it'll break your heart.

The animosity unleashed by one game forces the players to switch to a round of long-distance Scrabble. Of course, these epitomes of culture achieve no smoother communication through the word game than they did through their sublimated war. They play on in blind and raging fury. Civilization does not elevate man above his aboriginal savagery; at best it provides a system of games or rituals that provide a safer outlet for it than war.

Despite a certain skepticism about civilization and culture, Allen relishes the mystery of art. He is particularly intrigued by the question lightly posed in the aesthetics course description in "Spring Bulletin": "Is art the mirror of life, or what?" In its dangling uncertainty, Allen's art clearly mirrors life. Allen's prose humor also suggests a confusion between art and life. For instance, in "A Twenties Memory" the narrator reports that F. Scott Fitzgerald based the protagonist of his latest novel on him, and that he based his life on Fitzgerald's previous novel and was sued by a fictional character. Similarly, in "The Irish Genius" we learn of Lafferty, Synge's podiatrist who "had a passionate affair with Molly Bloom until he realized she was a fictional character." [14] This situation is reversed later on the page when we read of O'Shawn's Celtic epic of two lovers transformed into a set of *Encyclopaedia Britannica.*

The fertility of this confusion between art and life is explored most fully in "The Kugelmass Episode." A C.C.N.Y. English professor escapes from dull life into lively literature when a seedy Jewish magician, Persky the Great, uses a magic machine to project him into the novel of his choice. As Professor Kugelmass has been suffering from a case of lingering Bovarysm, he chooses Flaubert's *Madame Bovary.*

But even Kugelmass's affair with Madame Bovary does not enable him to escape the pressures of his real life:

> He held Emma's face cupped in his palms, kissed her again, and yelled, "O.K. Persky! I got to be at Bloomingdale's by three-thirty."

The idyllic life and the real contaminate each other. When the novel registers Kugelmass's presence, students ask "Who is this character on page 100? A bald Jew is kissing Madame Bovary?" Of course the professor reduces this miracle to platitude: "the mark of a classic is that you can reread it a thousand times and always find something new." Even Emma Bovary is contaminated by her modern contact—she wants to hear more about O. J. Simpson, to study acting with Strasberg, to win an Oscar. So Persky brings her into Kugelmass's world for a luxurious weekend. When Persky has difficulty returning her to the world of fiction, the prolonged idyll destroys the romance for Kugelmass. Fantasized bliss cannot survive in reality. Though Kugelmass resolves never to cheat again, once he is secure from Emma Bovary he succumbs to temptation, this time in the form of the redoubtable Monkey in Philip Roth's *Portnoy's Complaint.* When Persky dies of a heart attack, Kugelmass is stranded in *Remedial Spanish,* where he will spend eternity being pursued across a desert by the word *tener* (to have), a large and hairy irregular verb.

That particular monster embodies the theme of the story: possession. Kugelmass enters literature to achieve a romance missing in his real life. But the possession of romance is different from the prospect. As his compulsion persists, he will be eternally hunted by the predatory "to have."

"The Lunatic's Tale" is a variation on the same theme, but the literary aspect is omitted and the romantic possession stressed.[15] The affluent Dr. Ossip Farkis is driven to ruin because he loves one woman's body and another's mind. Inspired by a Bela Lugosi movie, he achieves a transplant that will give him the preferred mind in the preferred body. But again, possession destroys satisfaction. Farkis perversely abandons his ideal woman for a stewardess "whose boyish, flat figure and Alabama twang caused [his] heart to do flip-flops."

Both stories chronicle man's desire to have life imitate art, and both inevitably end in failure and dissatisfaction when the lovers achieve their desire. As is characteristic of much of Allen's work, the tales draw on such disparate sources of art as Flaubert and Lugosi to dramatize man's hunger for fantasy, his desire to transcend his physical nature, and his unhappiness with what he has.

That Allen's work combines the energy of popular culture and the ambition of high art is dramatically evidenced in "The Whore of Mensa." [16] In this story Allen's private eye, Kaiser Lupowitz, is assigned to crack a blackmail ring that operates in an unusual manner: it furnishes call girls who provide intellectual stimulation. Lupowitz's client is a man whose profession involves physical sensations ("I build and service joy buzzers") and whose name combines intellectuality and phallicism (Word Babcock). He is easy prey to these blackmailers because, as he explains, "I need a woman who's mentally stimulating. . . . I don't want an involvement—I want a quick intellectual experience, then I want the girl to leave."

As in the other Lupowitz saga, "Mr. Big," Allen reverses his usual technique of parody. He establishes a seamy setting (call girls, blackmailing, and private eyes) in which to consider a lofty aspect of human nature (the intellect). This reversal again suggests a society with inverted values. Here the physical is respectable and the intellectual is furtive and forbidden ("I got caught reading *Commentary* in a parked car. . . . I can get you photographs of Dwight Macdonald reading"). Once he has solved the case, Lupowitz cleanses himself with an old account named Gloria, a *cum laude* graduate who "majored in physical education. It felt good."

With Draconian precision Allen defines the range of intellectual sins available. Thus "symbolism's extra," and "a comparative discussion" of two works costs a hundred dollars. There is the jaded girl who "rattled off her ideas glibly, but it was all mechanical. Whenever I offered an insight, she faked a response: 'Oh, yes, Kaiser. Yes, baby, that's deep.'" Allen enumerates these intellectual activities with a detailed enthusiasm ordinarily reserved for the carnal. Moreover, the intellectual sins lead to similarly lurid sins of emotional connection. Here Allen summarizes the emotional lives of modern urban intellectuals, as seen through his brothel glass darkly:

> For fifty bucks, I learned, you could "relate without getting close." For a hundred, a girl would lend you her Bartok records, have dinner, and then let you watch while she had an anxiety attack. . . . Nice racket. Great city, New York.

This passage incidentally satirizes the New York intellectual scene, but its primary thrust is Allen's reversal of the legitimate and the forbidden.

Considerations of man's double nature traditionally place greater value on his intellectual life than on the life of the senses. By reversing this, Allen demonstrates the arbitrariness involved and suggests that injustice is done to the unity of man by preferring one aspect of his nature to the other.

Part Four

Woody's Films: Guilt-Edged Cinema

Woody Allen's work in the mass media began when he became a gag writer while still in high school. Later he was one of the brilliant stable of comic writers for Sid Caesar's *Your Show of Shows*, a group that included Mel Brooks, Carl Reiner, and Neil Simon. Unfortunately, with the exception of a script parodying Ingmar Bergman's *Wild Strawberries*, reproduced in Eric Lax's excellent study, *On Being Funny: Woody Allen and Comedy*,[1] almost none of Allen's work for television is available for study.

Once Allen had established himself as a successful monologuist and playwright, it was logical that he should return to try his hand—and his persona—in television, but the results were disappointing. In 1962 Allen made "The Laughmaker," a half-hour pilot starring Louise Lasser, Alan Alda, and Paul Hampton, but ABC declined to develop the program into a series. Allen could not yet attract audiences large enough to satisfy a national sponsor. Even his two television specials—one with Billy Graham, Candice Bergen, and the Fifth Dimension in 1968; one with Liza Minnelli in 1970—were not commercial successes.

Furthermore, television was too squeamish for Allen's wit, even when he appeared on late-night shows. For example, he was ordered to remove the word "God" from a skit on the Jack Paar show. Allen was describing a South Sea island where sex is normally conducted on an open, shameless basis, but eating is covered in shame and secrecy.[2] The censorship proved his point about the arbitrary nature of social prohibitions and decorum.

Allen's biggest effort for television—and his biggest disappointment with the medium—was a 1971 special, "The Politics of Woody Allen," that he wrote, directed, and starred in for the Public Broadcasting Service. The program was never shown. Publically, the PBS explained that the show was canceled because it dealt with presidential candidates who could then have demanded equal time. However, since the replacement featured Pat Paulsen, a comedian who was contesting the New Hampshire presidential primary at the time, it seems likelier that the program was canceled because it was considered offensive to the Nixon-Agnew administration.

According to Eric Lax's summary, the show centered on a mock-heroic version of Henry Kissinger. Allen played Harvey Wallinger, a lawyer who began as the president's errand boy, rose to eminence in the administration, and acquired a reputation as a playboy. "He's an unbelievable swinger, a freak," opined one of his dates, Sister Mary Elizabeth Smith. In addition to Allen's usual jibes about sex (the average American thinks sex without guilt or shame is not good; "it becomes almost pleasurable"), there were also standard political quips (Rockefeller's farm in Venezuela is bigger than Venezuela itself). But PBS producers were reportedly concerned about three scenes in particular: the Sister Mary quotation, a shot of Hubert Humphrey making a suggestive motion with his finger (out of context), and Wallinger claiming that Pat Nixon would have him over when Dick was out of town. When Allen refused to remove these jokes, the telecast was canceled. Allen later admitted that the show was "in enormously bad taste," but he noted that it was "hard to do anything about the administration that wouldn't be in bad taste." He did not claim any "great political depth or insight" for it; it was "an innocuous but insulting show" that was funny—and censored.[3]

In any case, Allen's disenchantment with television was reinforced by his concern about the ephemeral nature of the medium. "Somebody who is terrific on radio or television is like a Renaissance painter who worked on sand." [4] In film, however, Allen had already found a measure of artistic permanence and more openness than the broadcasting media would provide. It is in film that Allen's major artistic achievement lies and in which his development has been both the most noteworthy and the most promising.

A laurel wreath on the headboard hails Victor, the would-be conquering hero in *What's New, Pussycat?* (United Artists).

In a fantasy, Allan Felix (Woody Allen) submits to an aggressive Linda (Diane Keaton) in *Play It Again, Sam* (Paramount).

After the ball is over, Allan Felix (Woody Allen) and Linda (Diane Keaton) lie together, separated and dwarfed by a Bogart image (Paramount).

Above: Robbed of his robbery by a rival gang, Virgil Starkwell (Woody Allen) tries to *Take the Money and Run* (American Broadcasting Companies). Right: The ubiquitous Howard Cosell (himself) interviews the assassinated president of a *Bananas* republic (United Artists).

Above: The King (Anthony Quayle) is not amused by his jester (Allen) in *Everything You Always Wanted To Know About Sex* (United Artists) Left: In disguise as San Marcos' president, Fielding Mellish (Allen) enjoys FBI protection but fails to come clean in *Bananas* (*United Artists*).

The passionate doctor (Gene Wilder) and his sheepish love, Daisy, steal a furtive moment in *Everything You Always Wanted to Know About Sex* (United Artists).

In *Sleeper* the disguised Alien (Allen) has a ball on drugs at his employer's radical chic party (United Artists).

Boris (Allen) and Sonia (Diane Keaton) enjoy an interlude of bliss in *Love and Death* (United Artists).

The balcony chat (*sans* the revealing subtitles) between the recently met Annie (Diane Keaton) and Alvy Singer (Allen), in *Annie Hall* (United Artists).

The isolated sisters—Renata (Diane Keaton), Flyn (Kristen Griffith), and Joey (Marybeth Hurt)—gaze out on the sea at the end of *Interiors* (United Artists).

While they shop for grocery staples, Tracy (Mariel Hemingway) shrewdly explains life and love to Isaac Davis (Allen) in *Manhattan* (United Artists).

8

What's Up, Tiger Lily? (1966)

To make *What's Up, Tiger Lily?* Woody Allen took a Japanese spoof of the James Bond films, reedited it, and replaced the original sound track with a comic one supplied by some friends and himself. He also cut in unrelated footage of the Lovin' Spoonful singing in a disco. The result was a one-gimmick film, but it had a remarkable range of effects. Moreover, it embodied Allen's basic comic stance—the outsider's detachment.

The original Japanese film, *Key of Keys* (1964, directed by Senkichi Taniguchi), was already a tongue-in-cheek affair, but Allen converted it into a mock-heroic parody by imposing his own *schlemiel* persona on the characters and the events.

Thus Allen's hero is Jewish, "Phil Moskowitz, lovable rogue," however Japanese he may look. His quest is merely to retrieve the stolen recipe for the world's best egg salad. The hero's every speech and action are comically undermined, as in his comic-strip epithets when he fights: "Saracen pig! Spartan dog! . . . Russian snake! Spanish fly!" He childishly pauses to tickle his would-be assassin and enjoys such bad jokes as: "Did you hear the one about the cross-eyed snake who married a rope?" Moskowitz is unfamiliar with the basic conventions of espionage—and the film genre it has inspired. When shown a diagram and told "this is Shepherd Wong's home," Moskowitz asks: "He lives in that piece of paper?" The typical Allen outsider does not understand the jargon of the in-group to which he aspires, so he takes the phrase literally.

Phil Moskowitz is also a coward: "No threat will ever make me tell that the plans are in her hairpin." This incompetent agent must depend on two shapely aides, sisters Terry and Suky Yaki. In Phil's adolescent slavering over the women, Allen parodies the sophisticated sexuality of the Bond heroes, but even when a superspy the Allen hero is rejected. In one scene Terry suddenly says to him, "I'd like to tear your clothes off and make violent love to you right now." But when Phil reaches for her, she pushes him away with "Oh, Phil, all you ever think of is sex. Look at the smokestack on that ship!" By the time Phil is allowed some measure of sexual heroism at the end of the film—Suki tells Terry, "Here's Phil bringing with him the constant promise of joy and fulfilment in its most primitive form"—he has, alas, retreated into a private fantasy. The sexual reward escapes him when he becomes convinced that he is a Pan-Am jet; we watch him fly away.

In keeping with Allen's typically mock-heroic strategy, all the other characters in the film are reduced accordingly. In the middle of a gunfight the villainous Wing Fat pops out of a manhole, cries "I bet you can't tell I don't have any pants on!," and retreats under fire. Two lesser hoods sulk about the comparative sizes of their bandages after the battle.

The minor characters also share Moskowitz's sexual anxieties. Even the handsome Wing Fat: "The last time I made love on a ship was on the *Titanic*. Unfortunately, we never finished." Safecrackers are fooled by Shepherd Wong's alarm system, which includes a recording of a female voice saying "Shut the door, I'm naked." As the ads for the film show, these jokes are related to the sexual ineptitude of Allen's persona. One ad announced "He's not the world's greatest lover . . . but 8th place isn't bad." Others show him as a combination trenchcoat spy and flasher.

Two patterns of irregular sex are also developed in the film. Moskowitz is obsessed by homosexual anxieties. His exchanges with Wing Fat suggest a romance that begins with the villain's "Is this the body of a killer?" and ends with his "I love you in my own way" (when he has left Phil tied, beaten, and prey to a cobra). Two henchmen are dragged out of the hold in which they have been caught committing "crimes against nature." At the start of the film a mysterious woman warns Phil: "I never sleep with a man who owns a dress." "Me neither," he replies. "I feel the same way."

The second pattern of irregular sexuality is sadomasochism. In this respect Allen's comedy breaks with American film traditions and opts for the headier Japanese eroticism. Such sadomasochistic scenes in the original as the binding and torture of the heroes are woven into a major pattern of comic play. Thus Terry remarks: "I'd call him a sadistic masochistic necrophile, but that's beating a dead horse." Shepherd Wong's promise to "use Miracle Whip" for the prized egg-salad sandwich is given in sinister tones. A scene in which a chicken is fed to a cobra becomes a wedding here, with the chicken the fluttering bride. Even lovable Phil is associated with kinky sex. After driving off with his date's vibrator, he tells another girl to meet him in the bedroom in five minutes "and bring a cattle prod."

As pervasive as the Allen persona's sexual interest is its Jewishness. The egg-salad objective has Jewish associations, particularly as the man who commissions the quest is introduced as the "high *macher*" (Yiddish for "big wheel") of "a nonexistent but real-sounding country," that faintly recalls the pre-Israel Jewish homeland: "Yes, we're on a waiting list. As soon as there is an opening on the map, we're next." Yiddish speech rhythms are clear in the *macher's* description of the villains—"They kill, they maim, and they even call up Information for numbers they could easily look up in the book"—who are themselves given a Yiddish accent. Wing Fat declares the egg salad "so delicious you could *plotz*" (Yiddish for "split"). When he finds his mother among a boatload of call girls she has a Jewish-mother explanation: "You never write . . . so I decided to take an ocean cruise."

As he lies dying, Shepherd Wong calls for his rabbi—and then requests that instead of being embalmed, he be stuffed with crab meat. The film abounds with clichés about Orientalism that relate to Allen's Jewish, sex, and loser jokes. All four patterns constitute a central theme: a narrow perspective is being imposed on an alien reality.

The all-Oriental cast is given lines of dialogue that are ludicrously Occidental. For example, the Oriental Phil is surprised by the fact that an escaped convict is "Hmm! An Oriental!"—rather than by the more surprising fact that the convict is a woman. Later Phil's idea of the "ancient erotic poetry" of Japan begins, "There once was a man from Nantucket." A croupier tries to delay a customer with "answer for yourself the question: 'Is it true what they say about Oriental girls?' " Later two jokes converge when Wing Fat and Shep-

herd Wong argue over whether Wong looks Chinese or Japanese:
the tradition of "But you don't *look* Jewish," and the Occidental's
inability to distinguish among Orientals. All these Western-bias jokes
about the East emphasize the fact that this film imposes an outsider's perspective on the action, and that such a perspective can only
distort its material.

As though further to distort perspective, the film often refers to the
fact that it is a film by offering film parodies. For example, Cobra
Man not only speaks in a Peter Lorre voice but at one point complains, "Oh, my throat. This Peter Lorre imitation is killing me."
In the jailbreak scene, the warden addresses the prisoner over the
loudspeaker, as in countless Big House films. Suddenly his warning
turns into a television parody: "We'll have more reasons why you'll
never get away in a moment, but first, here's Len Maxwell with the
weather." As Len Maxwell is one of Allen's friends who kibbitzed
the soundtrack, this line refers to the dubbers' real world as well
as to the television context.

The characters even refer to the fact that they are in a film. For instance, Phil complains that "I was almost shot and killed just before
the opening credits." Later he warns Terry, "Don't look now, Baby,
but this is the obligatory scene where the director has to walk by with
his wife. Egomaniac." In the same spirit, Wing Fat forces the others
—at gunpoint!—to hear his James Cagney impersonations. As he
beats up Phil for expecting an Oscar for his performance, Wing Fat
invokes his thespian gods: Sonny Tufts, John Wayne, and the Flying
Wallendas. Finally, the hero triumphs by reverting to the simpler
tradition of James Barrie's *Peter Pan*. Left with an empty gun, he
asks for audience support: "If all you in the audience who believe
in fairies will clap your hands, then my gun will be filled with bullets." Thus supported, Phil shoots four villains with three bullets
and saves the day.

This formal self-consciousness works in several ways. It is another
example of the film's disjunction. Just as the soundtrack is always
at madcap odds with the action, so the film references undercut any
lingering pretense to realism. Furthermore, the obvious disparity between character and role is a variation on the basic point of the film's
structure, which is the imposition of an Occidental viewpoint on the
Oriental world. This gives a special relevance to the words "Foreign

Version," which appear in the top left-hand corner of the screen during the opening sequence. The words are accompanied by a large red arrow pointing toward two small red Xs that bob around to conceal the breasts of the topless dancer. By so blatantly proclaiming its censorship, the film reminds us that we are the foreigners for whose benefit special adjustments have been made. Allen is at his familiar game of making insiders identify with outsiders.

Finally, by demonstrating how an ironic perspective can subvert, or even reverse, one's impressions, the film becomes quintessential Allen. Thus a girl's innocent calisthenic exercise is completely redefined by her line: "Boy, I'm a great piece." The familiar closing shot of a plane taking off is completely revised by the hero's claim that he is that plane. The image is undercut by the dialogue. To put it another way, Allen stands apart from the material which he presents in *What's Up, Tiger Lily?* Moreover, he transforms everything he shows by what he says. This interplay between the serious image and the reductive tone is the basic element in all his work—in his parodies, his mock-heroic pretenses, and his ironic persona projection. Seen in this light, almost everything in Allen's later comedy can be found in embryonic form in his first film.

Allen himself appears in the film four times. The first is during the Murakami-Wolf credits. Here a cartoon Woody dons glasses and cavorts across a variety of pin-up pictures. Though he ogles these large ladies, lies on their breasts, and pulls credit lines out of their navels and cleavage, he nevertheless remains generically removed from them. He is an animated, moving figure while they are still-life images. This is a visualization of Allen's common pretense to frustration with women, who seem to exist on another level and are unresponsive to him. The animated sequence presents Woody as literally an Outsider, locked out of the life of the beauties.

Allen appears again as the film proper begins. He is interviewed in his book-lined study, where he explains how he made the film. His heroic pretense is deflated by the bookish glasses and setting, and by his struggle with language. He claims that he was invited to make this, "the definitive spy picture," because "death is my bread and danger is my butter." As this does not sound quite right, he fumbles through variations (e.g., "Danger is my bread and death is my butter") before settling on "Death and danger are my various breads and various butters." Our man of action is snarled up in his own words.

Allen's most remarkable appearance is in the midst of the film's most thrilling scene. When our heroes are attacked by a cobra, a shadow hand reaches across the screen to remove a hair from the projector gate. This is followed by two male hands doing clumsy hand-shadows on the screen; then male and female hands reach across the screen and caress. A male and a female silhouette meet and kiss on the screen. Allen and Louise Lasser play lovers enjoying a supposedly private tryst in the projection booth. "Dolores, we can't keep meeting here like this," Allen says. "My wife is getting wise. It's against Union rules" (the projectionists' union, that is, not the marital). As the drama of these lovers unwinds, the action of the film is arrested between frames. The projectionist and his love project themselves on the action. Like the Allen dubbing, they are an alien projection on the original film.

In his final appearance, Allen lies on a sofa, eating an apple. He is detached from and unmoved by the striptease performed by China Lee on the right side of the screen. The camera pans right to exclude Allen. As the strip continues on the left side of the screen now, on the right we read the usual statement about everything in the film being fictitious. Then comes another statement that condemns the audience for having read the first one: "If you have been reading this instead of looking at the girl, then see your psychiatrist, or go to a good eye doctor." An eye-chart helpfully follows. By blaming the audience for reading the words instead of watching the Oriental dancer, Allen provides a reprise of the entire film, in which he imposed bathetic Western dialogue on Oriental characters and action.

In all four appearances, Allen emphasizes his detachment from the work. More than just a comic romp, *What's Up, Tiger Lily?* is the essential Woody Allen work, because the *kibbitz* is Allen's essential stance. He stands apart from the game of life and jokes about the players.

9

Take the Money and Run (1969)

Woody Allen's first complete feature film, *Take the Money and Run,* derived from the style of his monologues. It comprised a series of absurd skits depicting a nebbish's comic attempts to become a master criminal.

The film pretends to be a documentary about the criminal hero, Virgil Starkwell (Allen). His Christian name evokes Allen's familiar associations with virginity and bookishness; his surname alludes to Charles Starkweather, a famous marauder of the late 1950s. An authoritative narrator (Jackson Beck) gravely intones the Starkwell saga in Allen's familiar mock-heroic mode. Hence the incongruous pride in his voice when he declares: "Virgil is an immediate failure at crime."

More specifically, the film parodies the *cinéma-vérité* documentary film form. Popular in the 1960s, it characteristically attempted to convey the impression of recording life as it happened, without staging or distortion by editing. In such films as *Chronique d'un Été* (Jean Rouch, 1961) and *Lonely Boy* (Koenig-Kroitor, 1962) and in the documentaries of Richard Leacock and the Maysles brothers, *cinéma-vérité* made use of interviews, hand-held cameras, natural sound, and a frank acknowledgment of the filming process in an attempt to record reality objectively. Allen's film parodies the technique and questions its validity by selecting as its subject a man whose manifest incompetence is magnified by the heroic rhetoric employed. By his very choice of Virgil as the subject of his film, the filmmaker has distorted his subject.

This point is made explicit in an interview with Virgil's friend Kay

Lewis (Louise Lasser). She is astonished that such "an idiot . . . such a nothing" should prove to be a famous criminal. Actually, his fame is due solely to the fact that a film is being made about him; this alone leads Kay to dismiss her sensible disdain for him and decide that only a genius could have successfully convinced everybody that he was so incompetent.

The film often makes us question the source of the footage we see. Whereas fiction films assume the convention that characters in a shot are alone, that no photographer is present, watching, and filming, in *cinéma-vérité* the convention was to acknowledge the presence of the photographer and the processes of making the film. This question is raised twice in *Take the Money and Run*. The first occasion is on Virgil's honeymoon with Louise (Janet Margolin). The narrator remarks that "when these innocent pictures were taken, they were both unaware of the unhappy events that were to come." We must assume that they were also unaware of the photographer for we are not told who was along to record the couple's culinary fumblings in the kitchen—scenes of charred roast, coffee poured over a teabag, and steak fried in its cellophane (standard illustrations from what could be called The New Bride's Cookbook)—nor do the words "innocent pictures" apply to the next scene of torrid passion and nuptial acrobatics during which Virgil's glasses end up on Louise. The reversal embodies a tension that makes us wonder who is making a documentary record of that intimate scene. The second instance occurs at the end, when we are informed that Virgil's last robbery was accidentally recorded by a passing amateur photographer, "Stanley Krim, a cretin." Krim is an intrusive filmmaker, for he attempts to divert the discussion away from Virgil and onto the subject of his own laundry.

This acknowledgment of the filming process challenges the *cinéma-vérité* assumption that the subject being filmed is not altered by the fact of filming. And since the film record of Virgil's criminal mishaps as a boy are of doubtful documentary origin, they even cast suspicion on the authenticity of *cinéma-vérité* itself.

The question of film realism also arises in Allen's treatment of Virgil's grandfather. Home-movie shots of Virgil and his grandfather playing catch on a rooftop are followed by stock footage of a Washington Senators baseball game. An injured fan carried out on a stretcher is said to be Virgil's grandfather, beaned by a foul ball. The consequent brain damage leads him to believe he is Kaiser Wilhelm. In the next newsreel footage, the real Kaiser Wilhelm and his associates are identified as Virgil's grandfather and "other inmates" at the sanitarium.

Here film from three different sources is forced into continuity. The most realistic footage, the newsreel shots of the real Kaiser, represents the grandfather's delusion; the staged home-movie footage of the rooftop game depicts his real life. The footage means not what it actually shows but what the narrator claims for it. As in *What's Up, Tiger Lily?*, Allen shows one thing but says that it is quite another. The sound track alters the meaning of the documentary and newsreel footage; there is no stable truth in the image. Indeed here, as in *What's Up, Tiger Lily?* and *Play It Again, Sam*, Allen is saying that the image lies.

This parody of *cinéma-verité* in *Take the Money and Run* relates to the central point in the hero's characterization: Virgil is a pathetic creature who spends his life trying to live up to unsuitable models of success. Some of these he takes from real life. For example, as a boy he sees a black shoeshine boy spit on and polish a man's shoes; Virgil incompetently emulates him, but spits on the client's pantleg. And so it goes. Woody Allen's first appearance as the adult Virgil is significant. He has sufficiently overcome his hopelessness at the cello to be "good enough to play in a local band." Enter Allen as the cellist—in a marching band! Virgil scampers along, trying to seat himself for a few strokes of his cello, but the band marches on, leaving him behind. Virgil cannot keep up with the image he has adopted. When Virgil later tells Louise that he is a cellist with the "Philharmonic," he is not just reviving an old ambition, but attempting to sustain a respectable identity. It collapses when she visits him in prison. In a voice throbbing with pathos and sincerity he confesses—not that he robbed a bank, but—"I'm not with the Philharmonic." With this confession he loses the whole fabric of illusion and ambition upon which he has based their relationship.

Most of Virgil's models, however, come not from real life but from the movies. Although we do not see him going to films, Virgil's life is a pastiche of films whose values, illusions, and life styles he has absorbed as if by osmosis. For example, when Virgil joins a street gang to "prove his manhood," Allen parodies a scene in *West Side Story* (1961). One by one, the boys click their switchblades open. When Virgil's turn comes, his blade shoots out altogether; Virgil's "manhood" is deflated in an image of premature ejaculation. Similarly, in his first bank robbery Virgil is politely asked to show his gun. He modestly flashes a small pistol from the center-front of his pants. This gesture of phallic weaponry alludes to the sexual play with a more prominent gun in the second scene of *Bonnie and Clyde* (1967). Virgil's admixture of pretended power and true shame shows Allen's characteristic touch.

In the same vein, Virgil's career as a pool hustler is prompted not by ability but by the probable influence of Robert Rossen's film *The Hustler* (1961). And when he removes his suit from the refrigerator and his shoes from the freezer, Virgil is identifying with another dream figure, the Marilyn Monroe of *The Seven Year Itch* (1955). In all these examples, Virgil ludicrously tries to live up to images from the movies.

Sometimes Virgil is stuck in film parallels not of his choosing. For instance, the chain-gang sequence relates back to *I Am a Fugitive from a Chain Gang* (1932). The prison-camp scenes, especially those involving the short, sadistic warden, recall *Cool Hand Luke* (1967). More specifically, Virgil's punishment by three days isolation with an insurance agent is a parody of Luke's solitary confinement in "The Box".

In a more complex film reference—a *hommage* to the Groucho Marx of *Monkey Business* (1931)—when the warden asks "Any questions?" Virgil responds with "Do you think a girl should pet on her first date? I mean if both parties are mature and liberal?" Behind the incongruity of this question lurks the implication of homosexuality in prison life. Moreover, Virgil assumes the female role (as he did in emulating Monroe, not Tom Ewell, in *The Seven Year Itch* reference), and his question suggests that he expects to be sexually victimized. The quip reveals not only his own psyche and dreads, but the fact that he seems trapped in the situations and rhetoric of other films.

Nor is Virgil the only one to project false images. Because they are so ashamed of their son, his parents wear Groucho Marx masks during the filming of their interviews. Paradoxically, their masks only relate them to Virgil all the more profoundly. The metaphor of the false image is also dramatized during Louise's second prison visit, when another prisoner and his visitor converse through ventriloquist dummies (mouthpieces), instead of speaking to one another directly.

Thus Virgil, who spends his life trying to live up to the image of a Hollywood gangster, is surrounded by minor characters who also pattern themselves after film stars. His fellow convicts include Neville Brand and Edmond O'Brien lookalikes, and Virgil is blackmailed by a Bette Davis type. Perhaps the most telling confusion between fact and film is in the prison camp scene, where we see in shadow play a guard whipping a convict. The guard is surprised to learn that he should be whipping the man and not the shadow. And like Virgil, those around him are also unable to sustain the tone of their Hollywood models. We see this in Allen's ludicrous lists of crimes. Virgil is wanted for "assault, armed robbery, and illegal possession of a wart." One cohort is charged with a list of crimes that descend from murder to "getting naked in the presence of his in-laws." Another is wanted for dancing with his mailman. The third is sought for arson, robbery, assault to kill, and marrying a horse. In each case what begins as a list of serious crimes dwindles into kinkiness.

At two points, the minor characters explicitly relate their criminality to their film experience. In the first, a convict is a Von Stroheim type "known for his detail work." For a jailbreak, he wants Virgil to steal the guards' underwear so that the escaping prisoners can wear it and feel like guards. In the second, Virgil plans to rob a bank with a gang pretending to shoot a film. An ex-con and former filmmaker is added to the gang and assigned the role of director. (His name is Fritz, in obvious *hommage* to Fritz Lang, whose *You Only Live Once* [1937] is a classic in the crime tradition from which Allen's film derives.) In this scene Allen most clearly roots his hero's aspirations in the Hollywood dream factory.

The entire robbery is handled in the context of film. Virgil cases the bank by "surreptitiously" filming the layout through a large rye bread. When the gang meets to view the films, the evening begins with the obligatory boring short ("Trout Fishing in Quebec," produced by Allen's agent-producers, Rollins and Joffe). In the rehearsal for the robbery, Fritz's line, "Up with your hands. This is a shtick-up," locates the scene in the comedy of the *shtick* (Yiddish for a routine) as well as in the tradition of film rehearsal. In the actual robbery, just as Virgil and his cronies draw their guns and prepare to say their line, some off-camera voices steal their role. Another gang is robbing the same bank.

Even after his role has been usurped, Virgil remains dominated by the influence of the media. In the manner of a television-contest master of ceremonies, he asks the bank patrons to indicate through applause the gang by whom they would prefer to be robbed. He loses. In an earlier, related scene, Virgil's job interview drifts into a game show, at the end of which Virgil pays the interviewer a ten-dollar consolation prize. In both scenes, Virgil is victimized by his emulation of a television format.

Virgil Starkwell's problem is his compulsion to live up to false images. From film he learns to be a criminal; from film he adopts heroic images that do not suit him. Hence his false bravado: "The prison hasn't been built that can hold me. I'll get out of this one if it means spending my entire life here." Not stone walls, however, but his unsuitable life models imprison Virgil, so he can never be free. When he wins an early parole by volunteering for a medical experiment, the test is "a success except for one temporary side effect: for several hours he is turned into a rabbi." (Virgil is shown as an orthodox rabbi carefully explaining Passover as the celebration of the Israelites' escape from bondage, of which his parole is a parodic echo.) Ironically, Virgil goes from one inapt model to another. For the experimental drug achieves what his father had failed to impose upon him ("He was an atheist. I tried to beat God into him, but . . ."). Virgil has merely escaped from one inappropriate model into another.

However earnest his commitment to the ideal of the gangster, Virgil never enjoys a sense of community with those who live outside the law. For example, no one tells him that the planned jailbreak has been postponed and he is the only one to show up—a small figure in long-shot under the prison walls, he is raucously laughed at by his mates. Similarly, in the escape from the chain gang, the image of six linked convicts is only a parody of outlaw fraternity. While Virgil runs, the other five ride bicycles. Only the moronic Deputy Lynch could take this crew to be "just a close family." Nor is the Allen persona's sexual naïveté in any way diminished by the outlaw role he has adopted. When frisked by guards, he dissolves into helpless giggles. Describing his reaction to Louise he says: "I was so touched. After fifteen minutes I wanted to marry her. After half an hour I completely gave up the idea of snatching her purse." Sentimentality impedes his work.

Virgil's failures continue: A "gun" he steals from a pawnshop turns out to be a cigarette lighter when he "fires" it. When he tries to murder a blackmailer, he grabs the wrong end of a hot poker and then "stabs" her with a turkey leg by mistake. In a jewelry robbery he forgets his objective; ignoring the jewelry, he makes off with the window-pane that he cut out. In perhaps the best scene of the film, his first bank robbery is thwarted because his hold-up note is illegible. The bank staff argues over how to read two words; there is one confusion between "act" and "abt" and another between "gun" and "gub." This lesson lingers in Virgil's mind, but not in a helpful way. When he prepares for his last bank job, he pronounces "gun" as "gub." He does not learn from his mistakes; he learns mistakes.

Virgil's failings usually reflect the absurdities in the world around him. The bank that he robs has its own silly rituals: "You'll have to have this note initialled by one of our vice-presidents before I can give you the money." Modesty and decorum are seen as only social pretenses when his prim-looking teacher first recalls Virgil "feeling the girls," and then becomes flustered at the idea of being interviewed: "Can I say 'feel'?" Virgil's former psychiatrist recalls Virgil's love for Louise—"genuine, clean, not like some patients I know" —and sneers at his present patient. Virgil finds a bra among the male prisoners' laundry, proof that his sexual anxieties are shared by others. And his concluding description of his former cohorts—"Many have become homosexuals and some of them have entered into politics and sports"—implies that respectability can be a front for irregularity.

The scene of Virgil's last arrest draws together several absurdities of conventional society. For one thing, the scene is recorded by a "straight" citizen, Stanley Krim, who is "crooked" (what "krim" means in Yiddish) and a cretin. More important, as the man Virgil robs turns out to be Eddie Haines, the trombonist in his old marching band, the conventions of the robbery are mixed with those of nostalgic reunion. As they part, Haines remembers his own role:

"Virgil, I just realized. I'm a cop."
"Really? How are you doing?"

Now the scene is reversed; Virgil goes through the conventions of being pleased at his friend's success, while Haines performs the role of arresting officer.

Thus, even though Virgil Starkwell is Allen's familiar loser, the central tension in *Take the Money and Run* derives from Allen's juxtaposition of the supposed realism of *cinéma-vérité* with the romanticism of the gangster-film tradition. Allen contrasts the glories that his hero wishes to emulate with the failure that is his lot. The fact that Virgil may be vulnerable because he wants to be what his myopic eyes see may explain the running gag in which various people—urchins, an iceman, hoodlums, a judge, and finally Virgil himself—smash his glasses. In his lovemaking scene, Virgil's glasses pass onto Louise as if to signify the passage of his essence or passion. Virgil's poor eyesight makes him vulnerable so he often cowers with his hands over his eyes. Whereas most films encourage us to believe what we see, *Take the Money and Run* warns us against the deceptions and seductions of the visual experience.

In its structural similarity to the monologues, this film suggests that Allen was feeling his way into the medium. His parodic themes enable him to exercise the language of film rhetoric and conventions while he learned how film works. Allen's simple but efficient shooting style is characterized by three types of shots. One is the straight-on interview, which places the film in the *cinéma-vérité* tradition. Another is the slow track, often circling, that suggests a hunter stalking his prey and relates the film to the crime genre. The third shot may derive from *What's New, Pussycat?*—an image is undercut by our changed perspective. In one example, Virgil preens for a dinner date, steps out, and then immediately returns; a new camera distance shows us he had forgotten to put on his pants. Similarly, when Virgil's gang flees a robbery, through the rearview mirror of the getaway car we see the police in hot pursuit. After this familiar shot, a long side-view reveals that the getaway car is being towed. As director,

Allen plays against the false security that we draw from a conventional film image.

Allen speaks of *Take the Money and Run* as a rough, spontaneous, and unshaped work.[1] Actually, it shows a thoughtful artist learning his craft and intrigued by its conventions and techniques. The film examines the effects of film values on life styles, indeed the very nature and function of the film image. Clearly Allen was turning to film not to take the money and run, but to stay and to explore the medium further. Each of his later films would deepen his investigations.

10

Bananas (1971)

Woody Allen's second feature film seems to have the same loose structure as his first, a series of comic misadventures starring Allen as a fumbling failure. As Allen explained his working methods at the time, he liked "to have a thin story to hang the comedy sequences on." [1] The story in *Bananas* is certainly thin. Allen plays Fielding Mellish, a products tester, who falls in love with Nancy (Louise Lasser), a C.C.N.Y. student activist, who is petitioning against the Latin American dictatorship in San Marcos. When Nancy breaks off their affair, Mellish holidays in San Marcos, where he becomes embroiled in a revolution and eventually becomes the country's president. When he returns to the United States to plead for foreign aid, he is arrested and charged with treason. However thin the story and free the narrative, *Bananas* is a significant advance in Allen's artistry. Beneath the apparent disorder is a remarkable coherence. More ambitious in its subject matter, its comedy has a serious social and political underpinning.

Many of the comic turns are variations on a single theme—the contrast between Inside and Outside. Allen plays his usual role of an outsider who wants to come in from the cold, but here this motif is varied and amplified to become the film's dominant theme. Thus Mellish is much concerned with doors and doorways, symbols of admission/exclusion. A doorknob comes off in his hand when he prepares to ask a secretary for a date. To admit Nancy to his apartment, Fielding must undo a battery of locks. Later he pointedly leans against a doorway as he tries to impress Nancy—"I love Yoga. I love Eastern philosophy. It's metaphysical and redundant and abortively pedantic"—with an onslaught of passwords by which the Outsider hopes to gain entrance.

Most of the comic scenes involve variations on the problems of the Outsider trying to establish himself on some Inside. Clashes over parking spaces, for example, occur twice. In one scene Mellish guides a motorist into a collision; in another he dreams he is being carried on a cross by monks, who are beaten out of a parking space by another group of monks carrying another man (Allen Garfield) on another cross. Mellish's attempts to win acceptance are always inadequate because he simply cannot fit in. His one successful attempt at camouflage—by becoming one with a bush—results in the indignity of being watered by a soldier.

The In and Out metaphor is most explicit in the scene in which Mellish regains consciousness in the rebel camp—"Blood! That should be on the inside"—but the motif occurs everywhere. Invited to dine with the president, Mellish arrives in an unfinished suit that shows the basting marks; it "seams" to be inside out. Later, when the rebel chief Esposito wins power and becomes a tyrant (i.e., a turncoat) he orders all citizens to wear their underwear on the outside, and makes Swedish the new official language (thus turning the entire population into outsiders in their own land).

Allen's fullest treatment of this theme is the trial scene. The Insider is typified by the glossy Miss America, who sings an operatic aria ("Caro Nome") and then rejects Mellish as "a subversive mother." As she explains, "Differences of opinion should be tolerated but not when they're too different." The use of the prefix "mother" by this WASP-ish porcelain doll relates to two other jokes in the film. In the first, Mellish rued the fact that he dropped out of college: "I was in the Black Studies program. By now I could have been black." In the second, one of the witnesses at the trial is a huge, black lady, who is introduced as FBI director J. Edgar Hoover. ("I have many enemies. I rarely go out unless I'm in disguise.") These three black jokes underline the futility of Mellish's attempts to join a group: He cannot be black, but J. Edgar Hoover, without taking any courses at all, can testify under oath as a black woman. Those who are *that* In can be any Out they want.

Mellish is on trial for having attempted to be both In and Out. That is, he is charged because he is an Outsider who has come In,

or an Insider (American) who has presumed to establish an identity on the Outside, or an Outsider (a loser) who presumes to the
establishment status of an Insider (a president). In this respect
Mellish is an apt representative for San Marcos. After the revolution,
the United States rejects it as Communist, the Communists reject
it as sympathetic to the United States, and the only person to recognize the new nation is jailed on a morals charge.

Mellish describes his trial as a tangle of In and Out, not just a
travesty of justice, but "a travesty of a mockery of a sham of a
mockery of a travesty of two mockeries of a sham." Mellish acts out
this confusion when he cross-examines himself on the question of his
citizenship in two countries. He dashes in and out of the witness
box to ask and to answer his tricky questions. Some of these seem
dragged in from another movie (or two) altogether: "Does the code
name Sapphire mean anything to you? . . . You swear to God and
yet you have no compunction about teaching evolution?" The trial
culminates fittingly: Mellish's fifteen-year sentence is suspended on
the written promise that he will never move into the judge's neighborhood. In other words, Mellish must remain an Outsider.

The theme of In and Out is also presented through aspects of
Allen's film technique. For instance, *Bananas* opens and closes with
telecasts of Howard Cosell's *Wide World of Sports*. In the first, Cosell
broadcasts the advertised assassination of the president of San
Marcos. In the last, the consummation of the Mellishes' wedding
night is telecast as if it were a championship prizefight. As both events
are presented as live television, the film viewer is neither at the event
nor discreetly distanced from it, but in the compromised situation of
a vicarious witness.

Allen uses and then exposes not only the conventions of live television, but those of film as well. For instance, Mellish's reading of the
dinner invitation from President Vargas is accompanied by dreamy
harp music. But then Mellish finds an actual harpist playing in the
closet. Similarly, when Mellish makes love to the rebel woman, Allen
uses the conventional pan away from the nude lovers to suggest the
passage of a respectable period of time, but then he jump-cuts to
the girl smoking, bored, and alone, his usual joke about his persona's
limited sexual staying power. Finally, one sequence between Mellish
and Nancy is replete with the rhetoric of a lovers' idyll—blurry

foliage, earnest conversation, and sweeping lyrical downshots—but they're breaking up! In all three examples, the scene's traditional form is undercut by its content. The viewer is left wondering whether the rhetoric is bringing him into the frame, or keeping him out. In other words, we have a technical analogue to the film's inner tension between the In and the Out.

To compound the confusion between In and Out, a number of gags set up whirligigs that permit no easy grip. For instance, in the television news report of Mellish's trial there is the traditional shot of the defendant hiding his face behind his hat as he enters the courtroom. But then this defendant turns and uses his hat to hide a face other than his own—that of a rather homely woman in the crowd. Then comes the topper: the woman resembles Eleanor Roosevelt. In this bananas world, the hero covers the symbol of exemplary citizenship; but is he concealing it or is he protecting it from the shameful events about to be revealed? Similarly, just as Mellish pronounces what we might have taken to be a central theme of the film— "To me the greatest crimes have been crimes against human dignity"—he steps out of his car and down a manhole. And again: "Life is so cruel," Mellish avers as he slams his locker door on a friend's hand. "See what I mean?" The visual joke undercuts the initial statement: the first line draws us into the frame, and then the gag pushes us out.

In addition to this theme, *Bananas* is unified by the implications of its title. In its working stages, it was called "El Weirdo"; the title change shifted the focus from the hero to the world. More precisely, the film depicts a lunatic world, a world gone bananas. Thus President Mellish and the United States Ambassador converse in clear English but they accept the intercession of an awkward, accented translater—afterward identified as an escapee from an asylum. In addition to implying a general madness, the title relates the film to the noble tradition of banana-peel slapstick comedy.

The most important implication of the title, however, is its association with exploitative politics. San Marcos, a nation of marks or victims, is a banana republic. As the film details the political machinations between America and San Marcos, and between the mutually exploiting factions within the nation itself, this aspect of the title is the most important unifier. For *Bananas* satirizes different kinds of imperialist exploitation. The most obvious kind is political: the cyclical tyrannies of Vargas and Esposito; the American government's abuse of the nation's citizenry; and American interference in San Marcos affairs. Although Allen claims that *"Bananas* was coincidentally political," [2] it has very clear political implications. From Mellish's first appearance in a red-white-and-blue striped shirt, he functions as the muddled, idealistic American citizen. For the bulk of the film he is manipulated and victimized by his own government and that of San Marcos.

Some of Allen's gibes may be lightly humorous—for example, Vargas mistakenly contracts for aid from the United Jewish Appeal instead of from the CIA—but most of it is biting. Mellish's trial is a funhouse reflection of the trial of the Chicago Seven. Thus the judge has the lean and bitter look of Judge Hoffman, and the gagging and binding of Bobby Seale are echoed in Mellish's being gagged and bound during his trial. Even gagged, such is Mellish's eloquence that he breaks down a witness's lying testimony, until she cries "Don't put words in my mouth!" Though Allen is disillusioned with politics, *Bananas* is a film of political concern.

The political satire shades off into religious satire when the UJA is embroiled in the revolution. Underlining established religion's susceptibility to imperialist impulses, Mellish remarks: "The Vatican did so well in Rome, they opened in Denmark." The religious satire climaxes in the television news report on Mellish's trial: a commercial promotes New Testament cigarettes. "You stick to New Testament cigarettes and all is forgiven," a priest advises his coughing communicant. Co-opting the language at the left, the establishment ad lays claim to a "revolutionary" incense filter. "I smoke 'em. *He* smokes 'em," the commercial concludes ambiguously. (It was presumably for this mordant bit that the National Catholic Office for Motion Pictures gave *Bananas* its "Condemned" rating.)

Allen also satirizes cultural imperialism—especially the spread throughout the world of the callous and inescapable American media. The implication is that the whole world has become a banana republic subject to the marauding media of the United States. The most obvious media satire involves the self-burlesquing Howard

Cosell (who will be identified in *Sleeper* [1973] as a punishment for twentieth-century traitors). In the assassination telecast Cosell expresses America's smiling indifference to its unpopularity; he reports "the traditional bombing of the American embassy, a ritual as old as this city itself." Cosell combines grammatical fastidiousness ("It's he.") with insensitivity, as in his remarks to the murdered president:

> Sir, you've been shot. When did you know it was all over? . . . Of course, you're upset and that's understandable under the circumstances. I guess now you'll have to announce your retirement.

Cosell uses his media role as a password to make his way through the mob: "Would you please let me through. This is American television. American television. Let me through." In the turmoil of San Marcos politics, he is an intruding Outsider with the authority of a supreme Insider.

The shot that kills the president is fired from the same perspective that the camera takes—implying perhaps that the American media may have direct political effect around the world. Several jokes establish the political uses of the media and art. For example, one prisoner is tortured by being forced to listen to a recording of *Naughty Marietta*. In addition, Allen uses the occasional film parody—a tumbling carriage from *Battleship Potemkin*, the runaway gadgetry from *Modern Times*—to recall the political art of his masters. Finally, the use of television to report Mellish's trial implies a society that is led, shaped, perhaps even governed, through its media.

In the last sequence Cosell applies his boxing rhetoric to the Mellishes' wedding night. Again, a private moment is violated by the presence of the media. Moreover, the hilarious confusion of sexual and boxing terms converts the lovemaking into a competition. After the match Nancy tells Cosell that she had trained so well that "there wasn't any time that I didn't think I was in complete control." Mellis thought he "had her in real trouble with the right hand up early." In the presence of the media, even the intimacy of love becomes violent and competitive.

One sentimental refuge from the film's satirical tone can be found in the Liebling-Hamlisch song that closes the film. The singer declares that he is taken for a fool because he believes in loving, giving, and sunshine. The nebbish hero of *Bananas* would like to live by this idealism, but the bananas world does not nourish those values. *Bananas* satirizes the variety of ways that man conspires to exploit others—politically, religiously, culturally, and romantically. The sense that this exploitation is a lunatic waste of life gives this chaos of comedy its remarkable and sober cohesion.

11

Everything You Always Wanted To Know About Sex (*but were afraid to ask) (1972)*

In its scale, complexity, and wit, Woody Allen's next feature film is an astonishing advance on his first three. The film is an adaptation of the best-selling sex manual by Dr. David Reuben. In seven short sketches, Allen purports to offer sex information in the manner of the original book. But the film is not a simple adaptation. Indeed Allen claims to have "thrown out the contents and based the script upon the title." [1] More exactly, Allen satirizes three major targets: the very notion of instruction by sex manual, contemporary culture's obsession with sex, and the distortion of our perceptions and values by the all-pervasive media, especially movies and television.

The phenomenon of sex education manuals drew Allen's satire elsewhere. In the movie version of *Play It Again, Sam* (1972) Allan Felix prides himself on his night with Linda: "I never once had to sit up and consult the manual." In the third sketch of the present film, after a bout of exhausting foreplay, a husband (Allen) instructs his wife to "Turn over . . . I want to do a quick check on some parts I missed." The bookish mode of lovemaking reduces the act to a mechanical operation.

This point finds full expression in the last episode of *Everything You Always Wanted To Know About Sex*. Allen dramatizes the psychological and physiological aspects of the male orgasm as if it were a space launching. Penelope Gilliatt has noted Allen's sensitivity to Dr. Reuben's tendency to technological jargon.[2] After all,

Dr. Reuben described ejaculation as "roughly comparable to a missile launching into outer space," with the erection comparable to "blowing up a balloon" and with "situation reports" constantly "relayed to the sexual centers in the spinal cord and brain." [3] As Gilliatt observed, "Allen's closing sketch seizes with beady-eyed lucidity on the good doctor's mechanistic view of sex and makes it as lunatically anti-sensual as it is in the book." [4] Obviously Allen's film is not an adaptation of the book but an ironic reaction against it—and against sex manuals in general.

The film also reflects on the phenomenal success of the book, for it dramatizes society's obsession with sex. The tension between curiosity and shame that characterizes modern sexuality inheres in the two-part structure of Reuben's title. The first part addresses Everyman's sweeping interest in sex. Allen spells this part out slowly on the screen in uncapitalized single words, as if we were reading a lesson in a children's primer: "every thing you always wanted to know about sex." (There is a coy bawdiness in the two-word treatment of "everything.") But the second part of Reuben's title expresses Everyman's timidity and shame where sex is concerned. A lurid red asterisk directs the viewer to the postscript: "but were afraid to ask."

This red softens into the spray of pink in the first shot: a horde of rabbits, pink in ear and eye. The rabbits represent innocent, animal sexuality. While the credits appear against the backdrop of rabbits, the sound track gives us a scratchy recording of Cole Porter's risqué classic, "Let's Misbehave." The song suggests that as we are not above the animals, we should emulate them and joyfully misbehave. But, alas, man is kept from the delights of animal sexuality by a socially imposed sense of shame, and his instinctual life is hobbled by a self-consciousness from which animals are happily free. That is why man buys sex manuals. But if rabbits don't need them, why should man? The variety of sexual yearnings, mysteries, frustrations, and impediments depicted in this film suggest the answer.

In addition to satirizing man's sexual self-consciousness, the film develops a consciousness of its own nature as a public medium. Each section parodies a specific type of film or television program. As a result, this is not a film about sex, but a film about films about sex. Moreover, it demonstrates the tensions that have led Western culture to develop cinematic and television programming that is at once obsessed with sex and too inhibited to deal with the subject openly. This might explain—and invalidate—Leonard Maltin's complaint that the film "strays so far from reality that there is nothing tangible for the audience to grab onto and *feel*." [5] Allen's film is not about reality but about our media's mediation in our apprehension of reality. As Harry Wasserman observed, Allen's parodies here show "how motion pictures can stretch human emotions out of proportion, while television packages them into commodities of merchandise." [6]

In this respect it may be useful to remember that Allen got the idea of filming Reuben's book while watching a late-night-television talk-show. Someone remarked that Woody Allen was the only person who could film this book; Allen immediately had his agent buy the rights from Elliott Gould. His approach to it was clearly by way of the media's fascination with the topic and tensions of sex. However, Allen made it clear that this film would not be another coy "sex comedy" like *Pillow Talk* (1959) or *It Happened One Night* (1934):

> I'm talking about real sex, about sex unashamedly and un-equivocally . . . rampant sexual topics treated in an extremely broad, surrealistic way. I may never get another date.[7]

In order to confront the topic directly Allen had to deal with the ways in which the media avoid dealing with it directly themselves.

Do Aphrodisiacs Work?

In the first episode Allen plays a medieval court jester, Felix, who fails to amuse the king (Anthony Quayle) and who lusts for the queen (Lynn Redgrave). The ghost of Felix's father ("who died in childbirth") orders Felix to seduce the queen. With the aid of an explosive aphrodisiac, Felix is about to succeed. He is delayed by the queen's chastity belt, however, discovered by the king, and beheaded.

The setting and amber hue suggest the tradition of Fred Zinneman's *A Man for All Seasons* (1966). But unlike the Sir Thomas More of Robert Bolt's original play, Felix is neither a figure for all times nor an ethical constant against a world in flux. An exceedingly narrow figure who simply does not fit into his setting, he is a man for just one season—and this is not his time.

The fact that Felix is a misfit is expressed in the abundance of anachronisms that Allen gives him. To wit: "I must think of something quickly because before you know it the Renaissance will be here and we'll all be painting." Felix's very appearance—his glasses and neurotic face—mark him as a modern figure who does not fit into his medieval setting. In this spirit, too, he tricks the queen's guards and then addresses the film audience: "Did you like the way I fooled those guys?" He is amazed that the queen "sleeps with the king and *he* wears leotards." This medieval jester has a modern perspective upon his own period. But rather than giving him a practical advantage over his contemporaries, it merely confuses him and makes him an outsider in his own time.

This affliction of modernity is also expressed in the jester's excruciatingly bad jokes. A poor combination of Bob Hope and Milton Berle:

> I know you're out there. I can hear you breathing. But seriously, ladies and germs. . . .

Though he has the whole range of comedy from which to draw, this jester's jokes are so bad that the king explodes with "Not funny," a dog slinks away nauseated, and two sentinels leave with a disgusted "Oh Jesus." Felix is almost the personification of television. Indeed his key speech, a parody of Hamlet's famous meditation on the nature of existence, centers on the medium:

> TV or not TV, that is the congestion. Consumption be done about it? Of cough, of cough.

Being is reduced to television, and our hero contemplates its choking pollution of man. It is in this scene that he is ordered by his father's ghost to seduce the queen. At first Felix rightly doubts the feasibility of his assignment: "But I am a baseborn fool. I cannot screw above my station." But he allows himself to follow the task set by the spectral visitor. This necessarily leads to his doom, for such is the fate of anyone who seeks to transcend his true nature by using artificial aids (such as aphrodisiacs) or by emulating images from the media ("that is the congestion").

Felix cannot quite be taken to represent television. For one thing, he enjoys a bawdiness more familiar in film and theater. Thus he uses a monstrous pike to undo the chastity belt, vowing: "With most grievous dispatch, I will open the latch and get to her snatch." Moreover, he seems to be a pastiche of various dramatic references. The scene with his father parodies *Hamlet;* his beheading parodies the ending of Orson Welles's film of *Macbeth.* His life and character are completely shaped by the myths of his culture, its art, and its media.

Do aphrodisiacs work? Dr. Reuben suggests that the only ones that work are such things as alcohol and marijuana, which tend to free our inhibitions. Allen's answer to the same question is that we are the victims of myths, one of which involves the magical arousal of passion. Our media's obsession with sexual conquest is the modern aphrodisiac.

What Is Sodomy?

Gene Wilder plays Doug Ross, a Jackson Heights general practitioner who is happily married and cozily affluent until an Armenian shepherd, Milos (Titos Vandis) comes for help with a romantic problem. Milos is in love with Daisy, a sheep, but she rejects him. Despite his sense of the absurdity of the affair, Dr. Ross agrees to meet Daisy and immediately falls in love with her. The doctor and the sheep enter into a passionate affair that brings him to ruin.

This episode parodies the conventional moral fable in which a prominent citizen is ruined by an unconventional passion. Thus we get the love-at-first-sight, the obligatory hotel tryst, the suspicious wife—she catches her husband fondling his lamb's wool sweater; later, she wonders why he smells of lambchops—and the lovers' traditional conviction that their passion can overcome social differences:

> I know this must all seem very strange to you. You from the hills of Armenia and me from Jackson Heights. And yet, I think it could work. If we give it a chance.

—Daisy looks away demurely. Then the lovers are exposed. Ross loses his home. Driven together, the lovers find their relationship weakening. In a parody of the famous breakfast sequence in *Citizen Kane* (1941), their estrangement is imaged in the lengthening dinner tables between them, as well as in their increasingly dark and cheap rooms. Finally Ross is a broken man. Daisy deserts him. At night Ross slinks through the slum streets alone and unkempt. He is last seen crouching in the shadows, taking a swig from a bottle of Wool-ite. All this is familiar romantic melodrama, "except instead of

Jennifer Jones, it's going to be a sheep" that brings our hero to ruin, as Allen noted to Wilder.[8] These conventions convey the traditional moral: the man who gives All for Love can expect ruination.

We are never told exactly what sodomy is. Instead we are given a story of high passion in which the female is a sheep. This episode presents sex with animals as a love story because the film industry cannot admit the possibility of sex without love. Nor can the industry conceive of sex with animals per se, so it couches the answer in the coy but lurid formulae of conventional, moralistic melodrama. This prurience is typical of the manner in which the media deal with illicit sex: everything is reduced to conventional rhetoric.

The episode of Ross's destructive passion for an Armenian sheep not only parodies melodrama but suggests the fragility of our social codes. The doctor is characterized as being supremely cultured, civilized, and well mannered. Hence Wilder's brilliant fifteen-second reaction to the news that Milos loves his sheep. Unflappably, Wilder registers the information, overcomes his considerable surprise, seems proud that he has controlled it, and after briefly considering the possibility finally says, "Oh, I see." This civilized cool will crumble before his passion.

Dr. Ross lives in a de-natured world. His suits and home are gray; abstract posters by Picasso and LeCorbusier and feebly cheery "Smile" and "Help" signs adorn his office walls. In contrast, Milos represents nature and the essential life. To Dr. Ross's astonished "With the sheep?" Milos replies, "Naturally." In Dr. Ross's passion, then, the tamed middle-class spirit is rudely confronted and over-whelmed by stirrings from man's primitive past.

As the complacent doctor discovers his humanity in an affair with a sheep, this episode relates to the frame of rabbits and Cole Porter's invitation to animal misbehavior. On its formal level, the story exposes the failure of our fictional forms to confront directly elemental and discomfiting facts of human experience.

Why Do Some Women Have Trouble Reaching an Orgasm?

Allen and Louise Lasser play Fabrizio and Gina, Italian newlyweds. Despite Fabrizio's reputation as a lover, Gina cannot achieve orgasm—

until she experiences sex in a public place. The sketch concludes with a series of such successful, public performances.

The episode parodies modern Italian cinema, especially the films of Antonioni with their screen-filling empty, white walls, splashes of color, plastic-and-chrome furniture, and abrupt changes of perspective and tone. Specific shots recall *La Notte* (1960), *Red Desert* (1964), and *Blow-Up* (1966). Allen declares that one shot of Venetian blinds, purple flowers, and shadows is designed to be "a totally satirical Bertolucci shot." [9] Finally, the plot recalls a similar episode in *Boccaccio '70* (1970).

The Antonioni parallels raise both directors' concern with social anomie, ennui, and the lingering, obsolete morality by which their jaded, sensitive characters try to live. Since the episode is in Italian with English subtitles, an additional effect is to impute sexual frustration and inhibition to the excessive intellectuality of the art film audience.

A second effect of the subtitles is to make language itself a theme of the episode. Through the subtitles Allen points up the communications gap between people of different backgrounds. For example, on the wedding night the mellifluous Italian is translated into such phrases as "Go easy on my hymen" and "Now take off your pants." Similarly, when Fabrizio says his wife is unresponsive, "Come un salmon freddo," the translation is even harsher: "You just lay there—passive—like a lox." True, one man's meat is another man's *poisson*, but the English translation suggests that the husband's cherished delicacy is not just dead but processed! In a similar vein, "Are you —small?" is the subtitle translation for a friend wiggling his little finger at Fabrizio and leering, "Piccolo?" These comic instances of culture gap and failures in translation suggest one answer to Allen's question about difficulty of orgasm: fulfillment may be impeded by gaps in communication.

The incongruous casting of Allen as a slick Italian lover is another kind of translation joke. In his English-language roles Woody Allen is an incompetent lover, but in this Italian sequence, he plays a Mastroianni type—suave, elegant, and proficient with the ladies. Fabrizio has one scene of fumbling to remind us of the Allen persona: at a moment of high passion he produces an impressive vibrator, which promptly shorts and breaks into flames. Otherwise Fabrizio is Allen's opposite.

This disparity between actor and role relates to the question that gives the episode its title. For to ask why women have difficulty achieving orgasm is to imply that it is solely the woman's problem. Moreover, macho complacency is implied in the "answer": some women are so jaded as to require the added thrill of danger. By casting himself as the macho hero (instead of using, say, Burt Reynolds), Allen underlines the question's shallow assertion of masculine vanity.

The sketch also reflects on the function of films. Like Gina, our jaded society craves thrills. By casting his own *schlemiel* as the great Italian lover, Allen dramatizes the wish-fulfilling function of movies and movie stars.

Are Transvestites Homosexual?

Sam and Tess are a middle-aged, middle-class couple who accompany their daughter to dinner at the home of her fiancé's parents. During dinner, Sam excuses himself, sneaks into the master bedroom, dons his hostess's clothing, and cavorts joyfully in front of a mirror. When he hears the host coming in, Sam jumps out the window. He is robbed by a purse snatcher. In the ensuing hubbub with passers-by and police, Sam is exposed to his family and to his daughter's prospective in-laws as a transvestite.

The sketch opens and closes with scenes of family intimacy, as Sam and Tess first dress for dinner and then undress for bed. Despite this intimacy, however, there is a telling harshness in the wife's expression of sympathy for her humiliated husband:

> I love you and you love me. You could have come to me and said "Tess, I have a diseased mind. I'm a sick individual. I need help. I need treatment. I'm perverted. I'm unfit to function with normal, decent people." I would have understood.

While ostensibly expressing sympathy, Tess is actually attributing to her husband the revulsion that she truly feels. In effect, we are given a verbal variation of transvestism. Tess "puts on" Sam's voice to reveal her true feelings, and "puts on" the tone of an understanding wife to project her socially required image. This speech is thus a variation on Sam's own dilemma, for he must don unconventional clothing in order to project his true nature.

Allen is careful to develop a charm and sympathy in Lou Jacobi's performance as Sam. For example, Sam clearly feels inadequate by comparison with his host, who is a successful executive, an expert gardener and pianist, and a shrewd and lucky art collector. Moreover, Jacobi's Sam is a figure of physical coarseness; his penchant for female dress expresses his aspiration toward delicacy. There is something touching as well as comic in his swirl before his hostess's mirror, in his attempt to veil his mustache, and even in the pseudonym that he gives the police. It combines a European family name with an exotic and improbable individuality: Jasmine Glick. As "Glick" is Yiddish for "luck," the surname is an ironic reflection on his misfortune and on his inability to sustain his desired image of delicacy.

The element of film parody is not as obvious in this episode as in the others, because what is parodied is not so much a matter of genre conventions as of tone. Sam's tragic exposure occurs at a family dinner; his frustrated sexual nature is revealed at an event that celebrates the marital union of two families. Allen could have called the episode "Guess What's Coming to Dinner?" because it sets an unaccepted outsider into a situation of rigid conventions. That Sam's exposure occurs on the corner of Arden Boulevard may give him the respectability of the tradition of sex-role changes in Shakespeare, but it also suggests the unreality of the tranquil, uniform neighborhood.

Finally, one should observe two ways in which this episode fairly represents the original book. By dramatizing an example of a transvestite who is not homosexual, it covers Dr. Reuben's answer to the question: "Not necessarily." [10] More importantly, in Tess's revulsion and in the hosts' shock, Allen dramatizes Reuben's shrill attack on homosexuality.

The transvestite sketch has more emotional impact than any other in the film, but Allen originally intended the spot to be filled by a different question, "What Makes a Man a Homosexual?" In it Allen played a spider on the make, and Louise Lasser played a black widow spider who seduces and then devours him. At the end the camera zoomed back to reveal that the drama had been witnessed by an entymologist, peering through his microscope. The entymologist was a lisping homosexual also played by Woody Allen. This episode was filmed, but Allen was unsatisfied with its ending. He replaced it with the transvestite story.

To judge by the script, as published in Eric Lax's valuable study of Allen,[11] this episode was extremely funny, especially as it projected onto insects human habits of thought and speech. The conclusion reversed this and showed a scientist unfairly projecting onto the human female the predatory sexuality of the female spider. This set of projections would have related the episode to Allen's media satire in the film, for it shows man defining human nature according to the images he has been watching.

What Are Sex Perverts?

From his most sensitive story, the transvestite sketch, Allen goes to his most vulgar. From the episode most free from obvious associations with the media, he goes to the one that is most explicitly related to television. This entire episode is presented as a television show, with the image in the flickering grain of television and framed as a television screen.

Television star Jack Barry hosts a panel show, *What's My Perversion?* Sophisticated real-life panel-show stars Pamela Mason, Regis Philbin, Toni Holt, and Robert Q. Lewis try to guess the perversion of guests. Other contestants vie for the honor of having the most fascinating sexual hang-up. On this particular program the winner is a lovable old rabbi, who gets to act out his favorite fantasy—he is bound to a chair and whipped by a beautiful woman while his wife sits at his feet gobbling pork. This unconventional subject matter is packaged in the inane normalcy that characterizes television quiz shows.

Allen's television show renders openly the sexual obsessions that genuine television generally deals with by coy indirection. This is clearest in the commercial for Lancer hair conditioner. Two male athletes in a locker room discuss the product, then fall into a passionate embrace in the background, while the price appears in sharp focus in the foreground. Moreover, by presenting perversion within the context of an open, normal television show, Allen is making the point that the distinction between what is normal and what is a perversion is strictly a matter of cultural choice. Allen dramatizes Dr. Reuben's point that perverts are not necessarily "wild-eyed drooling maniacs, lusting for an innocent victim," but "anyone who isn't interested in the penis-vagina version of sex." [12] Thus the prize-winning rabbi hails from the heartland of innocence, Muncie, Indiana, and his libertine fantasy climaxes in a forbidden something that is not sexual but dietary—his wife eating pork.

Are the Findings of Doctors and Clinics Who Do Sexual Research Accurate?

This question is not in Reuben's book, so it is a significant Allen addition. His answer is obviously "no," for this episode finds lunacy in a mad scientist, Dr. Bernardo (John Carradine), and his sex research.

The sequence parodies two distinct types of horror film. The first is the cycle of mad-scientist Gothic thrillers. On a dark, isolated country road, a young sexuality researcher, Victor Shakopopolous (Allen) meets an attractive Sunday supplement reporter, Helen (Heather MacRae), and takes her along to interview Bernardo. The couple are horrified to find that the doctor plans to use them in his mad experiments. During the course of their escape, the laboratory explodes. At this point the second genre begins: the marauding, murdering monster movie. A forty-foot-high breast escapes from Bernardo's lab and terrorizes the countryside. Only after our hero has lured the breast into a huge bra is order restored.

The three central characters represent the basic issues. The reporter stands for the popularization of sexual research through journalistic simplifications. The mad Dr. Bernardo represents lunatic attempts to reduce the mystery of sex to scientific data. As he reports, he was considered mad by Masters and Johnson because he discovered: how to make a man impotent by hiding his hat; the connection between excessive masturbation and entering politics; and the principle "that clitoral orgasm should not be only for women." His current projects include studying the premature ejaculation of a hippopotamus and building a 400-foot diaphragm to provide birth control for the entire nation at once.

Victor struggles to reduce the strange events to a pattern he can handle. Hence his two responses to the obligatory hunchbacked servant, Igor (the misshapen product of a four-hour orgasm that "backfired"): "There's a big problem with domestics these days," and "Posture. Posture." When he and Helen flee Bernardo's exploding castle, Victor observes: "Now we owe *them* a dinner." The young researcher cannot adjust to the infusion of horror-film elements into his life. Bernardo is a scientist with a warped imagination, but Victor is a scientist unequal to the products of the imagination.

Victor proves more capable in the second part of the story because there the threat is less a reflection of movie horror and more an extension of his own anxieties. When the monstrous mammary menaces the countryside the dangers remain rooted in realistic details of life. There is a difference in scale, not in kind, in the sheriff's warning, "Be on the look-out for a large female breast, about a 4,000 with an X cup." Victor explains the death of a little boy: "The cream slowed him up and the milk killed him. . . . We're up against a very clever tit. It shoots half-and-half." In the only joke that derives from movie-reality, Victor borrows from the vampire film tradition and tries to fend off the advancing monster by wielding a cross. This film convention fails so Victor must draw his solution from reality—he deploys a giant bra. The sheriff remains worried: "They usually travel in pairs."

The monster is a projection of familiar anxieties. Victor's conquest of the breast is important to him because as an infant he was breast-fed from falsies. On a social level, the breast's first victims are two lovers petting in an open convertible. As the man fondles his girl friend's breast, the giant nipple looms up in his rearview mirror, as though reflecting his thoughts. Later the breast dwarfs a billboard of a bikinied beauty selling the idea that "Every body needs milk." These details of language and imagery relate the danger of the breast to realistic anxieties, whereas the earlier Dr. Bernardo sequence derived from the conventions of the horror film. (For all its greater realism, the image of billboard and breast is also an ironic allusion to Fellini's contribution to *Boccaccio '70,* in which Anita Ekberg comes down to life full-blown from a billboard advertisement for milk.)

The giant mammary is not only an expression of the American breast fetish but—true to the monster movie tradition—an externalization of the characters' unreconciled anxieties. By rooting the episode in popular film genres, Allen shows that the powerful force in human sexuality is the imagination and not those physical aspects subject to scientific control and verification.

In other words, we can learn more about human sexuality from the arts than from the sciences. The poetic or imaginative insights are more accurate than those of science when it comes to dealing with the tensions and impulses of human sexuality. This point would have been even more obvious had Allen retained the earlier sketch in which a homosexual scientist studied the devouring sexuality of the black widow spider. That scientist's narrow, indeed microscopic, perspective would have contrasted with the dominant gigantism motif in the drama of Victor and Helen—the woman on silicone, Igor's back, a man fornicating with a giant rye bread, the 400-foot diaphragm, and the huge breast and bra. But whether reduced or amplified, the sexual response is inevitably distorted when the human scale is lost. Victor pessimistically concludes: "When it comes to sex, there are certain things that should be always left unknown—and with my luck they probably will be." Even after scientists and artists have had their say, sex remains a matter of personal discovery, personal mystery.

What Happens during Ejaculation?

Allen explains the psychological and physiological processes in male orgasm by converting Dr. Reuben's analogy of a missile launching into a space film. As in Richard Fleischer's *Fantastic Voyage* (1966), the inside of the human body is explored in the language of the outer-space genre. Consistent with his usual mock-heroic stance, Allen deploys the massive technology of science to depict what happens to the prosaic Sidney and his dinner date in a romantic tussle on a car seat.

Allen's point is again the folly of treating man's emotional and sexual aspects as if they were scientific mechanisms. Hence the gruesome spectacle when Mission Control (or more properly, Emission Control) orders "Roll out the tongue" for a kiss. Sidney's passion fades with lines like "Maintain hands on breast."

By casting two well-known actors in significant roles, Allen relates the episode to the way we internalize our screen models. The ever-fastidious Tony Randall plays the operator who receives messages from the body. The macho Burt Reynolds is responsible for Sidney's physical reactions to those messages. Thus Randall hears that the leg itches, but Reynolds sends out the order to scratch it.[13] Similarly, it is Reynolds who determines to "try to ball her right there in the car."

Woody Allen himself plays a sperm cell who has all the anxieties and fears that we associate with the Allen persona. As a sperm cell, Allen represents the basic unit of human life. That essence of humanity is already fraught with fears. "Do you know what it's like out there?" he asks another sperm, "I'm scared. I don't want to go." When he's not worrying about his nemesis—"the pill"—he's worrying about slamming his head against a wall of hard rubber, and worse— "What if it's a homosexual encounter?" This sperm forgets his training school oath, "to fertilize an ovum or die trying," and broods over the entire range of possible disasters: "What if he's masturbating? I'm liable to wind up on the ceiling."

All these quips suggest that nervousness, squeamishness, and dread are sperm deep. The expansion of man's technological prowess (to which the space-launching imagery attests) and the refinement of his artistic skills do not reduce his sexual anxieties but only give him new ways to express them.

In *Everything You Always Wanted To Know About Sex* Allen parodies a variety of film styles to demonstrate man's obsession with sex and his frustration by the conventions of art and science. Allen jocularly made this point in a promotion piece in *Playboy:*

> I had a choice of filming this or the Old Testament and chose the former because it made more sense. There are probably a lot of people who will think [this] is a dirty movie, and it's those people I'm counting on.[14]

In spite of its episodic nature, *Everything You Always Wanted To Know About Sex* has an astonishing unity that confirms our sense of Allen's new sophistication in technique. One source of unity is the historical range of the settings—from the medieval opening to the futuristic conclusion, all within the framework of the eternal rabbit.

Another derives from Allen's choice of his own roles, which stand out because he is the only performer to appear in more than one episode and because the audience recognizes him as the film's creator. Even the Allen characters' names recall his earlier films. His jester is "Felix," from *Play It Again, Sam,* and his "Victor Shakopopolous" is from *What's New, Pussycat?* Since his sperm is the human essence, it is appropriately unnamed, but his smooth Italian is "Fabrizio," which means "the maker" and so relates both to sexual success and to Allen's function as author-director.

Allen's first appearance is closest to his familiar persona—the misfit monologuist, the sexually frustrated neurotic. His second is the antithesis—the suave Italian lover, Fabrizio. The third synthesizes the first two. As Victor, he is the average citizen who heroically battles a monster and in the process resolves a childhood trauma. His fourth appearance returns him to his persona of nervous maladjustment, the squeamish sperm. These four roles allow Allen to begin and end with his familiar image as a nervous failure. A doomed jester at the beginning and a terrified sperm at the end, Allen has intermediate film-inspired careers as Fabrizio the virile lover and Victor the giant tamer (or breast beater). This sequence of roles suggests that films permit viewers to enjoy interludes of vicarious success. Allen's double role in the omitted episode, a homosexual entymologist watching himself as a successful but doomed heterosexual spider, would have been his middle role in five and would have emphasized the process embodied in the other four. The outside two roles are of sexual failure, while the inner two are successes based on fantasies related to film viewing.

Finally, the sequence of Allen's roles suggests two kinds of progression. Allen advances from the incompetent jester, through the smug, pleasure-seeking playboy, through the paranoid homosexual, through the horror-film hero, to the nameless sperm, which is the most modest and yet the most heroic character of all—the germ of life. In one respect Allen's roles trace the emergence of the life instinct despite cultural obstructions and man's pleasure-oriented sexuality. Allen's role as entymologist would have been pivotal—and it remains so in the conception of the film—because it presented an inner story of natural reproduction with an outer story that involved a man's horrified recoiling from it.

In addition, there is a development in the four roles' inflection of Allen's persona. After his first appearance as a horrid stand-up comic, Allen moves through a variety of models, of types of film hero, until he finally appears as man's most essential self, the sperm cell. In this respect the sequence of Allen's roles embodies his growth from formulaic, conventional comedy through the mock-heroic attempts to emulate inappropriate models, to the ultimate simplicity of essential self-expression. From routine through mock-heroic pretensions to self: Allen's four roles reprise his development as a comic artist. Of course, the "self" that remains after Allen has stripped away the inapt and inept images is the core of the Allen persona—a nervous Everyman terrified by the prospect of life.

12

Sleeper (1973)

After his series of short parodies in *Everything You Always Wanted To Know About Sex*, Woody Allen made a feature-length parody of the futuristic science-fiction film (Rip Van Winkle subtype). *Sleeper* was an ambitious undertaking—a social satire intended to delight children as well as adults. "It bothers me that I would be confined to intellectual humor," Allen noted.[1] As a result, the film provides a hilarious slapstick adventure story with a serious underpinning. As the title alerts us, Allen's central metaphor is sleep, which can be taken to represent noncommitment either in one's political or emotional life.

Allen and Diane Keaton play characters who are awakened from hedonistic apathy into both political and emotional engagement. Allen is Miles Monroe, part owner of the Happy Carrot Health Food Restaurant in Greenwich Village. When his 1973 minor ulcer check-up ran into complications, his cousin had him frozen into suspended animation. The film opens with two scientists thawing Miles out 200 years later. They need an unregistered citizen to help them overthrow the tyrannical government, which seems to be modeled after Aldous Huxley's *Brave New World*. When the state pursues Miles as a dangerous alien, he poses as a robot valet, and then kidnaps his employer, Luna (Diane Keaton). Miles is caught and brainwashed. But Luna escapes and is politicized by the rebel underground. She then involves Miles in the rebels' uprising. At the end Miles and Luna pretend to be doctors; summoned by the government, they are assigned to clone the state leader, whose nose is all that remains after an assassination attempt.

In the tradition of negative utopias, the world to which Miles awakens in 2173 is a cautionary extension of our own; the country is called the Central Parallel of the Americas. The central parallel between Miles's new world and ours is its hedonistic apathy. Lost in the stupor of pleasure, Luna's society literally has a ball (large and silver) on drugs. Sex has been reduced to a mechanical convenience—the orgasmitron—to which a character can repair in mid-sentence for an orgasm—partner optional. As the characters are lost in their pursuit of pleasure, the joke about the cloning of the leader quite literally posits a society that is led by the nose.

Luna's pleasure-seeking friends are contrasted to the rebels and to the activists who revive Miles. While they do not convert Miles to political commitment, they do awaken him to the realization that his own survival depends on awareness and activity. Formerly Miles engaged only in faddist causes: "For twenty-four hours once I refused to eat grapes." He pleads insignificance: "I'm not the heroic type. I was beaten up by Quakers." But he is forced into activity in order to survive. In the process he awakens Luna's emotional life and sense of responsibility. At the end Miles doubts even their new leader, the rebel captain Erno: "Don't you understand? In six months we'll be stealing Erno's nose. Political solutions don't work." Miles opposes to political faith a belief in the two basic facts of life—sex and death, two things that happen once in his lifetime, "but at least after death you're not nauseous!"

Earlier, Miles's flawed humanism had been expressed in a remarkable scene with Luna, just after he has convinced her to side with him against the state.[2] He counters Luna's proposal of mechanical sex by suggesting an alternative:

LUNA: Do you want to perform sex with me?
MILES: Perform sex? I don't think I'm up to a performance, but I'll rehearse with you if you like.

Miles prefers human imperfection to the nonhuman efficiency perfected by Luna's society, where they "don't have any problems. Everybody's frigid." *Sleeper* warns against the loss of human personality, individuality, and vulnerability, by positing an age of imposed equality, technological dominance, and the replacement of human responsibility with the debasing efficiency of the machine.

The fact that Miles fondles his clarinet throughout this delicate scene gives it a personal weight, for Allen is known to play the clarinet and he plays with Dixieland musicians on the *Sleeper* sound track. This personal touch in Miles's characterization suggests that Allen is beginning to shed his *schlemiel* persona. The clarinet is the loser character's first public assertion of the creator's talent. In *Sleeper*, Allen told Eric Lax, he began to "come out aggressively a little bit." [3]

Despite this new assertiveness, Allen's dominant image in *Sleeper* is still the fumbling loser. Our first laugh is at the sight of Woody when he's drawn out of the deep freeze. His aluminum-foil booties, his glasses, and his protruding nose give us the comfortingly familiar Allen image. In addition many of his jokes are based on familiar routines. Thus he hasn't had sex for 200 years—"204 if you count my marriage." Being dead for 200 years is "like spending a weekend in Beverly Hills." Threatened (implausibly) that his brain will be "electronically simplified," he replies in terror: "My brain? That's my second favorite organ." This is the Allen persona in full weed.

One distinctive set of jokes shows the persona unable to adjust to his new situation in the world of the future. He is staggered to learn that all his friends have been dead for 200 years: "But they all ate organic rice." A series of one-liners show him clinging to old associations for support against the mystery of his new world:

> I want to go back to sleep. If I don't get at least 600 years I'm grouchy all day . . . What kind of government you got here? This is worse than California . . . I knew it was too good to be true. I parked right near the hospital . . . You know, I bought Polaroid at 7. It's probably up to millions by now.

As he later admits to Luna, "I'm always joking. It's a defense mechanism." These jokes show him trying to apply his obsolete experience to his new situation.

The film suggests that the plastic society of 2173 needs the nervous energy and imperfect humanity of the *schlemiel* in order to recover a sense of what is human. To this end Allen makes the future society's citizens and their robots of equal character and worth. Both man and robot are said to be "reprogrammed." The equivalence is confirmed when Miles first meets Luna. His face is covered in white so that he will pass for a robot; she has her face covered in green face cream, as she prepares for a party with her vapid, radical-chic friends. He is a human pretending to be a robot; she is a virtual robot but thinks of herself as a human, though she does not recognize her responsibilities as such. Thus she refuses to spoil her party with news of a friend's arrest for underground activities: "This world is so full of wonderful things, what makes people go berserk and hate everything anyway?" They have the drug orb, the two-way telescreen, and the orgasmitron—"What more do they want?" A mechanical imperturbability is also found in the robot butler: "Excuse me, sir. The security police are here and they are surrounding the house. When will you be wanting lunch?" When Allen models his robots after such human types as the designer's limp-wristed and bitchy valet, the robots are not just extensions of their masters but an index of their masters' disappearing humanity and a metaphor for man being replaced by machine.

Ethnic jokes affirm the need for quirkish human individuality. Luna remarks, for example, that most of the men in 2173 are impotent, "except for the ones whose ancestors are Italian." And Miles has a scene with two Jewish robot tailors assigned to make his uniform. Ginsberg and Cohen are a delightful contrast to the traditional robot impersonality, and to their own function, which is to make something *uniform!* Their warmth, humor, and bickering deprecation express Allen's faith in the survival of human character in an age of technology and uniformity. There is even something reassuringly human in their failure to make Miles a uniform that fits reasonably well. ("Okay, okay, we'll take it in!")

By maintaining their spirit and their ethnic character in such an antipathetic world, the Jewish robots perform the same function that Allen's Jewish hero does in the Gentile world. As Barry Gross has observed in a fine study of the tension between Jew and Gentile in recent American popular culture, the Jewish figure challenges the values and assumptions of the WASP society. He releases the WASP from his inhibitions and conventions, enlivens his existence, and raises new possibilities for the WASP's life, by providing an example of a "vital, energetic, passionate, committed, in all respects hyper—hypercritical, hypersensitive, hypertense, hyperkinetic, hyperbolic" spirit.[4] Gross's thesis is firmly supported by Allen's work from

Play It Again, Sam through *Interiors,* and especially by Miles Monroe and the Jewish robots in *Sleeper.*

In a culture drifting toward bland homogeneity, strong individual personalities of the past are preserved on film. For example, among the twentieth-century artifacts that Miles is asked to identify are film clips. In one, Howard Cosell prematurely blathers on about Muhammad Ali's retirement. In another, we have Richard Nixon's Checkers speech. (Interestingly enough for a pre-Watergate film, Nixon is known to the 2173 doctors as an American president who did something horrendous and of whom all traces were therefore erased.)

Allen also makes use of a number of classic film-comedy routines that draw on the past tradition of his art. Hence the running gag of the state police firing at Miles with a bazooka. First their gun explodes, then their control box, then their van. Like the Jewish tailors, the spirit of the Keystone Kops manages to survive in an age of technological perfection. The sole function of another scene—one involving a gigantic garden—is apparently to set up the ultimate banana-peel pratfall.

Allen's performance as Miles also draws on film precedents. His robot disguise makes him resemble Harry Langdon, an earlier clown-innocent befuddled by a sophisticated, strange world. The scenes in which Miles and Luna attempt to clone the dead leader recall Bob Hope's comedy: "We're here to see the nose. We hear it's running." Cowardly but brash Miles escapes by holding a gun to the nose and threatening to shoot it between the eyes. When a steam roller runs over the nose it is massively flattened out like the victim in a Chuck Jones cartoon. These jokes relate the film to a noble tradition from which it derives character.

Allen also revised the past in details of the design of the film. The furniture styles mix in a representation of the old with the new. Although the rooms are ultramodern, almost each one contains one antique piece of furniture—a washing stand, a grandfather clock—as a remembrance of times past. In the same spirit, the musical score is not futuristic but Dixieland. These examples of the past have a warmth and sense of human connection that express optimism about the survival of human values in the world of the future.

In four scenes Miles Monroe is confronted with his own past. The first is when he is brought back to life. His infantilism—he dribbles his drink, splatters his food, and generally cavorts like a zany infant—is underscored by the sound track: "Yes, Sir, That's My Baby." When he relearns to walk, he takes his first steps backward. In the second example, he is asked to identify a variety of relics from his earlier life (in his confusion he identifies Charles de Gaulle as a famous chef and Bela Lugosi as a mayor of New York City). His third return to his past is the government brainwashing session, during which he is electronically projected into situations summoned from his subconscious, for "assimilation into society." Thus he is Miss Montana in the Miss America contest—and he wins. He must be purged of his past character in all its absurd humanity if he is to achieve robotlike conformity.

Miles's fourth return to his past is the most significant. Luna and Erno undo Miles's reprogramming by performing a psychodrama from his past. The first part is rooted in Miles's personal experience. The two Gentiles assume unconvincing Yiddish accents for a 1962 Flatbush dinner scene in which Miles comes home and tells his parents that he and his wife are getting divorced. This episode frankly dredges up Miles's Jewish identity ("Vot vill the *goyim* say? . . . Stop whining and eat your *shicksa*") as the means of reviving Miles's individuality. The second part of the psychodrama involves Miles's experience of art. He breaks into a parody of Blanche DuBois from Tennessee Williams's *A Streetcar Named Desire*. Luna responds with a creditable version of Marlon Brando's Kowalski. Here a classic work of creative imagination bridges two centuries to make a profound connection, purging Miles's mind of the government interference and restoring the individuality of his imagination. When Miles quotes Blanche's famous "Whoever you are, I have always depended upon the kindness of strangers," he in effect cites the function of art to overcome man's alienation, to bring the artist and his audiences in all times and places into a community based on the human values of the work.

As *Sleeper* is about art as well as life, not surprisingly it includes a variety of false artists. For example, the stirring connections caused by the Tennessee Williams play have a comic parody in Miles's recollection of Lisa Sorenson, a Trotskyite who became a Jesus freak and was arrested for selling pornographic connect-the-dots books. More importantly, Luna's boyfriend Harold represents the art of the apathetic hedonist. Detached from the responsibilities of living, Harold cannot "understand the criminal element," that is, the rebel underground, because "We're artists. We respond only to beauty." This simpleton is enchanted by Luna's puerile poem ("So obviously influenced by McKuen") about a cloying little boy whose butterfly turns into a caterpillar when the lad pledges himself to universal understanding. Luna is brokenhearted when she learns that a caterpillar really turns into a butterfly; her shallow faith and unreal art cannot survive the onslaught of truth.

Miles may have slept for 200 years, but the more significant sleeper is Luna, who has remained dormant for a lifetime and who—thanks to Miles—awakens to a fuller life. The caterpiller evolves into a butterfly.

13

Love and Death (1975)

In its design, complexity of script, and philosophical import, Woody Allen's next film was his most ambitious project to date. *Love and Death* is a comic epic that confronts the classical Russian literature and cinema. Its very title evokes *Crime and Punishment* (though not necessarily in that order) and *War and Peace*. Allen's new somberness is confirmed in the opening voice-over monologue. His character wonders how he ever got into his incredible predicament:

> To be executed for a crime that I never committed. Of course, isn't all mankind in the same boat? Isn't all mankind ultimately executed for a crime it never committed? The difference is that all men go eventually; I'm supposed to go at 6 o'clock tomorrow morning. I was supposed to go at 5 o'clock but I've got a smart lawyer. Got leniency.

The Dostoyevskian opening dwindles into bathetic comedy. This device, bathos, is the primary source of unity and meaning in the film. Throughout *Love and Death*, an elevated expectation is established only to be comically deflated. As a result man seems too small a creature to assume the mantle of heroic philosophy woven by the great writers.

Allen plays a nineteenth-century Russian peasant named Boris Dimitrovitch Semyonyovitch Grushenko. Despite his sensitive and cowardly nature, he is forced into the war against Napoleon. Boris's compelling ambition is to win his sweetheart, his cousin Sonia Petrovna Pavlovna Volkonska (Diane Keaton). She marries him on the eve of his duel with a jealous count, because she assumes Boris will be killed. But he survives. At exactly the halfway point in the

film, Boris and Sonia consummate their marriage. At first their relationship is tense, but eventually it settles into an idyllic romance.
This is disrupted when Sonia decides that they should assassinate
Napoleon. When their plot fails, Boris is arrested and sentenced to
die. The film relates the condemned man's remembrances of the
incidents that led to his imminent execution.

Allen's very presence as a bespectacled Jewish intellectual loser in
a nineteenth-century Russian and Christian community is a bathetic
anachronism. His somber concerns and the classic aura of the setting
are deflated by his modern presence and his remarks to Sonia: "Hey,
you've been going to finishing school!" and "Have you been dating
any Russians?" So too the battlefield cheerleaders, the man selling
red-hots (blinis), and Boris's black, army sergeant who rails, "You're
the worst soldier I ever seen." Boris is as striking a misfit in the past
as the Miles of *Sleeper* was in the future.

But this time Allen's character is the moral superior of those
around him. The anachronistic qualities that make him lose his contemporaries' respect win him ours. We respond to the sensitivity behind his attempt to take his butterfly collection when he goes to war,
and the morality that urges him to avoid going to war altogether.
Allen underlines Boris's superiority by defining his character through
modern tones, allusions, and values. A misfit in nineteenth-century
Russia, Boris has stumbled in with the values and perspectives of the
modern Western world. Thus he is brave enough to be a coward in a
society that values only mindless combativeness ("Yes, but I'm a mili-
tant coward").

Part of Boris's character and modernity derive from traditions of
film comedy. For example, his struggles with a loose, wilting, jam-
ming, and goosing sword recall the Chaplin of *Soldier Arms* (1918)
and *The Great Dictator* (1940). In Chaplinesque spirit, too, he becomes a hero when the cannon in which he has fallen asleep fires
him into the enemy headquarters. This soldier thrives by asserting
pacifism and by rejecting false representations of honor and manliness.

Boris also draws on the Bob Hope style (as Allen admits to Eric
Lax).[1] For instance, his courtship of the Countess Alexandrovna is
in the tradition of the slavering, cheeky Hope: "I'll bring the teabags.
We could run a quick check on your erogenous zones. But what about

the dybbuk?"—the latter referring to the jealous Count, listening agog and afume. In the manner of Hope, Boris's doubletalk assumes audience complicity. When Boris is awaiting Napoleon's entrance and admits that he is "Scared? I'm growing beak and feathers!" the Hope inflection confirms that his sense and perspective differ from the other characters in the film.

This same point is made visually. For one thing, Allen plays a small man in a country of robust giants: "I grew to full manhood—five-foot-six . . . Under five-foot-three you need special permission from the Czar to hold land." Allen's first entrance is a futile attempt to follow his brothers in a *kazatsky* dance. A related device is Boris's direct address to the cinema audience when he wishes to dissociate himself from the surrounding ethos. The first time is when his mother refuses him sanctuary from war: "Thanks, Ma. My mother, folks." The second is when the Count pledges to reform. Boris tells the audience, "He's got a great voice, eh? I should have shot him." In both instances he refuses to be swept along by the false heroism of the moment.

Much as Boris relates to other comic heroes, the film as a whole draws on other films. For example, the score is taken mainly from Prokofiev's composition for Eisenstein's *Alexander Nevsky* (1938). This allusion establishes a heroic context that further diminishes Boris's activities. Other film references relate *Love and Death* to political and philosophical cinema. In the first case, the generals' view of the soldiers as a herd of sheep is shown literally. This combines two famous shots, cattle being led to slaughter as metaphors for the workers in Eisenstein's *Strike* (1924) and Chaplin's comparing of the workers to sheep in *Modern Times* (1936). The philosophical cinema is recognized in the many references to Bergman. There is an echo of *Persona* (1966) in the blending of Sonia's and Natasha's faces. More importantly, as Gabriel Miller has demonstrated in detail,[2] *Love and Death* often parallels Bergman's *The Seventh Seal* (1956), in which a more heroic knight than Boris, similarly searching for a material sign of God's existence, traverses a landscape of death and disillusionment before finally being caught up in the Dance of Death. Because of the discrepancy between Boris's image and that of the Bergman hero, there is a comic effect even in these somber cross references.

Allen's funniest film allusion occurs during the hero's wedding night. The montage of stone lions is an obvious parody of the famous sequence in Eisenstein's *Battleship Potemkin* (1925). In the original sequence, the awakening stone lions signify the arousal of the dormant masses into action and the emotional conversion of stone into flesh. But Allen's collage has an aroused lion collapsing into Boris's postcoital exhaustion. The parallel establishes a cinema of political and philosophical commitment, but Boris is defined in terms of the weakness of the flesh. The parody is another example of Allen's mock-heroic deflation.

Similarly, the film's title promises the profound ether of the Russian novel but Allen's literary expressions in the film are reductive. In Boris's jail-cell chat with his father, Dostoyevsky titles are reduced to flat counters of gossip. Boris's father reports hearing from one of the Karamazov brothers that "that nice boy next door, Raskolnikov," murdered a woman:

> BORIS: He must have been *Possessed*.
> FATHER: Well, he was *A Raw Youth*.
> BORIS: *Raw Youth!* He was an *Idiot*. . . . I hear he was a *Gambler*.
> FATHER: You know, he could be your *Double*.
> BORIS: Really. How novel.

Here the film assumes a literary tone only to deflate it. This trivializing of the classic titles points up Allen's major theme in *Love and Death*: philosophical and literary speculation are essentially irrelevant to the business of living. To this end Allen continually introduces philosophical passages only to turn away from them in favor of man's basic appetites—food and sex—the drives by which man ensures his survival both individually and generically.

Allen's deflation of profundity often involves religious subjects. Thus Boris demands that God prove His existence with a miracle, like the traditional parting of the seas or—more practically, perhaps —by making "my Uncle Sasha pick up a check." In the same vein, Boris observes that the virtuous man will "dwell in the house of the Lord for six months with an option to buy." Or, "If Christ was a carpenter, I wondered what he charged for bookshelves" and "If God is testing us, why doesn't he give us a written?" What begins as a traditional statement of religious quest is deflated by the practical concerns of the modern, urban intellectual's struggle to reconcile old faith with his present education and needs. As in Bergman's work, the voice of God cannot be heard; but Allen fills the silence with one-liners.

Allen deflates secular abstractions as well as religious ones. When Boris's brother Ivan dies, his wife and Sonia, his lover, divide his letters. But Allen takes the phrase literally—Sonia takes the vowels and the wife the consonants. Similarly, when Boris's father treasures his "small piece of Russia," we see that it actually is a small hunk of turf, on which he proceeds to build his own model farm. In these jokes, a sentimental abstract is reduced to a comic materialization. Allen's point is that for all the traditional respect paid to abstractions of love, death, patriotism, and philosophy, life remains a matter of immediate sensation, of carrying on in the physical experience of living regardless of what may (or may not) lie beyond.

The film is therefore generally suspicious of philosophy. Boris and Sonia have long debates that may at first seem to luxuriate in the powers of man's intellect, but are ultimately exposed as irrelevant to life. For one thing, man exists in a fundamentally absurd, irrational world to which the orders of logic and language are inappropriate. Thus "Young Gregor was older than Old Gregor," Old Nehamken dies trying to erect a lightning rod during a storm, and Ivan is "a fatality of war . . . bayonetted to death by a Polish conscientious objector." Man's language, science, and logic are weak against the illogic that seems to be the principle of creation.

In this illogical world, man's philosophical bent leads only to confusion. For example, Boris attempts an elementary syllogism to justify assassinating Napoleon: "A: Socrates is a man. B: All men are mortal. C: All men are Socrates. That means all men are homosexual." But Boris's personal anxiety subverts the ostensibly objective course of his logic. Hence the brief scene in which Boris and Sonia somewhat enviously pass the Idiots Convention: "It's easy to be happy, you know, if your one concern in life is figuring out how much saliva to dribble." Logic and philosophy are an affliction.

The lover's intellectualizing even leads them into a ludicrous confusion over their own identities. For example, their first meeting with Napoleon dissolves into a confusion over who is who:

NAPOLEON: You can call me Napoleon.
SONIA: You can call me Napoleon, too.

Boris and Napoleon similarly bog down in an exchange of "No, it's a greater honor for me." The comic convention of impersonation (another Bob Hope favorite) works here as a metaphor for a confused sense of identity.

For his part, the pragmatic Napoleon, briefly confused by the presence of a convincing double, wrestles with the double in the background in order to determine which is the bona fide Napoleon. Because such a direct, physical approach to a problem is uncharacteristic of Boris, this joke is played out on the periphery of the shot. The foreground is occupied by the ambitious Sidney Applebaum, who plots an alliance with the crown to ensure his place in world history (not with the king, note, but with the crown—another abstraction comically literalized). Napoleon's wrestling with his double parodies the self-analysis of classic Russian heroes and the danger attendant on unbridled speculation.

Often in *Love and Death* the characters are isolated from each other by their meditating. When Boris and Sonia become engaged, he pours out his passion for her while she calculates his (negligible) chances of surviving the impending duel. In a later close-up, Boris eulogizes wheat while Sonia describes her dreams of a happy family life and her more apposite dread of suffocation. Earlier, while her first husband carried on an earnest dispute with a herring, Sonia conducted illicit affairs.

The same point is made when Boris declaims a "review" of the army's "little hygiene play," a nineteenth-century stage version of the present-day practice of using films to warn soldiers about venereal disease. As Boris sinks into wrong-headed critical jargon—"A droll spoof aimed more at the heart than the head"—the other soldiers go off to the brothel. Here art as well as philosophy are remote from the business of life, and Boris's analytical disposition increases his isolation.

The most serious case of the philosopher's isolation is Boris's compulsive speculation about the existence of God. Boris is too obsessed with logic and philosophy to be able to accept God's existence on faith, but he is not confident enough to be agnostic. Thus in Boris's duel with the Count, when both duellists are blessed ("God be with you both"), Boris looks heavenward with his usual naïve literalism: "You listening?" Boris fires his gun up into the sky—the shot drops and wounds him in the arm. By addressing the vacant heavens Boris merely wounds himself.

When Boris is engaged in his "favorite pastime"—awaiting his execution—he receives a vision that convinces him there is a God. An angel appears and promises Boris that he will be pardoned by the emperor. To this our hero reacts with an outburst of repulsively righteous confidence:

> . . . the wicked man shall have all kinds of problems. His tongue shall cleave to his mouth and he shall speak like a woman. And he shall be delivered to his enemy whether they can pay the delivery charges or not.

While an angelic choir swells behind his voice, Boris becomes increasingly smug in his religious confidence. But the promise of salvation proves as false as his religious fervor. Boris's quest for communication with God is parodied when (the false) Napoleon wonders whose voices he heard when he entered Sonia's room:

"NAPOLEON": I heard voices.
SONIA: I was praying.
"NAPOLEON": I heard two voices.
SONIA: I do both parts.

In *Love and Death* man's conversation with God is a soliloquy in which he either wounds himself with misdirected faith or inflates himself with false confidence.

Against this fruitless philosophizing Allen posits the more vital activities of the flesh. Hence the many jokes relating sex and death. Some could appear in any Allen routine, such as his observation that Jewish women don't believe in sex after marriage. In context, however, this quip parodies the film's larger concern with the possibility of a life after death. In this film the familiar Allen bawdiness expresses a more pressing need, one that cannot be satisfied or controlled by philosophical digressions.

Boris's mind inevitably moves from logical and moral concerns toward his sexual anxieties. Thus he tells Sonia that he's not the army type: "I can't shower with other men." Later, poised to kill

Napoleon, he waffles on about moral imperatives, Socrates homosexuality, and, ultimately, his concern over a herpes on his lip. When
he is invited to name his seconds for his duel over the Countess, his
reply betrays his primary interest: "Seconds? I never gave her
seconds."

The other characters share Boris's obsessions. For instance, the
sage whom Sonia visits for The Answer reveals that "the best thing
is twelve-year-old blond girls, two of them whenever possible." The
false Napoleon, when he sees Boris aiming a gun at him, leaps to a
sexual conclusion instead of the obvious, political one: "Put down
your gun. She's over eighteen." Boris rightly observes that everyone
is obsessed with sex except for "some men [who] don't think about
sex at all. They become lawyers." Even after they have died, the
characters in Love and Death persist in their sexual and material
anxieties. One dead friend gives Boris a ring to return to the Smolensk
jeweler for a refund, but the dead man insists on keeping the receipt
for tax purposes. Another dead man, Krapotkin, is with another
woman when he asks Boris, "If you run into my wife, tell her I'm
with you."

The numerous jokes about eating also deflate the philosophical
pretensions by affirming the appetites of life. Boris's mother is famed
for her blintzes, which are diagrammed like aeronautical blueprints
(aptly enough, for her denial of maternal security sends Boris to war).
In the same spirit Sonia rebuts Boris's qualms about murder: "And
if everyone went to the same restaurant [at the same time] and ordered blintzes there'd be chaos." In both gags, the domestic delight
of blintzes is corrupted to serve war. The characters' habits of speech
and mind are based in essential human appetites. Thus what Sonia
sees as "this best of all possible worlds," Boris regards as "an enormous restaurant" with "spiders and bugs and big fish eating little
fish and plants eating plants and animals eating. . . ." When Boris
returns from the dead he tells Sonia that death is worse than the
chicken at Tresky's restaurant. (One in-joke: one of the Prokofiev
pieces in the score is his "Love for Three Oranges".) In all these
jokes, good food is assumed to be the civilized norm against which
are measured the hungers and horrors of a world of war and violence. Thus on his first sight of the battlefield carnage Boris concludes: "That army cooking will get you every time."

Allen also translates politics into food. The Russian soldiers are exhorted to battle by a call to save their loved ones from unhealthy French cooking: "Do you want them to eat that rich food and heavy sauces?" The war is reprised as a race between Napoleon's pastry and beef Wellington. Boris receives the news of Napoleon's invasion of Austria with "Why? Is he out of Courvoisier?" The supposedly important reasons for war are reduced to matters of appetite. Conversely, the glories of food are proposed as a more vital point of living than politics or war.

Sonia's associations with food characterize her as a cold person. She cooks Boris meals of snow (including a snow steak that Boris finds "a little rare"!). Moreover, she causes coldness in others. When Boris sneaks up behind her to play "Guess who?" she infers from his touch that he is Old Nehamken, who is dead. On their first night of lovemaking, Boris emerges from under the blanket, dons a pair of fur gloves, and returns to the action. Their romance is a tension between the warm Boris, who craves the life of the instincts, and the chilling woman who is drawn to the cold consolations of philosophy and politics.

Sonia has an impossible quest. She wants a relationship that combines the three great aspects of love: the intellectual, the spiritual, and the sensual. When she finds this ideal difficult to achieve she compromises indiscriminately. For example, when Ivan spurns her, she quickly announces her marriage to one man and then to another when the first choice drops dead from the excitement. Later she has an alphabetical list of lovers; promiscuity is her analgesic for the impossible idealism with which she is afflicted. Her ideals operate at one level of her life, abstractly. But her immediate needs and instincts must be gratified more directly. We see this in the scene where her first husband lies dying. Sonia interrupts her impassioned valedictory with a cool question to the doctors: "What's he got, about eight minutes?" Then when the doctors console the new widow ("The dead pass on and life is for the living") Sonia proves amenable: "I guess you're right. Where do you want to eat?" Life must go on, regardless of our hopeless ideals and pointless speculations. The appetites must be served. Life is for the now, the world for the senses, and the hereafter (if any) for the then.

At the end of the film Sonia remains cooly detached from the torrid tangle of unrequited loves unraveled by her cousin Natasha (e.g., "The firm of Mishkin and Mishkin is sleeping with the firm of Tushkov and Tushkov"—the lurking "Tush" may imply buggery as well as interoffice incest). Natasha is innocent and inexperienced: "I never want to marry. I just want to get divorced." The young naïf wants the liberty without experiencing the restriction from which to be liberated. But man needs strictures in order to enjoy his freedom from them. In context, man needs his philosophical abstractions and processes in order to escape them into the enjoyment of life's riches and its appetites. The cold hand of philosophy must be known before it can be shaken off.

Boris makes this point in his concluding monologue. All he has learned from life is that man is divided into mind and body: "The mind embraces all the nobler aspirations, like poetry, philosophy, but the body has all the fun." Although Allen subordinates philosophy to the appetites and senses, only philosophy can explain this necessary priority. Philosophy also enables us to accept our doom without understanding it:

> The important thing, I think, is not to be bitter. If it turns out that there is a God, I don't think that he's evil. But the worst you can say about him is that basically he's an underachiever. After all, you know, there are worse things in life than death. I mean, if you've ever spent an evening with an insurance salesman, you'll know exactly what I mean.

In context, Allen's familiar satire of insurance agents signifies a shallow anxiety about death, the kind that insurance agents can address and assuage. Typically, Boris slips from the profound to the pressing:

> The key here, I think, is to not think of death as an end but think of it more as a very effective way to cut down on your expenses.

Inevitably Boris's philosophizing leads to considerations of sex:

> Regarding love, you know, what can you say? It's not the quantity of your sexual relations that count. It's the quality. On the other hand, if the quantity drops below once every eight months, I would definitely look into it. Well, that's about it for me, folks. Goodbye.

In closing on a plaint of sexual frustration, Allen encapsulates the philosophical frustrations that have collected through the film. Boris grows from being perplexed by his mortality in the opening monologue to warmly accepting man's lot at the end. His tender "goodbye" is resigned and dignified.

So too is the last image. For *Love and Death* ends as it began—with a view of the beautiful, clouded, but empty heavens and with an assertion of joy. The first character that we see in the film is Uncle Nikolai with his famous laugh ("God, he was repulsive," adds the unsentimental young Boris). The last we see is Boris dancing with Death along a placid lake. Boris entered the film with a pratfall *kazatsky*; he leaves in an elegant, graceful *pas de deux* (of sorts). As he tiptoes around the thin, majestic trees, he seems to have found with Death a grace of which he was deprived in life. Moreover, in the Hassidic flavor of his dance, Boris is telling us that in the face of our mortality we can do nothing better than snap our fingers, dance, laugh, and be hearty, our senses enlivened by art and our appetites sharpened for life. The opening laugh and closing dance provide a frame of hearty joy that dispels the futile philosophizing, politics, and religious tension in the body of the film. Death may take Boris away, but Allen has snatched from its jaws an affirmation of appetite, of life in laughter, and the immortal continuity of the human spirit, at least through its art. The beauty of the last shot, indeed of Ghislain Cloquet's stunning photography of the French and Hungarian countrysides throughout the film, bear mute testimony to the peace and delight potentially available to man if only. . . .

As Allen admits to Eric Lax, *Love and Death* is an extremely romantic film, because "any existential obsession, even as frivolous as my film, carries with it romantic overtones automatically." He quotes Malraux's remark that art is "the last defense against death." As the literary and film allusions and parodies in *Love and Death* demonstrate, man lives on through his art. Of course, Allen would rather not achieve immortality through his work: "I want to achieve it through not dying." [3]

Nevertheless, man's use of art as a support against his mortality is the main theme that Allen extended from *Love and Death* into *Annie Hall*. In addition, the last shot of *Love and Death* achieves the rare balance of laughter, emotion, and thought that was to make *Annie Hall* his masterpiece. Allen had left behind the limitations of commercial comedy, as he ironically announced in an *Esquire* piece:

> . . . a comedy about death and one's existence in a godless universe. The commercial possibilities were immediately apparent to me. Sight gags and slapstick sequences about despair and emptiness. Dialogue jokes about anguish and dread. Finality, mortality, human suffering, anxiety. In short the standard ploys of the professional funnyman.[4]

He wasn't kidding.

14

Annie Hall (1977)

Annie Hall opens with an even more intimate address then the voice-over narrative of *Love and Death*. As if he were doing a club monologue, Woody Allen faces the cinema audience directly and tells them that two jokes summarize his life. One is the classic from Freud and Groucho Marx: "I would never want to belong to any club that would have someone like me for a member." In the other joke, a tourist at a Catskills resort complains about how terrible the food is. "And in such small portions," her listener adds. As Allen explains, life is like that: "full of loneliness and misery and suffering and unhappiness and it's all over much too quickly." At the end of the film, Alvy Singer (the character now distinguishable from Allen) recounts another joke in voice-over. A man tells a psychiatrist that his brother thinks himself a chicken. "Why don't you turn him in?" asks the analyst. "I would, but I need the eggs." Both food jokes make the same point about life and human relationships: "They're totally irrational and crazy and absurd, but I guess we keep going through them because most of us need the eggs."

At the start of that opening monologue we do not know whether to take the speaker as Allen himself or as a fictional character. It could be Allen declaring that as he turned forty he found himself going through "a life crisis or something," and that he expects to become "the balding, virile type . . . unless I'm one of those guys with saliva dribbling out of his mouth who wanders into a cafeteria with a shopping bag screaming about socialism." Suddenly the clown's mask drops: "Annie and I broke up. I still can't get my mind around that." With the mention of Annie, the Allen monologuist gives way to the character, Alvy Singer. The film presents Alvy "sifting the pieces of the relationship through my mind—trying to figure out where did the screw-up come."

Alvy Singer is a neurotic but successful New York Jewish comedian. Diane Keaton plays Annie Hall, his WASP girl friend. During the course of Alvy's "sifting the pieces" we watch Annie develop from nervous country mouse to poised woman and polished singer. Their affair ends, is resumed, and ends again when Annie moves to Los Angeles to advance her singing career. At the end, Alvy writes his first play. He bases it on their love affair but he gives it a (for him) happy ending. These memories, mingling fantasies with real events, are recounted according to the vagaries of free association, rather than in chronological order. As a result the narrative suggests the character's ambivalent compulsion to confront and yet to avoid the traumatic memories.

One important element complicates the usual problems in interpreting comedy here. It is tempting to take this film as Allen's autobiography. We know that Allen and Keaton were lovers and then broke up, that Keaton was born Diane Hall (Keaton was her mother's name), and that Allen functioned as Keaton's mentor much as Alvy Singer does as Annie's. Our confusion over whether Allen is speaking as himself or as a character in the opening monologue is compounded by the fact that, objectively speaking, Alvy is the Allen character probably most like Woody Allen: a successful comic and playwright, indeed so successful that he has "been killing spiders since [he] was thirty."

Allen denies that the film is autobiographical, beyond the fact that "there have been a couple of true facts in nearly every movie I've done." His affair with Keaton was not like Alvy's with Annie; nor were their meeting and parting as depicted in the film.[1] To take the film as Allen's personal memoir would be to reduce it to what Aristotle defines as "history," the record of what happened once, instead of the more significant "poetry," what may not exactly have happened once but happens all the time.

Annie Hall seems more fruitfully located in the myth of Pygmalion than in Allen's life story. It is the story of an artist who falls in love with his own creation and loses her when she blossoms into full life. Like the Pygmalion myth, it admits a double sympathy: one can appreciate the artist's loss, but one can also understand his creation's need for freedom and independence. Accordingly, *Annie Hall* has a precisely defined double structure, despite its appearance as a random "sifting the pieces." The film has different points of climax depending on whether one considers the story from Alvy's point of view or from Annie's.

From Annie's perspective, the climaxes occur at the one-third and two-thirds points in the film—her two musical numbers. In the first Annie auditions in a noisy club. Of course, this scene is important from Alvy's perspective: after the audition they go out on their first date and have their first kiss. But the scene is more important to Annie because it marks her debut as a singer, the beginning of the career by which she will mature, ultimately to break away from Alvy. By virtue of Alvy's surname, this scene establishes her eventual choice as being between independence as a singer and dependence as Mrs. Singer. As if to point this alternative, her audition song is "It Had To Be You."

At the two-thirds point in the film Keaton sings "Seems Like Old Times." This scene is a turning point in several respects. First, it proves Annie's talent and growth. Second, the nostalgia implicit in the choice of song concentrates the emotional tenor of the entire film in this scene. (This song is heard again, faintly, behind Alvy's concluding monologue, and it swells up to provide the very last word that we hear in the film, Annie's warm "you.") Third, the scene marks a crucial point in Annie's life. It follows her reconciliation with Alvy, when they celebrate her birthday by revisiting Alvy's childhood home in Coney Island. Thus the scene is associated with her birthday, the resurrection of her affair with Alvy, and Alvy's own fixation on his past. But the song also leads to Annie's meeting Tony Lacy (Paul Simon), the California musician-producer who will lure Annie away from Alvy romantically, philosophically, and professionally. The song bridges her reconciliation with Alvy and her meeting his successor. At the very moment that it expresses the comfort of their reunion, it contains the beginning of their final separation.

Allen makes some significant contrasts between these two scenes. As Annie sings the first time, she is photographed from a distance, so she appears small and timid. The second time she is shot from a low angle and close, so she dominates the screen. Whereas her debut was drowned out in the clatter of plates, telephones, and an uninterested crowd, in the second performance the silence is such that she seems to be alone in the dark, until the camera draws back to reveal a rapt audience. Her fidgety isolation in the first number contrasts with her total control in the second. These contrasts show the growth in Annie's poise, sensitivity, and maturity that makes her leaving Alvy inevitable.

From Alvy's perspective, the narrative climaxes at the quarterpoints of the film. The first quarter is marked by his first meeting Annie at a doubles tennis game with his friend Rob (Tony Roberts). Of course, we have already seen Annie. Our first sight of her is in the scene in which she arrives late and irritable for a Bergman movie; her first line is "I'm in a bad mood." Here Alvy's perspective biases us against her; but the scene of their first meeting shows her to be completely charming and attractive.

Nevertheless, there are implicit tensions in their meeting scene. For one thing, a sexual tension carries over from the preceding scene in which Alvy rose frustrated from his conjugal bed. Because his wife has been upset by outside noises, he must go for "another in a series of cold showers." The next line is Rob warning Alvy that "My serve is going to send you to the showers early." On this bridge of "showers" Alvy moves from remembering the frustrations of his marriage to recalling his first meeting with Annie. The shower image also presents athletics as an alternative to marital sexuality. This is confirmed when Alvy suggests that he and Rob team against the two girls. Though the line is facetious, it implies a barely suppressed battle of the sexes. In the event, Rob and Annie team against Alvy and Rob's girl friend; in both couples the woman is perceived as her date's opponent rather than his teammate. Thus the one-quarter scene locates the protagonists' meeting in an image of physical opposition with an undercurrent of sexual tension. The other quarter-mark scenes express similar balances between connection and separation.

Half-way through the film we find Annie and Alvy enjoying a traditional Thanksgiving ham at the Hall family home. At exactly the half-point in the film, Allen splits the screen to compare the Hall family dinner scene with the Singers'. On the left third of the screen is the Hall family—gracious, healthy, affluent, quietly enjoying Grammy's ham. On the right two-thirds is the Singer family—sloppy, noisy, obsessed with sickness and jobs, slavering over their brisket. Across the division, the two families converse about guilt:

MRS. HALL: How do you plan to spend the holidays, Mrs. Singer?
MRS. SINGER: We fast.
MR. HALL: Fast?
MR. SINGER: No food. To atone for our sins.
MRS. HALL: What sins? I don't understand.
MR. SINGER: To tell you the truth, neither do we.

While the Singers chatter about disease and guilt, we faintly hear Annie refer to the Christmas play and Duane, her clean-cut brother with the All-American name, mentions his 4-H Club. The two families are, as Alvy puts it, "like oil and water." Thus Alvy may seem to be warmly accepted in the Hall bosom, but his radical alienation from them will inevitably surface. He suggests this separation in his fancy of Grammy Hall's vision of him as an orthodox rabbi. The vertical division of the screen to compare the two families expresses Alvy's sense of remoteness from the WASP world of the Halls. As in the tennis game at the quarter-point, the dinner scene at the half presents an image of unity with an underlying sense of division.

A similar separation within connection occurs at the three-quarter mark, where Allen's second split-screen shows Annie and Alvy with their respective analysts. As in the first split-screen shot, the self-centered narrator appropriates the right two-thirds of the screen, leaving Annie the left third. As in their tennis game and as in their ham dinner, Alvy and Annie are again engaged in the same activity but are separated by it. They even express contrary attitudes when they acknowledge the same fact. Asked how often they have sexual relations, Annie replies, "Constantly, I'd say three times a week," but Alvy: "Hardly ever, maybe three times a week."

The split-screen shot also expresses the basic differences between Annie's character and Alvy's. Her side is bright, his dark. Her analyst's office is furnished with modern art and furniture, his with old-fashioned, heavy furniture and traditional works of art. She sits, Alvy lies, for he is prone to stasis or regression, whereas Annie is perched to advance.

At the end of the film Alvy has reconciled himself to having lost Annie. This acceptance is emphasized by the contrast between the unflattering first impression Alvy gives us of Annie, and the loving esteem that finally supersedes his confusion, indignation, and frustration at having lost her. At this point, the tension between unity and division is reversed. Now Alvy no longer has Annie, but an underlying connection nonetheless remains: "I realized what a terrific person she was and what great fun it is just knowing her." Where the quarter-marks defined a separation underlying the appearance of union, the film closes with an unseen union underlying the separation. In addition, as the film ends with Annie singing the song of her success and happy memories, in its last moments Alvy's perspective and Annie's are reconciled. This peaceful union is the satisfactory conclusion of Alvy's sifting the pieces.

Within Alvy's quarter-structure, the half-way point can be taken as a pivot upon which the entire plot turns. There are subtle balances between the scenes that precede the Hall dinner and those that follow it. For instance, before the dinner Alvy encourages Annie to take continuing education courses and to meet exciting professors (arguably a contradiction in terms); after, he spies on her and ridicules the affected teachers and their pretentious courses.

Contrasting scenes are often given parallel spots in the plot. For example, the scene in which Annie moves into Alvy's apartment parallels the one in which she reports her analyst's analysis of her dream of first being suffocated by, then breaking the glasses of (castrating?) a Singer surrogate, Frank Sinatra. In both scenes Annie is unpacking incidental baggage (her belongings, her groceries) while she unloads her concerns on a flustered Alvy. The balance between these two scenes shows the shift from Alvy fearing restriction and commitment (when she moves in) to Annie fearing them (as is inferred from her dream). Similarly, their first meal together is paralleled by their last. The first is in the delicatessen, where Annie is out of place: she orders pastrami on white bread! with tomato and lettuce!! and mayonnaise-!! In the second Alvy is the misfit. At the Los Angeles health-food restaurant, with pronounced distaste, he orders alfalfa sprouts and a plate of mashed yeast.

One of the less obvious parallels is a kind of rhyme on the word "grammy," that expresses Alvy's Jewish paranoia. When he first meets Annie he is surprised to hear she has a "Grammy": "What did you do? Grow up in a Norman Rockwell painting?" As Annie admits,

Grammy Hall is "a real Jew-hater." Later Alvy is upset to hear that his successor Tony Lacy has been nominated for Grammy awards. Alvy's response shows his Jewish paranoia: "They give awards for everything. For the World's Biggest Fascist—Adolf Hitler!" These parallel references to an anti-Semitic "Grammy" confirm Alvy's sense of himself as a threatened outsider.

The film abounds with such incidental doublings. Thus the doctor who treats Alvy for his anxiety attack in California bears a striking resemblance to the Dr. Flicker in Alvy's first flashback, when he is treated for despair at the impending expansion of the universe. As if to validate the boy's gloom, Alvy does suffer from Annie's expansion and from the trauma of extending his own work into television.

One effect of these parallels is to suggest the extremely narrow range of Alvy's interest and activity. The repetition of details suggests Annie is right when she says he is like New York City, "this island unto yourself." Another effect of these parallels is to suggest that built into Alvy's every relationship is the seed of its end. We found this in Annie's two singing scenes. Similarly, Alvy's relationship with his first wife, Alison Porchnik (Carol Kane), begins and ends in parallel mixes of sex and politics. He meets her at a political rally where he jokes about dating a woman from the Eisenhower administration: "I was trying to do to her what Eisenhower has been doing to the country for the last eight years." His relationship with Alison ends when she realizes he is using his doubts about the Warren Commission report "as an excuse to avoid sex with me."

There is an especially illuminating parallel between Alvy's first scene in bed with Annie and his bedding of a *Rolling Stone* reporter (Shelley Duvall) after a yogi's performance. There are even parallel allusions to novelists. After making love to Annie, Alvy exults, "As Balzac said, 'There goes another novel.'" Creative energy has gone into sexual fulfillment. But after the reporter has made love with Alvy she says "Sex with you is really a Kafkaesque experience. . . . I mean that as a compliment." Whereas Alvy expressed the advantage of the sexual experience over literature, the reporter seems to retreat from sex to literature, perhaps for completeness or perhaps for comprehension.

Many of the parallels in the film relate to the idea that art and life are continuous, mutually feeding forces. Sometimes what is in the first half told as a story is in the second presented as an event. For example, in Alvy's university concert he tells of being expelled from college for cheating on a metaphysics exam: he peered into the soul of the boy sitting next to him. This "story" becomes an incident in the macabre scene in which Duane tells Alvy about his nightmare of a fatal car crash. That story in turn is threatened with realization when Duane drives an unconcerned Annie and a terrified Alvy through the night rain to the airport. Similarly, in the first half Alvy tells Annie that he does not use drugs because once when he puffed a joint he tried to take his pants off over his head. In the second half an event proves this maladroitness with drugs; Alvy learns that $2,000 worth of cocaine is nothing to sneeze at. Again, story becomes event.

A related kind of prophecy involves the adult Alvy's return to his childhood school room. The sequence is shot in a nostalgic gold that contrasts with the dusky grays of the New York scenes and the bone-bleached white of the ones in California. In the school room the children rise and say what they became as adults. "I'm into leather," a mousey miss reveals. One orthodox lad is now a *tallis*-seller, and another classmate is a methadone addict. As the scene pretends that the children can foretell what they will become, story again anticipates reality.

In the most affecting of these parallels, Alvy attempts to recreate a hilarious experience involving Annie and live lobsters in their summer home kitchen. The original event is shown some fifteen minutes into the film. About fifteen minutes from the end of the film, Alvy tries to relive that event with another girl. Of course, it does not work, for the girl does not understand what is happening.

Annie has that experience captured, framed, and preserved in photographs that we see on her wall when Alvy comes to kill her spider. In these snapshots, Alvy holds the lobsters in parody of a big-game hunter; he resumes this pose when he attacks the spider. Annie's photos preserve the lost moment but when Alvy tries to recreate the experience with someone else, he fails. However, Woody Allen can recapture and hold the experience better than either Annie or Alvy. For through the power of film he conquers the flux of time, the fading of love, the growing apart of lovers, and the variety of loss before which Alvy stands helpless.

Another parallel is set up by the scene in which Alvy produces Marshall McLuhan to squelch an affected twit in a movie ticket line. "Boy, if life were only like this," Alvy tells us, after McLuhan (played unconvincingly by McLuhan himself) has silenced the twit. But life is not like that. Only in art can one have such complete and satisfying control over one's situation. The McLuhan scene is recalled by the scene in which two young actors rehearse Alvy's first play. The scene is a reworking of his parting from Annie, only in the play the heroine comes back to the hero. As Alvy admits sheepishly, "You know, how you're always trying to get things to come out perfect in art because it's real difficult in life."

The power of art to compensate for the limitations of life is the primary theme of *Annie Hall*. This concern happens to be central to the first book that Alvy buys Annie, Ernest Becker's *The Denial of Death*. At the time Annie was buying *The Cat Book* because she was considering getting some cats as a buffer against her solitude. Alvy's gift obtrudes a solitude wider than the merely social one; it raises the specter of man's death, of his inability to resist the processes of time and loss.

That Annie has not contemplated death is dramatized in her emotionally uncertain story about the old man who died in a fit of narcolepsy while waiting in line for his free war-veterans' turkey. In this anecdote, death is an amusing, puzzling, vaguely unsettling continuation of the sleepy, passive life. As Annie does not see death as a unique and overwhelming problem, she is confused by her own story and uncertain both as to what it means and why she feels compelled to tell it.

Annie's suppression of her awareness of mortality is also paralleled in the Beautiful People whom Alvy interviews ("She is very shallow and empty and I have no ideas and nothing interesting to say," one man pleasantly replies) and in the scenes of California hedonism, typified by the one in which Rob explains that he wears a grotesque sun visor so he won't "get old." Even as a boy, Alvy was aware of man's doom. The lad's sense of not just man's mortality but the limited life of the universe resisted Dr. Flicker's advice that "We've got to try and enjoy ourselves while we're here, huh? Huh?"—he laughs, smokes, and coughs. Allen cuts to the Singer home, which quakes under the impact of hedonists blithely enjoying a roller coaster ride, while Alvy ponders his blood-red and quivering bowl of tomato soup. Alvy's consciousness of death prevents his enjoying the pleasures known by simpler souls. For Allen, the unexamined death is not worth living. Therefore he contemplates death and loss, and reaffirms the values of life, art, and love.

This theme is supported by the striking liberties that Allen takes with narrative convention in *Annie Hall*. As if to demonstrate man's need to control and to reshape reality, he violates various principles of film rhetoric. For example, his opening direct address denies the usual gap between film-image and audience. So do his addresses to the audience from within the action, as in the case of his McLuhan scene, or in his quarrel with Annie over whether she said "The only question is will it change my wife." Alvy turns to the cinema audience for support: "You heard that because you were there so I'm not crazy."

In the same spirit Allen often bends the film's realism to reveal something that would otherwise have been concealed. In one scene a double-exposure enables Annie to rise from bed while Alvy continues to make love to her. ("That's what I call 'removed.'") Perhaps the richest example is the balcony conversation between Alvy and Annie after their tennis game. While they exchange the usual banalities of strangers circling each other, Allen runs subtitles to reveal what the speakers are thinking. When Alvy says that photography is "a new art form and a set of esthetic criteria have not emerged yet," his pompousness is deflated by Annie's simple, "You mean, whether it's a good picture or not?" In addition, the subtitle reveals what he is thinking: "I wonder what she looks like naked." So much for Alvy's "esthetic criteria."

Alvy's statement on the fluid state of photographic rhetoric may also justify Allen's liberties with form: "The medium enters in as a condition of the art form itself." Both as he confronts death and loss, and as he contemplates his art form, Allen exercises the freedom of a life and art in flux. Alvy's young classmates admitting their adult failures, Annie's recollection of narcoleptic George, Alvy's closing montage of scenes with Annie from earlier in the film, Annie and Alvy revisiting scenes from their past, indeed all Allen's liberties with film rhetoric assert the power of art in the struggle against the transience of love and life. All are denials of death.

On the other hand, Allen demonstrates the dangers of reducing life to art. Alvy often comments on the passing scene as if he were interpreting a work of fiction. Sometimes he is very good, as when he summarizes the blabbermouth in the theater waiting line. But sometimes he is insensitive; Alison Porchnik is reduced to "a cultural stereotype." More amusingly, he entertains Annie by giving thumbnail analyses of passers-by—the lovers back from Fire Island, the Mafia linen supply man, and, finally, the winner of the Truman Capote Look-a-like Contest, who in another happy confusion of reality and fiction is the real Capote cast as a victorious imitation.

In addition, Alvy often retreats from emotional involvement to the detachment of his comic art. In his emotional scenes with Annie he habitually retreats to comedy. For example, when they walk along the dock at night, Annie stutters a bit but finally admits that she does love him. Unable to express his sentiment directly, Alvy breaks into a comic routine:

> Love is too weak a word for it. I *lerve* you. I *loave* you. I *luff* you, two F's. Yes, I have to invent, of course I—I do, don't you think I do?

He never does, simply and clearly, say he loves her. In the very next scene he again turns comic when he tries to convince her not to move in with him. He admits her apartment has bad plumbing and bugs, "But you say that as if it's a negative thing—Entymology is a rapidly growing field." As Annie correctly observed, "I don't think you like emotion very much." So, too, when he comes to kill her spider and she weeps from loneliness, he evades her emotional needs with a joke or three:

> What are you sad about? What did you want me to do, capture them and rehabilitate them? . . . What do you mean, "Don't go"? Are you expecting termites?

Although we are used to Allen portraying compulsive jokers, what is new is Alvy's accountability for being a relentless quipster. In *Annie Hall* Allen examines the limitations of the comic reflex. Hence his negative images of characters doing comic routines: the aging Aunt Tessie, the intolerable "ass-hole," Joey Nichols, and the pathetic entertainer who hires young Alvy to write material for him.

Finally, Alvy literally uses movies as a means of avoiding problems in his real life. A tension with Annie is deflected into a quarrel over whether or not to enter a theater showing Bergman's *Face to Face* (1975) once the screening has begun. Later he prevents a useful opportunity for her to see Tony Lacy by going yet again to see Ophuls's *The Sorrow and the Pity*. At this point Alvy's hoarding of her time is reflected in a Nazi quotation from the film: "The Jewish war-mongers and Parisian plutocrats tried to flee with their gold and jewels." Similarly, when Alvy imagines an animated scene from Disney's *Snow White and the Seven Dwarfs*, in which Annie is the wicked queen, he omits the very virtues by which Annie outgrows him. Again, Allen uses a film inset to undercut Alvy, for the cartoon suggests Alvy is being childish and regressive.

Indeed one could take all the film references in *Annie Hall* as the coordinates of Allen's relationship to film. If the *Snow White* sequence expresses Alvy's infantilism, it also expresses the abiding influence that art has on one's life. The Ophuls film relates to the hero's Jewish sense of alienation, but also represents one function of film: to confront issues of political and historical significance, and to provide an understanding of the past. The Bergman references represent the use of the medium to explore the artist's psychological nature. The reference to *Face to Face* is especially significant, for that film deals with a psychiatrist's own "sifting of the pieces" of her marital and mental breakdowns. Fellini affirms the validity of imaginative realism and Allen's exuberant, personal style.

Indeed, when the pretentious professor in the movie line-up complains that Fellini's new film is "incredibly indulgent," "lacks a cohesive structure," and gives "the feeling that he's not absolutely sure what he wants to say," Allen might well be warning us against making similarly shallow responses to the structural complexities and ironic ambiguities of *Annie Hall*. From Annie's perspective, it is Allen's *Juliet of the Spirits:* his free-form homage to his lady, in which he celebrates her mystery, her individuation, and her liberation from sexual, psychological, and emotional subordination.

More generally, the *Snow White* and Ophuls inserts represent the artist's social function, in which he speaks to and for his community, while the Bergman and Fellini context represents the use of art to express and to explore the artist's private tensions. These four coordinates embody the balance between personal experience and general metaphor that makes *Annie Hall* the culmination of Allen's work, especially in its inflection of his persona. The film references also confirm the self-reflexive stance of the film: "the medium enters in as a condition of the art form itself."

Annie Hall deals with the use of art as a means of confronting man's helplessness before time, loss, and death. This film reconciles us to man's imperfect lot. We cannot control our world, stop time, stop aging, avoid loss. As one stranger tells Alvy, "It's never something you do. That's how people are. Love fades." So Alvy sifts the pieces and eventually reconciles himself to the loss of Annie. That shows us how we can reconcile ourselves not just to our romantic losses but to our sense that our whole world is being lost. As Allen told Frank Rich in an *Esquire* interview, "The fundamental thing behind *all* motivation and *all* activity is the constant struggle against annihilation and against death," for even *"the universe itself* is not going to exist after a period of time." [2]

This is the subject of Becker's *The Denial of Death,* the first book Alvy buys Annie and the one he lingers over when they are separating. *Annie Hall* dramatizes Becker's argument that man's essential activities are a response to his sense of his inevitable death. So thoroughly rooted is the film in Becker's book that even incidental jokes are illuminated by it. For example, Alvy's admission that he has an "anal" personality sets up Annie's quip: "That's a polite word for what you are." But Becker's description of the anal personality fits Alvy exactly: he is "trying extra-hard to protect himself against the accidents of life and danger of death." Similarly, when Alvy compliments Annie as "polymorphously perverse" it is not just in Freud's sense of the child attempting to master his sexuality symbolically, but with Becker's particular refinement: "this kind of play is already a very serious attempt to transcend determinism, not merely an animal search for a variety of body-zone pleasures." Allen's double-exposure, which demonstrates how Annie is "removed" when Alvy makes love to her, demonstrates Becker's explanation of why sex is usually attended by guilt: "the body casts a shadow on the person's inner freedom, his 'real self' that—through the act of sex—is being forced into a standardized role." Annie expresses Becker's distinction between the woman's sense of "me" and "only my body." [3]

More importantly, Allen's use of art as a means of confronting death is consistent with Becker's argument that the artist's work "justifies" him by "transcending death by qualifying for immortality": "he lives the fantasy of the control of life and death, of destiny, in the 'body' of his work." This is Allen's objective in making the movie and Alvy's in writing his play. The "anal personality" tries to "use the symbols of culture as a sure means of triumph over natural mystery." [4]

As Becker defines it, Annie would represent Alvy's "romantic solution" to his anxiety about death. Man fixes "his urge to cosmic heroism onto *another person* in the form of a love object" and looks to that love partner for "the self-glorification" that he needed in his innermost nature. Alvy's bitterness at having lost Annie is caused by the sense that his beloved has failed him: "The shadow of imperfection falls over our lives, and with it—death and the defeat of cosmic heroism. 'She lessens' = 'I die.' " Here and in *Interiors,* a broken love affair shatters the lover because he has elevated his beloved to the position of God, and requires her to provide nothing less than "redemption . . . to be rid of [his] faults, of [his] feeling of nothingness . . . to know that [his] creation has not been in vain." [5]

The Becker context is confirmed by Allen's choice of title. At one level we can read it as Alvy's dedication to Annie. Further, in the romantic heart of the general audience, the title is Woody Allen's fond and touching salute to Diane Keaton. Either homage emphasizes the change in the man's attitude from the beginning of his sifting of memories to his final acceptance of his loss and the new terms of their relationship.

Allen originally intended to call the film *Anhedonia,* referring to Alvy's chronic inability to experience pleasure ("I don't respond well to mellow," he remarks). Changing the title from *Anhedonia* to *Annie Hall* reflects more than just an adjustment to the audience's vocabulary, however. It shifts the emphasis of the film from the bleakness of Alvy's character to the riches embodied by Annie—her beauty, her warmth, her youth, her stunningly eccentric charms, and her sense of growth, of human expansion. She is inevitably advancing, moving on and away, to be loved on the fly and to be held for only a short while, thereafter to be treasured in the memory. In this respect Annie is like life itself. Alvy loses her but learns to hold her in his memory and in his emotion. And through the art of film, Allen can hold her in yet another dimension; he can triumph over time and loss by transforming his experience into art. Alvy's treasuring homage to his lost love becomes Allen's melancholy but affirmative homage to lost life and time. Annie Hall is a character as charming, as absurd, and as elusive as life itself. She embodies Alvy's denial of death through romantic love, and Allen's through art.

15

Interiors (1978)

After the critical and commercial success of *Annie Hall*, Woody Allen undertook his biggest challenge: a noncomic feature that he wrote and directed but in which he did not appear. The film met a mixed response. Though many critics complained of its unremitting and sometimes risible somberness, sixteen of the thirty-one reviewers surveyed by *Variety* included *Interiors* in their lists of the ten best films of 1978; this made it eighth in the ranking (which was led by Terrence Malick's *Days of Heaven*, with twenty citations). The British monthly, *Films and Filming*, named *Interiors* the best feature film from any source.[1]

Like *Annie Hall*, *Interiors* concerns the various ways in which man responds to his sense of mortality and loss. But without the palliative of comedy, this film can be described as a Chekhovian vision of an O'Neill family, expressed with Bergmanesque rigor. Allen focuses on an apparently cultured and sensitive New England family that suffers unresolved anxieties and frustrations. The father, Arthur (E. G. Marshall), a sixty-three-year-old lawyer, announces one morning at breakfast that he has decided to leave his family and to begin a new life alone. His wife, Eve (Geraldine Page), has a nervous breakdown, then tries to come to terms with her new life, but is unable to accept the fact that her husband will not return. When he marries a life-affirming widow, Pearl (Maureen Stapleton), Eve drowns herself in the sea outside their summer home.

Arthur and Eve have three daughters. Renata (Diane Keaton) is a poet whose success has traumatized her novelist husband, Frederick (Richard Jordan). Flyn (Kristen Griffith) is a film and television

actress of great beauty, modest ambition, and seemingly easy satisfactions. Allen considers the third daughter, Joey (Mary Beth Hurt),
to be the central character in the film and—at least originally—the
healthiest.[2] But as Renata describes her, Joey "has all the anguish
and anxiety of the artistic personality with none of the talent." She
lives with a documentary filmmaker, Mike (Sam Waterston), but
rather than marry him, she aborts their child.

All three men, Arthur, Frederick, and Mike, are warm characters
who have been chilled and immobilized either by their encounter
with Eve—and the daughters of Eve—or by their various involve-
ments with art. While Joey admits that she is "too self-centered" to
join Mike in his political art, Mike himself is only "interested in the
masses as an abstraction," with a "strictly political" outlook rather
than a human interest in his subject matter.[3] Frederick chafes under
his intellectual frustrations and grows violent. At one point he tells
Flyn that he was frightened at the pleasure he took in savagely
reviewing a friend's book. Later he attempts to rape her, in a des-
perate effort to affirm his strength and existence: "It's been such a
long time since I made love to a woman I didn't feel inferior to. Am
I being tactless?" Here his callous self-awareness is as ugly as his need
is pathetic.

All the characters suffer from Eve's attempt to impose a placid,
pale, elegant, but lifeless world upon them. Eve is a compulsive
interior decorator whose ideal is a gray, monochromatic austerity.
She wears either the extremes of noncolor, black and white, or the
"ice-gray" color of the "ice palace" that she has decreed be the family
home. When she visits Joey and Mike, Eve rearranges their furnishings to maintain her design even at the expense of their convenience
and living needs. In tacit homage to her, everyone wears gray at her
birthday party. But as Mike and Frederick are both dark-haired men,
inclined to wear warm, earth colors, neither seems to fit into Eve's
design. And the people are elements in her formal design. After she
complains about Mike's aftershave, she admits that he "is not what
I had in mind for Joey, but I'm getting used to him." Eve considers
her husband her "creation" because she put him through law school.

Into Eve's stuffy, rigid elegance, Pearl explodes like a whirlwind.
Pearl wears reds, which soften into a sensuous pink on her wedding
night, and she plans to redecorate the beach house to enliven its

sepulchral spaces and pallid tones. In contrast to Eve's tight, high collars, Pearl's dresses are open, loose, and billowing. Whereas Eve on vacation visits churches and ruins, Pearl prefers to sun on the beach and to dance the night away: "How many ruins can you see?" Pearl's taste in art runs to sensuous black ebony from Trinidad; Eve collects gray vases. Indeed the vase is Eve's emblem—elegant, pale, fragile, harmonious within itself, unmoving, and empty. When Pearl, bopping alone at her wedding, accidentally breaks one of Eve's vases, we have an image of Eve herself being shattered by the loss of her husband. In contrast, Pearl has survived two marriages and is merrily dancing into a third.

Pearl's direct enjoyment of life is seen in her simple responses to art. In the family's dinner conversation about a recent play, Pearl reacts directly to the entertainment and its characters. Renata cites Schopenhauer, Aristotle, and Ecclesiastes to conclude that "it's hard to argue that in the face of Death life loses all meaning." Pearl replies simply, "They should know," and takes a hearty gulp of coffee. She eagerly shares her zest for life, as we see when she urges upon Arthur more gravy and then more cheesecake. Pearl embodies the joy of appetite that Woody Allen asserted in the face of death in *Love and Death*. In this spirit she observes that "you'll live to be a hundred if you give up all the things that make you want to," and "you only live once, and that's enough if you play it right." Little wonder that Arthur is eager to marry her although he has known her only one month. She is precisely Eve's opposite: "She's kind, affectionate, full of energy, demonstrative, and open." In spite of her vulgarity, Pearl is the only character in the film with a rich and harmonious relationship to life.

Not just lively in herself, Pearl causes liveliness in others. Arthur, Frederick, and Mike visibly brighten in her company. In her first appearance, Pearl is shown from the waist up, as if to emphasize her bosom, her maternal softness and abundance. When Joey runs into the ocean in her futile attempt to save Eve, it is Pearl who saves Joey by mouth-to-mouth resuscitation. As she breathes new life into her, we remember Eve's earlier sharp rebuke of Joey: "Would you please not breathe so hard!" Pearl brings full and exuberant breath to all. Her instinctive intimacy with her new family is poignantly expressed when she comes down after the wedding and finds Joey talking to Eve:

JOEY: Mother?
PEARL: Yes?
JOEY: What?
PEARL: You said "Mother" and I said "yes."

Despite its fatal consequence, the suicide of Eve, Pearl's entrance into the family introduces a note of warmth, generosity, and genuine maternal feeling.

Pearl's eagerness to reach out and embrace is contrasted with Eve's attempts to shut herself off from the outside world. Eve frequently closes windows to shut out noise. When she tries to kill herself by gas she tapes the windows and doors in her final effort to seal out the fresh air and sounds of life—and to seal in her poison. As the sound track amplifies the grating noise of the tape, it is harsher than the street noise. After the close-up of the taping, the camera draws back to reveal that Eve has been designing again, composing a formal symmetry in the room. She arranges herself as a posed element in the composition. But in the next shot we learn that her esthetic attempt at suicide has failed. As the ambulance speeds her through the night, she has become a part of the street noise that she tried to shut out.

Interiors opens in Eve's world but the initial shots contain ironic hints of the alternatives embodied by Pearl. It begins with several quiet, still shots of the living room in the family's beach house. In the first, the outside windows are prominent behind an overstuffed sofa. The second shot shows a row of Eve's elegant but empty gray vases. The next two shots are of doorways, one directing us inward and the second outside. In addition to establishing a contemplative mood, this sequence suggests the ideas of windows and doors, of viewpoints and escapes. The formal composition and the vases express Eve's touch, but the outward perspectives anticipate Pearl.

This sequence also establishes the paradox in the film's title. For "Interiors" refers to the family's *exteriors,* to the anemic estheticism of Eve's life. The opening shots of empty interiors suggest that the family has sacrificed its internal life for the composition of an austere exterior. They also suggest that the elements in the room are arranged with regard only to their relation to each other, not to the outside world. "Interiors" is thus a kind of pun by exclusion. By referring to Eve's art of formal arrangement of her living spaces, it emphasizes the characters' neglect both of their inner lives and of the forces that exist beyond their delicately composed rooms. The characters' insubstantiality is confirmed by the many shots in which they are either reflected off glass surfaces or filtered through windows. Furthermore, in key instances the characters seem to be looking at the world through windows, but are actually reminiscing introspectively. Finally, the title and its related imagery may derive from a passage in *The Denial of Death*, the book we found so important to *Annie Hall*. Ernest Becker explains the bitterness that comes about in family relations, when we are disappointed by a loved one, by noting:

> We feel diminished by their human shortcomings. Our interiors feel empty or anguished, our lives valueless, when we see the inevitable pettinesses of the world expressed through the human beings in it.[4]

As virtually all the characters in *Interiors* are disappointed by their loved one, the film is dominated by empty interiors: artificially composed rooms and anguished selves.

In the context of Becker's argument, Pearl and Eve embody man's two basic creative urges. Eve's attempt to impose an ice-gray form on her life represents the "powerful desire to identify with the cosmic process," to merge with the rest of nature. She finally achieves this fading away when she drowns in the sea, which is the archetypal source of life and the symbol for the unindividuated subconscious. Pearl embodies the opposite urge, "to be unique, to stand out as something different and apart," against all restrictive pressures.[5] In her resistance to her mother's influence, Joey says: "I don't want to be swallowed up in some anonymous lifestyle." On the other hand, Joey is repelled by Pearl's robust character.

In the context of Allen's other works, Eve and Pearl embody opposing impulses in the Allen persona. Eve represents the drive for control and success, usually expressed in terms of social (and especially sexual) acceptance. Pearl represents the Outsider's spirit, vitality, and independence. In this sense Pearl functions like Allen's Jewish hero in his comedies with Diane Keaton, in which the life-affirming Jew plays against and enlivens the controlled WASP. Just as Alvy Singer was the alien in Annie Hall's world, so Pearl is seen as a "vulgarian" in Joey's world. Allen told Yvonne Baby that "somebody so truly close to life will always be regarded as vulgar by cultivated, brainy people." [6]

Several details are consistent with the inference that Pearl is Jewish. For example, her wedding to Arthur is conducted by a judge, not a minister, and Pearl's attempt to dance with each member of her new family in turn, including the daughters, would seem more at home at a Jewish wedding. There is even an implicit anti-Semitism in Joey's attack when the "vulgarian" has accidently broken Eve's vase: "For Christ's sake be careful." Pearl is astonished by this outburst: the viewer may be additionally struck by Joey's Aryan appearance here—blonde, straight hair, thin-rimmed glasses, and tight, thin-lipped mouth. Earlier, the specter of the Jew was raised in Eve's consciousness, as if an omen of her replacement by Pearl: Eve was idly watching a Christian talk show on television. The guest, Roy Schwartz ("black" in Yiddish), is a converted Jew invited to testify how "it's an exciting thing to be a Christian" and to explain the Jews' part "in God's time-piece today." The question of the Jew's function in the Gentile society relates to the tension between Pearl and Eve; the mechanistic implication of the latter phrase relates to the film's broader concerns.

For *Interiors* is about characters who have been unable to find something that would replace God as a shield against their sense of mortality. The closest any character comes to being religious is Pearl, but her Jewishness is more a matter of class than religion, and her religious sense is primitive. To judge by her remarks about fortune-telling and seances, she has a superstitious sense of the powerful forces beyond man. In contrast, Eve brings Arthur to a· Catholic church but only to show him its artistic treasures. Allen recalls that originally Eve was to be an active Christian, but "my feeling about that sort of involvement is that it's crazy." He admits that the "religious thought" in *Interiors* may now be lost among the more obvious elements of "psychological family drama." [7] Nevertheless, the central characters represent different approaches to recognizing man's mortality. Specifically, they represent sensuality, romance, and art, which Becker enumerates as man's three ways to transcend his limited, mortal self if he lacks faith in God.

Flyn, the actress, represents the sensual response. But her image of beauty and easy satisfaction is undercut by several indications that her contentment is only skin-deep. She retires from the family reunion to snort cocaine alone in the garage. She complains at how uncomfortable her beautiful, expensive boots are. Her uncontrolled weeping at Eve's funeral suggests that her cool elegance conceals a deep despair and sense of loss. Clearly the drunken Frederick mistakes Flyn completely when he reduces her to a sex image: "You like to be looked at. Otherwise you don't exist." Flyn has a troubled existence that her appearance conceals.

Joey's romantic ambitions are her means of evading mortality. Thus she claims for women a mysterious interiority that takes precedence over marriage. Her stultified emotional life is one of Eve's negative effects on her; another is her desire to be an artist. This ambition has no talent to support it: "I feel a real need to express something but I don't know what to express or how to express it." Consequently, she drifts from one job on the fringe of the art world to another, unable to stabilize herself any more as an artist than as a lover.

Renata represents the attempt to counteract mortality with creativity. She is not only a success as a poet but has produced a child. Her creativity intimidates Frederick—whom she archly reminds of the fact that it is she who "turns things out"—and isolates her from the other members of her family (as Joey, Arthur, and Frederick complain). As Becker points out, "one of the ironies of the creative process is that it cripples itself in order to function," and "what we call a creative gift is merely the social license to be obsessed." [8]

Moreover, Renata's art has become blocked by her "increasing thoughts about death," especially her own. Unless she overcomes this "impotence" and "paralysis" she will be drawn into her mother's despair. This danger is suggested in the shot where Renata sits alone staring into the sea. Both as a professional artist and as someone who "can't seem to shake the real implication of dying," Renata is Allen's most direct representative in the film (a fact confirmed in his interview with Ira Halberstadt, and by his casting his familiar costar, Diane Keaton, in the role). But art is a feeble defense against death. Ultimately Renata's poetry is no more substantial than Flyn's television movies or Eve's anemic interiors. For Allen, "Art is like the intellectual's Catholicism, it's the promise of an afterlife, but of course, it's fake—you're only doing it because *you* want to do it." [9]

Of the three sisters, Allen's favorite is the ungifted but ambitious Joey. He regards her as a "middle ground type of person," who has an admirable intelligence, sensitivity, and the courage to question life despite her lack of talent.[10] The sister with the "deepest interior," Joey "gets closer than the artist to the source, the essence of life" and possesses a quality more important than artistic sensitivity: "courage in the face of concrete danger: suffering, or death." [11] For Allen the most courageous person is the one "who acts in spite of an almost paralyzing fear." [12]

Joey's centrality in the film is indicated in the fact that she is the first character we see (reflected on the glass of a family photograph). In addition, key scenes begin with a close-up of Joey's response to them: Pearl's entrance, Arthur's and Pearl's wedding, and Eve's reappearance and suicide. After a series of reminiscences (like the collage of flashbacks at the end of *Annie Hall*) Joey closes her diary: "I felt compelled to write these thoughts down. They seemed very powerful." Still lacking both the understanding and the skill to be an artist, Joey has made a statement for herself. In addition to fulfilling her need for self-expression, Joey's private diary has a courage and modesty that goes beyond the public arts of Eve, Flyn, and Renata.

In one scene Allen strikingly violates a convention of film narrative to demonstrate how Renata's poetry isolates her from reality and from other people.[13] Halfway through the film, Allen shows her writing a poem, scratching out words, struggling. After this establishing shot there is a close-up of her page. Appropriately, the poetry refers to the worth of old gray homes, but the lines are difficult to read because the page is shown upside down. The traditional sequence would be the establishing shot and then a close-up of the page from Renata's perspective. The shot of the page upside down suggests that we are standing across from her desk, intruding on her. This reversal suggests that Renata may share experience with her readers but she still keeps them at a safe distance. By its obscured offering, her poem raises more mystery than it clarifies.

This sequence is followed by another equally intriguing. Renata crumples up the poem and throws it away. She then appears on the right side of the screen, in a gray close-up, staring off. We are next given her view of the outdoors (the perspective from which we expected to see her poem), but the lens is altered in mid-shot so that the outdoors is lost and the intervening windowpane comes into sharp focus instead. We then see the outdoors again without the window, then a closer shot of the outdoors, then a jarring close-up of the bathroom faucet from which Renata washes her face. For a moment she watches her daughter playing by herself. Then Renata tells Frederick that she has just had a clear vision in which everything seemed awful and predatory; the world seemed out there and she seemed inside and unable to connect (precisely our feeling when we tried to read her upside-down poem). She felt hyperaware of her body and its organic operations. Finally, she is worried because she is approaching the age at which her mother first showed signs of strain and collapsed.

When we were deprived of Renata's view of her poem, we experienced her frustration. In the subsequent series we experience her disorientation, but its meaning does not become clear until she explains it to Frederick. After experiencing the frustrations of artistic block, Renata feels besieged by the outside reality and must tear herself away to refresh herself with a brisk wash. The interlude with her daughter suggests she must stabilize herself with a moment of domestic normalcy before she can articulate her experience. The entire sequence demonstrates the artist's detachment from normal experience, perception, and sentiment.

The sequence also typifies the film's tension between introspection and relating to the outside world. This theme was introduced in the opening contrast between the windows that open outside and Eve's self-contained vases. Furthermore, Allen often moves from within a character's emotion to a wider view of it, as if from an interior to an exterior perspective. In the sequence just discussed, we went from experiencing Renata's dislocation to overhearing her explanation of it.

A simpler example is Allen's variation in camera distance at the wedding of Pearl and Arthur. This scene opens with a close-up of Joey, the most agitated witness. For the couple's exchange of vows, the camera draws back to include side views of Renata and Mike as well as Joey. For the conclusion of the ceremony, the camera includes the antagonistic Frederick and Flyn. The shot of the newlyweds sealing their union with a kiss is taken across the laden wedding table, with a rear view of the officiating magistrate and with the family in the background. This expanding shot suggests that the private family tensions have been superseded by the celebration and ceremony; at least for the moment the family emotion has overcome the spirit of the single opposed member.

On the thematic level, Allen achieves a related effect by intercutting shots of the sea, especially in the series that begins when Arthur first tells Eve that he plans to remarry. A natural force, the sea represents the powers over which man has no control, the power in which Eve will eventually immerse herself. In Allen's use of the sea there is also a sense of expanding awareness. After the opening shots of interiors and secure doorways, Allen directs us through the windows as the characters look out upon the sea and recall their past lives. For most of the film the characters are defined by the tension between their inner nature and their living spaces, that is to say, between their true interiors and their merely designed interiors (or exteriors). But with increasing force and volume the sea asserts itself against these shallow preoccupations. After Eve has drowned, our last view of her stately beach house is dominated by the sickly yellow grass in the foreground; it diminishes the impression of stability that the house—and Eve's designs—made earlier and it mutely reminds us of the superior power of the sea.

Perhaps the key phrase of *Interiors* is the term by which Frederick initially dismisses Flyn and his own writing: "form without any content." The phrase does not fit the deeply moved and vulnerable Flyn, but it does apply to Eve's dignified but empty designs and vases. It also applies to the relationships between the family members, which seem to be formal rather than substantial. Eve favors Renata because she worships genius, but Renata is her least supportive daughter. Eve is helped most by Joey, whom she likes the least; Joey loves Eve despite her "rage" at her mother's "perverseness and willfulness of attitude." Similarly, Joey is her father's favorite child but she responds the most harshly to his new freedom. In Frederick's attempt to rape Flyn we have the most dramatic of the discordant family relationships that underlie the elegant exteriors. In contrast, Pearl enters the family circle without any formal connection but full of warmth and maternal love. Ultimately, however, form is content. To claim form without content is to be insensitive to the content—as Frederick is to Flyn—even if the content is emptiness—as in Eve's vases—or negative—as in the family's violent tensions.

Allen's film itself is a masterful harmonizing of form and content. Every nuance is expressive. In *Interiors* Allen achieves what he did in *Annie Hall*, a symbolic transcendence of "the darkness and dread of the human condition," [14] as Becker puts it, only this time he worked without the safety net of comedy.

The characters achieve different solutions. Flyn's tears at her mother's funeral are a rare expression of emotion and an abandonment of her image. Renata recognizes the need to subordinate her art to human relationships, as we see from her new warmth toward her sisters. Joey returns from her mother's path to accept her own limited capacity for understanding and expression. Before their mother's death the sisters were separated by their individual concerns. In exposing them to "the overwhelming reality" of their own mortality, Eve's death authenticated their lives and their relationships. Thus the last words in the film are of acceptance:

JOEY: The water's so calm.
RENATA: Yes, it's very peaceful.

The sea, of course, is pure content—the nature that exceeds all human efforts to impose form upon it. The effect of the sea—and the universal mortality for which it stands here—is to wash away the characters' individual differences and to unite them in a sense of common vulnerability. As Joey tells Eve, "we have no choice but to forgive each other." In the final image the three sisters still stand separate and apart, but now they are united: they gaze out upon the image of their common doom.

16

Manhattan (1979)

After the sombreness of *Interiors*, Woody Allen returned to the romantic comedy style of *Annie Hall*. The result is his most lyrical and emotional film to date. Although it may not be as complex as *Annie Hall*, *Manhattan* is a magnificent film, subtle both in expression and in feeling. It proves that Allen's genius is still growing and capable of fertile surprises.

In *Manhattan* Allen plays Isaac Davis (inaptly nicknamed Ike, as if an old Hebrew could become an icon of Gentile leadership), a TV comedy writer who suffers the slings and arrows of outrageous romance. For one thing, his ex-wife Jill (Meryl Streep) is a bisexual who left him for another woman (Karen Ludwig as Connie). Isaac is humiliated when Jill exposes their marital break-up in an "honest" book, *Marriage, Divorce, and Selfhood*. In addition, the 42-year-old Isaac feels squeamish about his affair with a 17-year-old high-school student, Tracy (Mariel Hemingway). He breaks off with her in order to have an affair with a nervous, chic journalist, Mary Wilke (Diane Keaton), but only after the collapse of Mary's affair with Isaac's best friend, a married English professor named Yale (Michael Murphy). At the end Mary goes back to Yale, Yale leaves his wife Emily (Anne Byrne), Isaac goes back to Tracy, and Tracy goes to England on a six-month theater scholarship.

This tangle of lovings and leavings demonstrates the theme of a short story Isaac is writing: "People in Manhattan are constantly creating these real unnecessary neurotic problems for themselves that keep them from dealing with more unsolvable, terrifying problems about the universe." More specifically, the film details the professional and romantic compromises by which man avoids confronting his insignificance in the cosmos and his inability to control his fate. Both concerns are familiar from Allen's earlier work.

The film's dominant theme is man's need for personal integrity in a decaying culture. In an empty anthropology classroom, Isaac attacks Yale for having undermined their friendship and his marriage by resuming his affair with Mary. "Well, I'm not a saint, okay," Yale admits, but Isaac holds fast: "You're too easy on yourself." Yale charges that Isaac is too rigid and self righteous: "You think you're God." Isaac replies: "Well, I've got to model myself after someone." In this exchange Isaac prefers to follow a remote, even impossible, ideal rather than adhere to the corrupt human norms around him. Behind Yale we see a showcase of skulls that suggest a kind of unsupported cerebralism or rationalization. Isaac's lecture is undercut by the 5'4" ape-man skeleton that stands grinning beside him. Compared to Yale's skulls, the skeleton associated with Isaac is the full man. "What are future generations going to say about us?" Isaac asks, as if the skeleton has reminded him of man's responsibility beyond his own desires: "Some day we're going to be like him. . . . It's very important to have personal integrity. I'm going to be hanging in a classroom someday. I want to make sure that when I thin out I'm well thought of." From the *memento mori* Isaac draws the need for an assertive morality. There may be a comical denial of death in the euphemism "when I thin out"—suggested by Allen's fear of the cold, analytic touch of film teachers who hang him in classrooms— but Isaac admits moral imperatives which Yale and Mary deny in their indulgent pursuit of pleasure.

Yale compromises himself in several ways. He betrays his marriage both by his philandering and by denying his wife's desire for children. He betrays his friendship with Isaac by resuming his affair with Mary. He compromises his professional principles when he neglects his book on Eugene O'Neill and when he buys an unnecessary Porsche with funds he was saving to start a small magazine.

Mary shares Yale's weak will. From reviewing an edition of Tolstoy's letters, she turns to novelizing a film, an example of the loss of proportion and values in this throwaway culture. Mary represents Isaac's obsessive target: the generation raised on TV, drugs and fatuous fashions, with neither a moral core nor a sense of responsibility. Thus she enthuses over Isaac's TV work, a show called "Human Beings—Wow!", which recalls the "Ferndale Tonight" and "Mary Hartman" shows in its absurdity and its appeal to modish sophisticates. Mary entrusts her quavering psyche to an analyst who phones her weeping at 3 A.M. ("He's unorthodox," she explains) and who is unavailable when she needs him because he's in a coma from a bad acid trip. Her flightiness is an emblem of her times—as is that of Isaac's first wife, a kindergarten teacher who became a Moonie and eventually found her way into the William Morris agency via drugs, California and est.

Mary often cites her roots in Philadelphia in a half humorous, half fraudulent claim to innocence. In contrast, seventeen-year-old Tracy projects a true innocence that is nonetheless insightful, responsible and warm. Isaac must ask Tracy not to be so precocious or mature, because she often acts with a wisdom beyond *his* years. For example, Tracy intuits the nervousness behind Mary's glib put-downs, to which Isaac reacted with anger. It is to Tracy that Allen allots his definition of love pure and simple: "We have laughs together. I care about you. Your concerns are my concerns. We have great sex." Unlike Mary—who when told that her affair with Yale will not last more than four weeks replies that she cannot "plan that far ahead"—Tracy assures Isaac that her London sojourn need not end their love affair: "What's six months if we still love each other?" Tracy has a more mature response to time and relationships than the older Mary has. She also has a more honest nature. In contrast to Mary's pretense to being a simple, virtuous kid from Philadelphia—and to society's fascination with the interchangeable glamor of Rita Hayworth and Veronica Lake—we have Tracy's wondering why people don't "let their faces age naturally."

Several scenes parallel Tracy and Mary. As Yale breaks off with Mary at a sidewalk cafe, Isaac breaks off with Tracy at a soda fountain. His romantic ride with Tracy in a hansom cab is in contrast with an earlier solitude: "On my prom night I went around this park five times, six times. If I'd been with a girl this would have been an incredible experience." Her youth makes this scene a recovery of the bliss that Isaac missed when he was young. But their ride also contrasts to Isaac's after-dinner taxi ride with Mary, during which his mad romantic fervor almost makes him abandon all practicality:

"You look so beautiful I can hardly keep my eyes off the meter." Almost, but not quite, for unlike Mary and Yale, Isaac does not forget the high cost of loving. This is the point of his quip when Mary tells him that Yale's furtive call was a prize from a dance studio: "They give you one free lesson and then they hook you for $50,000 worth." Life with Mary is a matter of games, cultural affectations and temporary commitments; Tracy provides simplicity, stability and integrity.

Over the course of the film Isaac grows from Mary's insubstantial promise to Tracy's real but unconventional riches. Isaac must overcome several obstacles to his fulfilment with Tracy. One is his sense of their disparity in age. Behind his jokes on the subject ("I'm dating a girl who does homework;" "I'm dating a girl wherein I could beat up her father") lies his reluctance to make a romantic commitment because of his fear of aging and death. Isaac's evasion of emotion is another obstacle, for he continually pushes Tracy away, urging her not to waste her feelings on him. She should consider him "a fond memory" or "a detour on the highway of life." His use of such clichés suggests that he is not saying what he deeply feels but is expressing a conventional point of view. Finally, Isaac must overcome the temptation to conform to society's manners. As Tracy is below the age of consent when their affair begins, their December-June relationship is so unconventional that it is illegal. In ending their affair, Isaac subordinates his emotions to those dangerous principles —logic and social custom.

In *Manhattan* Allen continues his satire against man's foolish applications of logic and culture. Hence the skulls when Yale rationalizes his betrayal of Isaac. Often there is a comical discrepancy between what the characters know and what they can effectively use in their lives. As Isaac admits, "When it comes to relationships with women I'm the winner of the August Strindberg Award." Although he still wants her himself, he warns Yale that Mary is "the winner of the Zelda Fitzgerald Emotional Maturity Award." Both quips combine intellectual knowledge with emotional deficiency. As Isaac tells the cerebral Mary, "Nothing worth knowing can be understood with the mind," for "the brain is man's most insignificant organ," and "everything really valuable has to enter through another opening." For example, when at the Museum of Modern Art reception the sophis-

ticates applaud a biting satire in the *Times* against the neo-Nazis
marching in New Jersey, the verbal and fragile Isaac expresses a
preference for persuasion by brick and bat. Man's culture is no defense against his greatest dangers. Greater truths are told by the heart
and the senses than by the mind. Not for Isaac the problem reported
by the dim-witted girl who finally achieved orgasm only to be told
by her analyst that it was the wrong kind! Isaac's orgasms are all
"right on the money" because they are experiences untouched by
analysis. He learns to accept his relationship with Tracy in the same
way. Tracy's last line, "You have to have a little faith in people,"
is really a call to trust his instincts. Tracy's own faith in her relationship with Isaac overrides her sense that "maybe people weren't
made for long relationships," but for a "series of relationships with
different links."

Though unconventional, Isaac is a character of exemplary integrity. He refuses to become involved with Mary ("never in a million
years") as long as Yale is involved with her—a courtesy not recipro-
cated later. Rather than accept the approval of an audience whose
"standards have been systematically lowered over the years," Isaac
quits his "antiseptic" TV show and undertakes a novel—about the
decay of culture. On a minor but telling level, Isaac rejects Mary's
and Yale's flippant consignment of major cultural figures to their
"Academy of the Over-rated" (*e.g.*, Lenny Bruce, Mahler, Boll,
Van Gogh, Ingmar Bergman). Resisting the easy temptation to smile
along, Isaac affirms that the attacked artists "are all terrific, every
one you mentioned." Here he supports his earlier claim (reminiscent
of Joey in *Interiors*) that "talent is luck; you've got to have courage."

In a parallel scene later, Isaac enumerates the things that make
life worth living. They vary from unpretentious popular culture
(Groucho Marx, Willie Mays) to various forms of the classical
(Mozart's Jupiter Symphony, Flaubert's *A Sentimental Education*)
and from art to experience, when he turns from Cezanne's apples
and pears to "the crabs at Sam Wo's" and, climactically, to Tracy's
face. This scene begins with a full-screen close-up of a tape recorder.
At first we do not know whether Isaac or the machine is reciting the
list. When we see Isaac speaking, we understand that values are due
solely to man, not to the things in his setting. The resolution of this
ambiguous opening establishes man as the center of values and

choice in his world. At the end of the scene, Isaac retrieves the harmonica that Tracy gave him at their last meeting. The harmonica is not just another thing, like the tape recorder; it embodies and revives the harmony between Isaac and his lost Tracy. In coming to accept his love for Tracy, Isaac receives his own sentimental education.

The theme of integrity relates to the feel of the film. As Isaac describes himself as "a non-compromiser" who is "living in the past," the film assumes a rigorous, classical spirit from its straightforward romantic narrative, its resolute black-and-white photography, and its George Gershwin score. Moreover, Allen's choice of songs provides specific settings in which to read the scenes. For example, the tunes over the scenes between Tracy and Isaac are direct expressions of love. Behind their first intimate scene in his apartment, "Our Love is Here to Stay" undercuts Isaac's detachment from her. Over their ride through Central Park we hear "He Loves and She Loves," which is reprised when Isaac's list of life's rewards concludes with Tracy's face. When he finds her in the apartment lobby, about to leave for London, his sense of her remoteness is suggested visually in the intervening door, a bar across its glass, and musically by the song, "They're Writing Songs of Love, But Not for Me." On the other hand, the music in Isaac's scenes with Mary are ominous: "Let's Call The Whole Thing Off" at the MOMA reception; "Someone to Watch Over Me," when they take her dog, "a penis-substitute," for a walk—and he mentions his short story about his mother, "The Castrating Zionist." When they drive in the country to " 'S Wonderful," it is at first unclear whether Isaac is with Tracy or with Mary. We hear "Embraceable You" when Isaac and Mary dance, enjoy a murky boatride, and walk in the city. When this song is repeated over the end credits, the emotion refers to the more embraceable Tracy. When Isaac frolics with his son, Willie, the song, "Love is Sweeping the Country," relates to the later scene of a football team of single fathers and sons, as if it is not love but the phenomenon of fractured families that is sweeping the country. When Isaac first sees Jill's book about their marriage we hear "Oh, Lady Be Good." In these ironic references, the songs establish a setting which either expresses or undercuts the attitude of the characters. The musical setting is analogous to Allen's use of Manhattan as the symbolic setting of his film.

Manhattan opens with a three-minute abstract sequence which establishes the setting and its characters, first the skyline, then individual buildings, then the streets and population. We hear Allen's voice, and the scene turns out to be one in which Isaac is choosing from a variety of openings for the first chapter of his novel. The different tones of Isaac's openings suggest the different meanings that Allen's Manhattan may carry. For instance, in one opening, the hero admits that he romanticizes Manhattan "out of all proportion." In another he presents it as a virile force, and in yet another as "the metaphor for the decay of contemporary culture." But the reading of the essential nature of the city depends upon the character of the reader, who may be "as tough and romantic as the city he loved," or a sexual power "coiled like a jungle cat." In describing the city, Isaac's hero—and so Allen's—projects his various moods and conceptions of himself onto the setting. When in the mellow dawn Isaac tells Mary "This is really a great city. I don't care what people say, I'm really knocked out," this is a tribute not to any real Manhattan but to the mood between Mary and Isaac, which the city at that point seems to embody.

Similarly the setting offers both elegant beauty and the rough streets, with a citizenry "desensitized by noise, music, drugs, and garbage." The city is in constant change, as one scene of a demolition crew at work reveals. But which of the innumerable and contradictory aspects will characterize the setting is the individual's choice. To both Allen's and Isaac's heroes, "New York still existed in black and white and pulsated to the great tunes of George Gershwin." But this is due to the idealism of the characters. When we hear "New York was his town and it always would be," we see a contradictory shot of the gleaming, modernistic highrises that are changing the city's physical nature. The setting is a projection of the human viewers. What one is and does, therefore, is one's own responsibility and not to be attributed to any influence from the setting. As Isaac works around to an affirmation of life's pleasures and his love with Tracy, the opening montage concludes by establishing an exuberant harmony between the climax of Gershwin's *Rhapsody in Blue* and the spectacular fireworks against the night skyline. The delicate and precise editing here discovers harmony in an ambivalent and discordant setting.

This point also lies behind the film's most striking visual technique. Allen often holds his stationary camera on a physical space after the actors have vacated it. The pretense is that the setting has its own personality independent of the human life that passes through it. But Allen's point is the opposite. The meaning lies in the human choice. In this spirit, the film does not have a title shot. We read "Manhattan" from a flashing hotel sign in the opening montage—but we also read a static "Parking" in the same shot. The film does not announce its name or identity, but rather seems to discover it in the setting. This is a formal equivalent to the characters' rooting their behavior in what they find rather than in their own ethical core.

Similarly, Yale joins Isaac and Tracy at the art gallery by stepping into the frame from an off-camera position and from behind a pillar; then Mary makes her first appearance by coming out from behind Yale. Here Allen uses the space of his shot to express the arbitrary framing of elements and the continuous life beyond the shot. In the marina scene, Isaac passes through a stationary shot while we hear the passage from his ex-wife's book in which she complains of his Jewish-Liberal paranoia, his male chauvinism, his self-righteous misanthropy, and his narcissistic obsession with death. The camera holds on the beautiful waterfront both before and after the harsh quotation and Isaac's sullen reaction. The shot establishes an ambivalence in the peaceful beauty. The calm waters seem to deny Isaac's gloom, but when in an earlier boating scene, Isaac reached into the water, his hand was covered with grime.

In *Manhattan* Allen's compositions avoid the sometimes obvious symbolism of *Interiors*. For example, in a single shot at the symphony we view a line of profiles. Isaac, Mary and Yale shift restlessly and shuffle to avert each other's eyes; Emily stares straight ahead. Later, we learn that she has known about Yale's infidelities but chose to ignore them; Emily's rigid stare may be as evasive as the shiftiness of the others. Similarly, when Mary phones Isaac to invite him out for an afternoon walk, Isaac is outside, but photographed from within his apartment. No, he tells Mary, he hasn't read the *Times* piece about the faceless masses in China; he's been too busy with the lingerie ads. As he chooses between two contrasting cultures of facelessness, his own face is obscured from us by the plants and venetian blinds through which he is seen. Moreover, the shot of him outside expresses his sense of remoteness from Mary, that he must not intrude upon his friend's affair.

The richest scene occurs in the planetarium, in which Mary and Isaac take refuge from the rain. The once antagonistic characters are drawn into an emotional attraction against a backdrop of the moon and stars. The location suggests that their love may require such an other-worldly setting. Moreover, as they grow more intimate Isaac and Mary assume more of the screen and the lunar landscape is allowed less. The setting disappears altogether for their most intimate exchange. Also, their inchoate love seems to be extravagantly literalized by the moon imagery, given the June-moon lyrical tradition over which Gershwin reigns supreme. This setting brings down to earth the "problems about the universe" that Isaac's Manhattanites avoid. Finally the force of human habit is comically imaged in the Japanese tourist who walks across the moon and pauses to take a snapshot (effectively of the cinema audience). This scene suggests that Manhattan contains the cosmos.

As an emblem of moral and aesthetic choices, Manhattan means something rather different in *Manhattan* than it meant when Annie Hall compared the insular Alvy Singer to it ("this island unto yourself"). In *Manhattan* Allen's hero reconciles a compromised, new Manhattan with his old idealized one and extends his rigorous ethics into a romance that exceeds logical and conventional limits. Despite the familiar Jewish, sexual and paranoia jokes, Isaac is Allen's most competent and confident role. He smokes, drinks, drives, has no trouble getting girls, and at one point invites his audience to share his self-acceptance. When Mary compliments his "good sense of humor," Isaac replies "Thanks. I don't need you to tell me that. I've been making good money off it for years now." Allen is still drawing his fictional character out of the limbo between his own experience and his public image. Thus the first sound we hear is the instrument Allen is associated with, the clarinet solo beginning *Rhapsody in Blue,* and the first scene is set in Allen's favorite hangout, Elaine's. (On the other hand, Yale warns us against confusing Isaac with Allen: "Gossip is the new pornography").

There are other echoes from *Annie Hall*. For instance, in her intuitive power, innocence, charm and growth, Tracy like Annie personifies the joys of life, the brief reward for suffering the failures and adversities the flesh is heir to. The racquetball game at which Yale sends Isaac to Mary recalls the tennis scene in which Alvy Singer met Annie Hall. Again the lovers disagree about an art movie; again the Keaton heroine keeps rotting sandwiches. In both films homage is paid to Jean Renoir's *La Grande Illusion*, another classic analysis of the decay of western culture. These echoes establish an experience that we seem to have shared with the artist.

Allen expands and inflects the vocabulary that his comedy has developed over the years. When Isaac comes home with shattering news from Jill—her book may be made into a movie and their son is taking ballet classes—and is about to hear that Mary is returning to Yale, there is a fleeting image of his vulnerability. When he closes his door we see that it has three locks and a security pole as defenses against the outside world. This passing joke is not even given the emphasis of a close-up. Because Allen developed it more fully in *Bananas*, the image can be quoted quickly. Similarly, the sidewalk cafe where Yale breaks off with Mary recalls the health-food restaurant where Annie Hall declined Alvy's proposal. The point of this echo is the common occurrence of such scenes. Behind Yale we see another couple lunching happily—at a rather early stage in their inevitable separation! Behind Mary we see another romantic mismatch, an elderly man and a young woman, that parallels both her situation with Yale and Isaac's with Tracy.

The familiar Woody Allen hero, for all his competence, remains shivered by the impossibility of justice. At one point Mary, before making love, asks Isaac what he's thinking. "I think there's something wrong with me," he replies, "because I've never had a relationship with a woman that's lasted longer than the one Hitler had with Eva Braun." Here Allen is at the peak of his artistry. He freezes in a one-liner the aspiration, compromise, horrifying history and rueful resignation that comprise the ethical man's response to the ambivalences of modern life.

Wrap-up 1:
Jester and Outsider

Although Woody Allen's performance in *Annie Hall* got him an Oscar nomination in 1977 as Best Actor, Richard Dreyfuss won for his
work in *The Goodbye Girl*. As it happens, Dreyfuss's career proves
Allen's influence on the changing style of film heroism. The typical
American film hero of the 1970s is a short, plucky, disenchanted,
candid, neurotic he-boy, with neither the prowess nor the confidence
that characterized the stars of past decades. Dreyfuss's debt to Allen
is most explicit in a scene in *Jaws* (1975). When the Robert Shaw
character demonstrates his manliness by crumpling a beercan, Dreyfuss cockily squashes his styrofoam coffee cup. The hero's combination of weakness, mock heroism, and self-acceptance in a single
gesture draws on the precedent of the Allen persona. Allen's influence
can also be seen in *The End* (1978), in which Burt Reynolds plays
a man who is obsessed with his death and candid about his sexual inadequacy. When such a macho star as Burt Reynolds accepts a role
as a sexual failure in a comedy about death, we see how deeply Allen
has influenced the comic film. Allen used to play losers who feebly
aspired to the style of a Bogart, a Peter O'Toole, or a James Bond;
now a Burt Reynolds expresses the flawed humanity of the Woody
Allen persona. Clearly Allen has articulated the spirit of our time.
Furthermore, his artistry has helped convert popular entertainment
media into modes of significant expression and apprehension.

From the prose humor in *Playboy* to the complex Kaiser Lupowitz stories and "The Kugelmass Episode," from *What's Up, Tiger
Lily?* through *Manhattan*, Allen's penchant for parody has both technical and philosophical implication. Technically, parody enabled

Allen to familiarize himself with a medium by exercising in a specific body of work. He could develop his confidence as a writer by following the forms of an established genre or style, adding his own satiric touch. Similarly, his first Broadway play, *Don't Drink the Water*, was admittedly modeled after particular plays (*Teahouse of the August Moon* and *You Can't Take It with You*).

In his film work Allen undertook a variety of technical experiments that enabled him to learn the craft while he parodied established forms. The most obvious example is *What's Up, Tiger Lily?*. Starting with a finished film, Allen explored the tension between a given image and an imposed sound track, between a situation and an alien perspective upon it. Allen developed more complex genre parodies in his next features: *Take the Money and Run, Bananas, Everything You Always Wanted To Know About Sex* and *Sleeper*. Having mastered the range of film narrative, he advanced to philosophical parody in *Love and Death*. From *Annie Hall* through *Manhattan* Allen established his independence from genre conventions and parody. But his career as a brilliant parodist had taught him his craft—and won him his audience.

The language of parody also had philosophical attractions for Allen. It expresses the extent to which we are deluded and tormented by the vainglorious dreams inflicted upon us by the romantic and commercial media. After all, Allen's losers live out a kind of parody of remote heroic images. This is the point of Allen's contributions to *What's New, Pussycat?* and to *Casino Royale*, in which the fumbling hero aspired to sexual prowess and to the all-around effectiveness of James Bond. Allen's Virgil Starkwell lives a parody of the heroism of the Hollywood gangster, Allan Felix the romantic efficiency of Bogart, and Eve in *Interiors* the gray, hollow elegance of her favored vases.

We find the same tension between an impossible dream and a frustrating reality in Allen's prose. In the *Playboy* pieces Allen represents himself as a sheep whose vanity leads him to strut about in a stud-wolf's clothing. In "The Kugelmass Episode" an English professor lives in his favorite fiction—which is, after all, what the Allen persona has always been trying to do, and technically what the parodist does—and finds that a dream come true can be a nightmare. Throughout the Allen canon, the failure exacerbates his frustration when he emulates the successes he has seen in art or in the media. In *Interiors* Allen expresses an even harsher view: art can be a sterilizing force if it walls out the consolations of human contact and obscures the direct experience of simple pleasures.

Allen's tendency to mock-heroic comedy embodies his sense of a small man reaching for an inappropriately heroic image that dwarfs him all the more by confirming that his reach is laughably beyond his grasp. Man seems to need myths and delusions of heroism to compensate for his feelings of insignificance. Hence the saga of the Earl of Sandwich, "Yes, But Can the Steam Engine Do This?," and the strained (and lumpy) rhetoric in the legend of Virgil Starkwell.

Allen seems early on to have arrived at Ernest Becker's conclusion in *The Denial of Death,* that "the problem of heroics is the central one of human life." As Becker argues, "Society itself is a codified hero system, which means that society everywhere is a living myth of the significance of human life, a defiant creation of meaning" by which man hopes to avoid confronting his mortality.[1] As Allen told Yvonne Baby: "Maturity has borne out my childhood. I'd always thought death was the sole driving force: I mean that our effort to avoid it is the only thing which gives impetus to our existence." [2] So the boy Alvy Singer refuses to do his homework because he knows the universe will eventually explode. In *Manhattan* Allen's hero more positively bases his sense of moral accountability upon his knowledge that he will someday be a skeleton in a classroom.

Allen's various losers and *schlemiels* represent man's attempt to conceal his own insignificance behind a fraudulently heroic pose. The involuntary celibate pretends to be a great lover, the bookish schoolboy a master criminal, and the befuddled misfit a philosopher. Allen's comedy of mock heroism demonstrates the falseness of social codes and images that obscure man's limits and thereby prevent his coming to terms with his fate. This idea is made explicit in *Manhattan* but it has lurked behind Allen's comedy from the very beginning.

Allen also demonstrates the danger of losing one's self in fantasy. In his routine about prolonging sex with thoughts of baseball and in his story about the wrong life flashing through the doomed man's mind, Allen dramatizes how man is disabled by his dependence on the fantasies of society's "codified hero system." Against all these dream images of success, acceptance, and glory, Allen establishes both the persistence of patterns of failure (as in *Take the Money and Run* and *Bananas*) and the inevitable limitations of man's physical nature (the need for "better housing" in *What's New, Pussycat?*, the debility in *Don't Drink the Water*, and the doom in *Love and Death*, where the hero's reprieve is trivial and his pardon a delusion). Allen's rare happy endings are severely qualified. For example, at the end of *Bananas* Mellish succeeds in winning Nancy but Howard Cosell warns that the couple may well not live happily ever after. Similarly, the romantic high point in *Love and Death* occurs half-way through the film and is destroyed by the hero's involvement in world politics. Allen's characters cannot sustain whatever satisfaction they may stumble into, because man's life is characterized not by achievement and permanence but by loss and change. In *Annie Hall* and *Interiors* Allen directly confronts the loss of love and life, but this concern was already implicit in his monologues and films about perennial losers. The ending of *Manhattan* raises the same anxiety but allows the aging hero and his teen-age love the possibility of renewal and success.

Allen's recurring use of deflating satire relates to man's attempt to substitute the satisfactions of delusion for the disappointments of reality. Thus in *What's New, Pussycat?* and "The Whore of Mensa" Allen examines the frustrations involved in the fact that man's spiritual nature is housed in a body obsessed by physical hungers. The religious and philosophical ambitions examined in *Love and Death* must similarly give way to the demands of the appetite. Perhaps the key moment in *Play It Again, Sam* occurs the morning after Allan Felix and Linda have made love. For here Felix avoids the unrealistic romanticism that has dogged him throughout the work. In the afterglow of love, Felix recalls: "I took you in my arms and we made love. Then we each got upset stomachs. The main thing is that we're honest." In this unconventional *aubade* the hero avoids the Allen character's usual mistake, which is to be so obsessed with pursuing a heroic image (to wit: Bogart) that he fails to acknowledge his own limits and his own worth. Rare for an Allen hero, Felix here achieves success but remains "honest" about his condition.

Interiors shows a cultured and self-conscious family that is unaccustomed to dealing with the truth either about their relationships or their own nature. Joey's conclusion, "We have no choice but to forgive each other," recalls Kleinman's warning to the warring factions in *Death:* "Co-operate . . . God is the only enemy." In her hearty warmth and simplicity, Pearl combines the invulnerability of Ackerman in *Death Knocks* with the expansive spirit and growth of Annie Hall.

Allen's choice of genres, tones, and techniques is always related to his vision of life. His parody, mock heroism, and ironic undercutting are matters of content as much as form. So too is his effect of seeming to remain outside his material. However much his persona may be rooted in his own experience, Allen always seems to stand apart from his work.

Indeed his first film, *What's Up, Tiger Lily?*, is based on his detachment from the material. Allen's appearances dramatize this detachment, and the very character of the work, in which a bathetic Occidental sound track is imposed on an Oriental imitation of an American heroic genre, suggests the stance of an Outsider. Here Allen is essentially the *kibbitzer*, the wise-cracking onlooker who stands apart from—and is irreverent toward—the game that others are seriously playing. This is also the stance of his parody, in which he plays against the conventions of a serious model, and his direct addresses to the audience in *Love and Death* and *Annie Hall*. This is also one effect of the deliberate anachronisms in *God, The Query, Everything You Always Wanted To Know About Sex,* and *Love and Death;* they show Allen standing apart from—and playing fast and loose with—his material.

His Outsider stance as an artist is reinforced by the Outsider figures he plays. In *Take the Money and Run* Virgil Starkwell is so isolated from the prison community that he is not told when a breakout is canceled; the other convicts laugh when he is caught alone outside. In *Sleeper* the Allen character is actually called The Alien, and in *Annie Hall* Alvy is persuaded that he is being treated as one. In Martin Ritt's *The Front* Allen plays an irresponsible middleman who matures into the dignified role of Outsider.

Allen's personification of the Outsider may be the most important way in which he expresses the spirit of his time. As Vivian Gornick recalls his nightclub years: "He made outsiders of us all." [3] He does just that in "Science Fiction Plot" when he imagines the world turned into Jewish tailors. He does just that in his story about the

Klan rally, when he reminds us that the cheer and innocence in Hollywood's image of a Kansas boyhood are not true for very many of us.

The Outsider expresses modern urban man's familiar sense of alienation and anomie. Involving more than just his comedy of the loser, it relates to Allen's feelings of persecution by an antipathetic society. For Allen defines life itself as a paranoid experience. In *Everything You Always Wanted To Know About Sex*, his climactic appearance suggests that anxiety and paranoia are sperm-deep in modern man. So, too, in *Annie Hall* "the worst kind of paranoia" is paranoia that is based on objective facts.

One shot in *Annie Hall* is set up to function as an act of paranoid perception. Alvy and Rob enter in the far, upper-right corner of a busy street view, then slowly walk into the foreground. Because of the characters' smallness and the many distracting details and movements in the shot, we hear their conversation long before we see them. That is, in order to see the speakers we hear, we must single out a peripheral detail from a crowded scene, emphasizing the one minute aspect that relates to our interest. We thus imitate Alvy's selective perception when he hears Tom Christie's elision of "Did you eat?" as "Jew eat?" Through the dynamics of this shot, Allen makes paranoids of us all.

As a Jew, Allen is the eternal Outsider. His moose story early in his career and the widow Pearl of his later *Interiors* suggest the range and consistency in this aspect of his work. For like Kafka, Allen makes Jews of us all. What he calls "the urban Jewish mentality . . . of being racked with guilt and suffering, of feeling one step ahead of trouble and anxiety" is no longer limited to the Jews: "Life is a concentration camp. You're stuck here, and there's no way out, and you can only rage impotently against your persecutors." [4]

Or you can laugh. The Hassidic spirit of laughter and dance that frames *Love and Death* is as characteristic of Jewish philosophy as the doom it defies. From it springs the modern phenomenon of the Jewish stand-up comedian. One thinks of Eddie Cantor, Al Jolson, George Jessel, Jack Benny, George Burns, Henny Youngman, Milton Berle, Totie Fields, Ted Lewis in one generation, and Lenny Bruce, Mort Sahl, Shelley Berman, Joey Bishop, Jackie Mason, Rodney Dangerfield, Don Rickles, Jack Carter, David Steinberg, Robert Klein,

Allan Sherman, Woody Allen in another. So who's watching the store?

There is something essentially Jewish about the act of stand-up comedy. The performer stands alone and without a prop before a crowd of strangers. By his wit he attempts to forge a sense of community with them. By his brain and humor he tries to gain their acceptance, the laughter that denotes approval. Without the protective cover of a dramatic role in a play, the stand-up comic must expose his own personality to an audience of strangers. Despite his strangeness and alienation, he must persuade them that he is one of them. He therefore stresses the foibles and failures common to humanity. He is motivated partly by a desire to reflect the humanity that he shares with his audience and partly by an eagerness to defuse their suspicion, fear, and potential animosity toward him. So he stands alone in front of a silent and alien audience, spinning out his line of self-deprecating patter or charming cheek (*chutzpah*). The stand-up comedian is the eternal Outsider, the Wandering Jew. He has no home or community except what he can establish with each house he faces. Two shows nightly, each performance is the drama of modern alienation. As the non-Jewish community grew attuned to its existential isolation from man and from God, the stand-up comedian came to represent not just the Jews but the general experience of modern urban man. The club comedian and Kafka converge in Woody Allen.

Allen's Jewishness serves other functions than establishing him as an Outsider. In his comedies with Louise Lasser, the Jew is a hopeless but unbowed loser. But in his films with Diane Keaton, Allen's Jew asserts positive values (that continue into the Jewish adumbration of Pearl in *Interiors*). Allen's Jew teaches the WASP heroine warmth, sensitivity, spirit, moral sense, and attunement to life— even as he frantically aspires to acceptance in her world. Allen's Jewish figures "improve" the envied WASPs just as Philip Roth's Portnoy teaches Monkey "to be compassionate, to bleed a little for the world's sorrow," in a word, to "put the *oy* back in *goy*." [5] Allan Felix helps Linda and her husband revive their lost passion, Miles Monroe awakens Luna to the responsibilities of human imperfection, Boris teaches Sonia to complement her compromised idealism and sensuality with warmth and emotion, and Alvy Singer brings about the transformation of Annie Hall. In all his comedies with Keaton, the Allen character—like Pearl in *Interiors*—is a "vulgarian," but he is also the spirit that breathes new life into the genteel, Gentile form. This cultural contrast is modified in Manhattan: Isaac warms Mary but is in turn steadied and gentled by the young WASP Tracy.

Not surprisingly, Allen's Jew is also a figure of moral rectitude. His Isaac assails Yale for being "too easy" on himself. Behind his recurring gibes at California lurks an Old Testament suspicion of easy pleasure. He satirizes not the state but the sunny state of mind that will settle for frolicking comfort and mindless cheer. Thus in *Bananas* a coffin with a stereo attachment is intended for the California market; already Allen identifies the state with irrational pleasure and obliviousness of death. In *Sleeper* the apathetic, hedonistic life under an autocratic government is declared even "worse than California." Finally, Alvy Singer is repelled by the bone-white pleasure palaces of California because life there is too easy; it is important to make an effort, he tells Annie.

Allen wears his moral purpose lightly, as we see in this monologue:

> I was involved [pause] in an extremely good case of oral contraception recently. I asked a girl to go to bed with me. She said no.

At the end there was a moment of silence before the audience realized that the joke was over, that they had been tricked into a narrow interpretation of what constitutes "oral contraception." It has come to mean The Pill, with all the attendant glories of sexual liberty. But the joke recalls an earlier time when liberty was less important than restraint. Though predicated on the persona's career of rejection, the joke reaffirms the primacy of the individual will. Allen's pause after "involved" reminds us of a double meaning in the term. People can be casually involved in sexual situations, or intensely *involved* with each other. This ambiguity implies that in the age of The Pill, the latter involvement is no longer a necessary element of the sexual experience. Here a racy gag conveys the spirit of an Old Testament conscience.

Though there is a large measure of fiction behind the persona's candid avowal of sexual inadequacy, neurosis, physical weakness, and cowardice, in so openly parading pretended weakness, Allen dramatizes the importance of man's knowing and accepting himself and his mortal limits. His *schlemielery* is an antidote to the dishonest dreams of glory and mindless pleasure by which modern man attempts to disguise the true nature of his existence.

Both in his admissions of inadequacy and in his transparent claims to being a stud, Allen expresses the sexual anxieties of modern man. There is, of course, the full-scale treatment of this concern in *Everything You Always Wanted To Know About Sex*. Elsewhere Allen often expresses a sense that man feels himself monstrous and vile because of his sexual stirrings. For example, in *Play It Again, Sam* Allan Felix recalls admiring his sleeping wife: "Once in a while she'd wake up and catch me. She'd let out a scream." The Peter Sellers role in *What's New, Pussycat?* is Allen's fullest representation of this view of sexuality as a monstrous, destructive urge.

But Allen seems to agree with Ernest Becker's point that not sexuality but *"consciousness of death* is the primary repression." [6] As early as 1963 Allen's jokes included "History will dissolve me." [7] (The gag is a pessimistic parody of Fidel Castro's "History will absolve me." For Allen there is no hope of absolution.) As he explained in 1969, his comedy of the loser was based on his sense of man's mortality: "Basically everybody is a loser but it's only now that people are beginning to admit it. People feel their shortcomings more than their attributes. That's why Marilyn Monroe killed herself, and that's why people can't understand it." [8]

Allen's appearance as a sperm cell in *Everything You Always Wanted To Know About Sex* owes less to Dr. Reuben's original book than to Becker's *The Denial of Death:* a child's questions about sex are not fundamentally about sex but "about the meaning of the body, the terror of living with a body." [9] Or as Allen's sperm puts it: "I'm not going out there. I'm not going to get shot out of that thing." The entire film demonstrates Becker's thesis that sexuality is a primary means by which man attempts to evade his mortality.

In *Love and Death* Allen explores a second of Becker's means of denying death. After transcending social and "merely cultural heroism," man assumes the "possibility of cosmic heroism" by believing in and serving God. [10] In *Love and Death* when Boris finally receives (as it happens, false) proof of the existence of God, he enjoys a very temporary religious refuge from his sense of mortality. "Yea, I shall *run* through the valley of the shadow of death." In *Annie Hall* Allen explores the use of art to deny loss and death. Finally, the various functions of art, romance, sensuality, and religion are presented in *Interiors* as examples of how man avoids confronting his mortality—and lives a life of hollow exteriors as a result.

Woody Allen's art moves beyond the comedy of mere laughter. Reaching into his own anxieties and the most frightened corners of the human psyche, this public artist has found a distinctive language and style with which to confront the human condition. From the grim grin of death the eternal Outsider snatches a laugh and a dance with which he reaches across the footlights, the page, or the screen to connect to his fellows in the dark.

Part Five

Through the Eighties

Even after *Annie Hall* and *Manhattan* Woody Allen continued to experiment. Rather than "be trapped" into complacency he undertook new challenges: "It's a healthy thing to fail a couple of times, because you know you're on the right track."[1] Far from failing, Allen produced an astonishing range of masterpieces—*Stardust Memories* (1980), *Zelig* (1983), *Broadway Danny Rose* (1984), *The Purple Rose of Cairo* (1985), *Hannah and Her Sisters* (1986), *Another Woman* (1988), and *Crimes and Misdemeanors* (1989)—plus a few works that were merely excellent.

Allen also appeared in Jean-Luc Godard's *King Lear* (1987) as a soliloquizing film editor named Mr. Alien. In 1991 he played charmingly against persona as a philandering LA lawyer in Paul Mazursky's *Scenes from a Mall*.

In his own films, throughout the decade Allen developed his familiar themes. For example, the magic he introduced in *Stardust Memories* was developed into a Broadway play, *The Floating Light Bulb* (1981), and a period comedy, *A Midsummer Night's Sex Comedy* (1982). Magic returns in the self-transforming heroes of *Zelig* and *Alice* (1991), and in "Oedipus Wrecks," Allen's part of the trilogy *New York Stories* (1989). In several nostalgic romances—*Broadway Danny Rose*, *The Purple Rose of Cairo*, *Hannah and Her Sisters*, and *Radio Days* (1987)—Allen's theme is the difficulty of finding an ethical center in a godless world. As Allen reduces the element of romantic comedy, his ethical concern dominates the decade end: *September* (1987), *Another Woman*, and *Crimes and Misdemeanors*. But each Allen film has the integrity of being both familiar and fresh.

The "family" man: in *Stardust Memories* Sandy Bates (Allen) lunches with Isobel (Marie-Christine Barrault) and her children (Orion Pictures).

In *A Midsummer Night's Sex Comedy*, Professor Sturgis (Jose Ferrer) prophetically pairs up with Dulcy Ford (Julie Hagerty), Maxwell Jordan (Tony Roberts) with Ariel Weymouth (Mia Farrow) (Orion Pictures).

Leonard Zelig adapts to the psychiatric environment by sprouting a mustache (Orion Pictures).

Broadway Danny Rose speaks sweet reason to an angry Tina Vitale (Farrow) (Orion Pictures).

The Ideal vs. The Real: Tom Baxter (Jeff Daniels) confronts Monk (Danny Aiello) in *The Purple Rose of Cairo* (Orion Pictures).

In *Hannah and Her Sisters*, Lee (Barbara Hershey) and her lover, Frederick (Max von Sydow), entertain a prospective buyer (Daniel Stern) and her would-be lover, Elliot (Michael Caine) (Orion Pictures).

Doubling reflections in *Radio Days*: Roger Daly (David Warrilow) trysts with Sally White (Farrow) (Orion Pictures).

The frustrated writer (Sam Waterston) and the frustrated wife (Dianne Wiest) flirt in *September* (Orion Pictures).

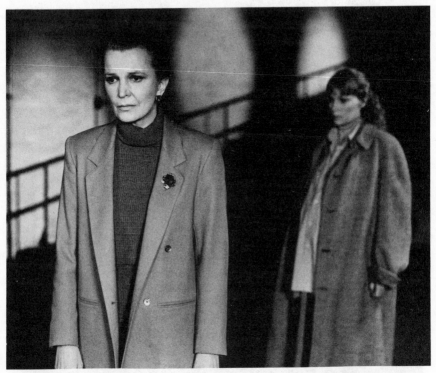

In *Another Woman* Marion Post (Gena Rowlands) meets Hope (Farrow) in a theatrical dream (Orion Pictures).

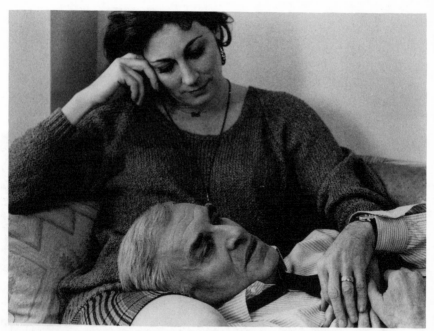

In the good old days, Dolores (Anjelica Huston) and Judah (Martin Landau) find mutual consolation (in *Crimes and Misdemeanors*) (Orion Pictures).

In *Alice* Dr. Yang (Keye Luke) prescribes and pours for Alice (Farrow) (Orion Pictures).

17

Stardust Memories (1980)

In *Stardust Memories* Allen pays homage to Ingmar Bergman and Federico Fellini, but his aesthetic references also have a moral dimension. Like Fellini's *8 1/2* (1965), the film mixes the chaos of filmmaking with a blocked director's fantasies. Sandy Bates (Allen) examines the "Proustian rush" (his putative cologne) that stymies both his love and his art. In Sandy's uncertainty—"I was thinking about should I change my movie? Should I change my life?"—he erases the distinction between life and film. So, too, the woman who "just did a definitive cinematic study of Gummo Marx . . . the one Marx brother that never made any movies."

In the opening episode Sandy appears trapped in a stifling train amid grim souls. He yearns to be in the party train across the tracks. This scene is revealed to be from Sandy's latest film. As *Stardust Memories* proceeds, Bates suffers a weekend retrospective of his films at the Stardust Hotel. In his more personal "retrospective," Sandy evades commitment to Isobel (Marie-Christine Barrault), who has just left her husband, and is drawn to a neurotic violinist, Daisy (Jessica Harper). Her "kind of lost quality" recalls his earlier love, Dorrie (Charlotte Rampling), who gave him two days of bliss for every twenty-eight of misery. The apparently happy ending of *Stardust Memories*, in which Sandy accepts Isobel's love, turns out to be the ending of Sandy's film. That is, Sandy has imposed a happy ending on his fiction (1) that he fails to make in his life, and (2) that is analogous to his producers' attempt to brighten Sandy's downbeat conclusion.

Allen's film concludes with Sandy's three women discussing their roles (including Sandy's/Allen's "irritating" French kissing). In a lyrical coda, Sandy studies the empty screen, then walks off the front corner, as if into our audience. The figure leaving could be Allen, not Sandy.[1] The exposure of illusion could logically culminate in Allen's departure from his character's world. For Allen is more likely than Sandy to pause in quiet awe at the power of the emptied screen and the ceiling arc of "stars," a stance Sandy nowhere takes.

As well as establishing contrary worldviews, the two trains of the opening scene represent the antithesis of the meditative Bergman and the frolicsome Fellini. The Bergman train is defined in bleak faces, a ticking clock, and a suitcase pouring out sand. The Fellini train is alluring hilarity. The trains also recall the moral contrast between the two male leads in *Manhattan*. Sandy, like Isaac, is stuck in Bergmanic abstemiousness. The alternative frivolity signifies Yale's world, which the same actor, Tony Roberts, now summarizes for Sandy: "You can play a little golf, get a little poon, you smoke some good grass, and that's what life's about, you know?" After Sandy's "death," a nurse affirms that life of simple appetite— "It's a shame. Poor fool, he's dead and he never really found out the meaning of life"—chomping an apple over her obsequy.

Despite everyone's demands (including space aliens') that Sandy return to making comedy, he is too preoccupied with anxieties. A psychoanalyst diagnoses Sandy's "Ozymandias Melancholia": "Faulty denial mechanism. Failed to block out the terrible truths of existence." Sandy is obsessed with mortality, as exemplified by his brother-in-law, who had two heart attacks before he began compulsively exercising—then another two after. His bicycle bell tolls for us all. Sandy is also troubled by violence. His wallpaper is shown to have changed from a Marx Brothers' poster to Eddie Adams's Pulitzer Prize newsphoto of the South Vietnamese police chief executing a civilian in Saigon.

The Bergman-Fellini axis continues in two moving close-ups of Dorrie. In Sandy's last meeting with her, a jagged montage, which suggests her cracked psyche, evokes the Bergman of *Face to Face* (1976). In the Fellini aspect, Sandy finds life's meaning in a treasured memory of a Sunday afternoon with Dorrie.[2] By "the combination of everything"—Louis Armstrong's "Stardust," the breeze, Dorrie's peace and beauty—"for one brief moment, everything just seemed to come together perfectly and I felt happy. Almost indestructible." Almost. Here Dorrie's repose feels more assuring because this shot is continuous, with Rampling farther away from the camera. In a related shot, Allen shows a Felliniesque line of tap-dancing nuns in the background while, in the Bergmanic fore, Sandy talks Dorrie out of her pre-filming anxieties.

In this light, the film's title is ambiguous. In naming the site of Sandy's retrospective, *Stardust Memories* refers to Sandy's suffering the business of his art. The title also suggests the mortality of artists, art, and our universe. In heaven as on earth, our stars turn to dust. Finally, in alluding to the Louis Armstrong song from Sandy's memory of Dorrie, the title subordinates the public life of art to its personal function.

This personal filmmaking explains Allen's frequent echo of his earlier films. A kitchen fire and an attack by killer pigeon recall the lobster and spider scenes in *Annie Hall*. In self-deprecation Allen replays old material, as when Sandy callously jokes at the raped woman's expense ("I'm sure you didn't resist, knowing you, Irene") and in his familiar masturbation jokes. Such Alleniana posits a limbo between Allen and Sandy that parallels the calculated confusion between Sandy's life and his films.

In the same spirit, Allen deflates (yet reaffirms) his own art through Sandy's critics. Even after the touching scene with Dorrie: "Cop-out artist!" "Why do all comedians turn out to be sentimental bores?" And further: "He's pretentious. . . . They try to document their private suffering and fob it off as art. . . . What self-indulgence!" The fans agree: "I like a melodrama, a musical comedy *mit* a plot but *nisht kein philosophia.*"

Indeed Allen seems to satirize Sandy's audience more than he does Sandy. The decor in Sandy's sister's home caricatures the middle class. Even his fans' gifts—script ideas, adulation, sex, a salami—are impositions upon him. Typical of how Sandy feels exploited by his fans, one man wants an autograph addressed "To Phyllis Weinstein, you unfaithful lying bitch." Despite Sandy's unpopular seriousness, another fan would include him in his "piece on the shallow indifference of wealthy celebrities." Even the saintly scholar dedicated to explicating the master's text is made vain and self-serving: "I'm Dr. Paul Pearlman. I did a paper on you and your films at a psychiatric convention. . . . It was very well received, you'll be happy to know. . . . Have you ever had intercourse with any type of animal?" English professor Jack Abel (John Rothman) seems funny for insisting that comedy is based on hostility, a theory denied by Sandy but exemplified by this film.

When viewers felt themselves Allen's target,[3] Allen denied having contempt for his audience: "I've always tried to play *up* to the audience," he told Tom Shales. He considers *Stardust Memories* "The best film I ever did." For one thing, "It was my least popular film. That may automatically mean it was my best film." Also, "It was the closest that I came to achieving what I set out to achieve."[4]

Although the film launched a "celebrity trilogy,"[5] it is more interesting for introducing Allen's childhood hobby, magic.[6] This theme unites Fellini with the Bergman of *The Magician* (1958). For Allen, magic is a metaphor for our attempts to overcome our helplessness in nature and in society. As a child Sandy wore Superman suits and tried to fly. "I would always practice to be popular," he tells Daisy. In his memories the frustrated adult artist often harkens back to his promise as a child magician (Robert Munk).[7] When young Sandy strokes his rod he produces a bouquet of false flowers. Making films is the adult's version of magic: "You can't control life. It doesn't wind up perfectly. Only art you can control. Art and masturbation—two areas in which I am absolutely expert." Even Sandy's surname evokes the apocryphal onanist (the Bates's son, Master Bates). Magic and art are associated with masturbation because they are solitary fantasies that do not improve the human condition. As the nurse reminds Sandy, "All those silly magic tricks you do couldn't help your friend Nat Bernstein." Nor Dorrie, adds Tony, though the filmmaker's craft suspends her in the life of the film's flashback.

When first reminded of Dorrie, Sandy retreats to a memory of a childhood magic act. He floats a white globe in the air, to Judith Crist's rave: "A born magician." The globe is an emblem of wholeness and illumination, both values Sandy finds elusive in life. When Sandy suspends Daisy in the air, she seems equivalent to his globe; Sandy suspends his real people to serve his imagination.

Though he controls Dorrie's role in his film, he cannot support her in life. Isobel is also lost as his love in life when she is made into the happy ending for his film. This magician perversely turns reality into illusion.

To one naif, Sandy's happy ending teaches that "Everybody should love each other. I mean, you know, he's telling us heavy, original things." Allen's point is rather that we use deluding art—the boy's magic, the man's films—to avoid facing our ephemerality. In life, unlike Sandy's college exam, we don't get 100 percent for leaving blank all the answers to an existential exam. While the audience prefers to ignore it, the artist feels compelled to make some mark on the blank page or screen, to confront the void.

18

The Floating Light Bulb (1981)

In his first Broadway play since *Play It Again, Sam* (1969),[1] Allen offered "a modest little idea" for "a good time."[2] *The Floating Light Bulb* premiered at the Vivian Beaumont Theatre on April 27, 1982, directed by Ulu Grosbard. In this bittersweet drama, set in a 1945 Brooklyn tenement, several characters fail to transform their lives.

The play loosely parallels Tennessee Williams's *The Glass Menagerie*. The sensitive Laura figure is sixteen-year-old Paul Pollack (originally Brian Backer), "awkward and gawky" with a serious stammer.[3] His life ambition is "T-to b-be a m-magician." Skipping school ("There are so many faces. I can't breathe"), he stays in his room, the apartment "reeking of hopelessness and neglect," to practice his simple tricks.

The father, Max (Danny Aiello), is a waiter who resents his wife's airs: "I was a bookmaker, you didn't like that idea. I drove a cab, you had a stroke when I parked it in front of the house." Resolving not "to put up a phony front anymore" and to "think of myself for once," he plans to flee to Florida or Nevada with his young mistress, Betty. Ironically, Max only switches from one fantasy to another ("Wear that little blue dress. It makes you look like a doll").

The mother, Enid (Beatrice Arthur), also wishes she "could vanish," she tells Paul. Her refuge in alcoholism only feeds the family's tensions. In contrast to Paul's floating light bulb, she works to "earn a few dollars and keep us afloat." Like Amanda Wingfield,

Enid Pollack tries telephone money-making schemes and recollects *beaux perdus:* "Herb Glass, a crackerjack foot specialist worshipped me. . . . In those days I wanted nothing more than to be a dancer in *The George White Scandals.*" Among her fantasies she treasures a girlhood escapade, "just like in the movies," with a hood she calls "the Kissing Bandit." Like Amanda, Enid depends on illusion, proposing a turban for her son's costume, pouring "the Christian Brothers into a decanter so it looks imported"—and placing excessive hopes on a gentleman caller.

In that role, Jerry Wexler (Jack Weston) is a small-time agent who yearns for one success: "I hear— 'A young magician'—and suddenly I'm off, and I think, My God . . . What if he's that one star I've been searching for my whole life?" In Paul, though, Wexler finds a kid too nervous for even basic tricks. When Wexler reenacts the best vaudeville acts he handled—a talking dog who sang "Little Sir Echo" and two Armenian boxers who performed "Ave Maria" while fighting—he reveals himself a performer *manqué*, another loser who dreamt stardom.

In Wexler Enid also discovers a romantic hope, but that is dashed by word he's moving to Arizona with his mother. Enid is realistic enough to see through her husband's deceptions. Hence her sarcasm: "Learn magic. That's exactly what we need around here— more tricks and illusions." But even she allows herself to be seduced by fantasy. She enthuses over Paul's card shuffle: "It's beautiful! You can hardly tell they're stapled together." She idealizes bigtime agents: "Take it from me, Paul—in this world, the bigger they are, the nicer they are." Later, her shrewd cynicism about Wexler dissolves before her need for romance. To Wexler, "Boy! This has turned out to be an evening of magic in its own way." But at play's end, Enid has reopened her heart to a man and been dashed. When Wexler, then Max, leave, Enid is left staring at Paul's false flowers.

Before the action proper begins, Paul floats a wireless light bulb that has materialized at his fingertips. But as this magic happens outside the action, it exists in theater, not in the characters' lives, like the "happy endings" Allen argues we seek in fiction because they are denied in our reality. As in *Stardust Memories*, magic represents for Paul the promise of power and social acceptance, dreamed in privacy but doomed in the real world. Enid describes

Paul as if he were an untalented Sandy Bates: "He's one of those people . . . that goes his whole life drifting, dreaming, dependent—in his own private world—with someone always having to take care of him." As Enid and Jerry draw pathetic hope from Paul's magic, they are an audience that craves illusionism.

In *The Floating Light Bulb* fantasies prevent the characters from coming to terms with their lives. Paul's magic is a debilitating retreat from reality. Max buys expensive fantasies of escape: he plays the numbers hoping for one big score and spends lavishly on Betty so he can "pretend [he's] thirty, not fifty." Betty, a cocktail waitress, fantasizes a steady provider (Max?!) leading her to a career in fashion design. Enid turns from one addictive refuge, her drinking, to another, her romantic fantasies first for Paul, then with Wexler. In their illusions the characters lose sense of who they are. So Max Pollack takes pride in having "hit a Polack the other night—a big sonofabitch. He don't wanna pay his check—I hit him a shot in the teeth." That unwitting identification makes Max's violence—like Paul's bedroom magic—another escapist form of self-abuse.

19

A Midsummer Night's Sex Comedy (1982)

In *A Midsummer Night's Sex Comedy* Allen emphasizes success over failure. Here the hero's magic works. It provides mysterious rewards beyond rational comprehension. Perhaps because such faith is archaic, Allen set this period piece in 1906. Nonetheless, his characters—except for his timelessly fossilized academics—speak and worry like Americans of the 1980s. As well as Allen's usual roots in Bergman—the romantic whimsy of *Smiles of a Summer's Night* (1955)—the title evokes Shakespeare's *Midsummer Night's Dream*, with its magical shuffling of lovers, and the opening music comes from Mendelssohn's version of that play. [1]

At an upstate New York country weekend, three couples discover their romantic natures. The agent for the transformation is a Wall Street broker and part-time inventor, Andrew Hobbs (Allen). Allen plays a worldlier man than usual but he still bumbles into his success. Andrew recovers his lost passion with his wife, Adrian (Mary Steenburgen), who feels guilty about an infidelity with his best friend, Dr. Maxwell Jordan (Tony Roberts). For the weekend, Maxwell brings his free-thinking nurse, Dulcy Ford (Julie Hagerty). But they become involved with the other guest couple, Professor Leopold Sturgis (Jose Ferrer) and Ariel Weymouth (Mia Farrow), who are about to be married. Andrew and Ariel revive an old passion but it proves dead. Ariel accepts Maxwell after he—heartbroken by her initial rejection—attempts to kill himself. He is wounded accidentally when the jealous Leopold attacks Andrew with a bow and arrow. In his newly discovered primitivism, Leopold ravages Dulcy and dies at the peak of his passion.

Allen's primary theme validates the nonmaterialist vision of life. In the opening scene the turgid Professor Sturgis afflicts his uniformly beige-suited students with materialist philosophy: "Nothing is real but experience, that which can be touched, tasted, felt, or in some scientific fashion proved. . . . Metaphysical philosophers are simply men who are too weak to accept the world as it is."[2]

Other characters believe there is more to life than the senses. Granted, both medics seek physical explanations for the mysteries of the emotions. Told that Raphael fainted at his first sight of the Sistine Chapel, Maxwell quips, "Had he eaten?" When Leopold marvels at living out his dream, Dulcy wonders what he ate before bed. But Maxwell believes there is more than the material because he knows the limits of his science. As Andrew teases, Maxwell has to believe in the spirit world because that's where his patients go.

Andrew is also defined by the tension between the material and the ethereal. As a stockbroker, "I help people with their investments until there's nothing left." For the wedding gift he invents a tool that removes the bones from fish—or that replaces them, if they prefer. He also invents a flying bicycle that works and wings that don't. That is, he harnesses human invention but not the power of another creature, like the Ariel of *The Tempest*. Andrew's key device is a spirit ball designed to "penetrate the unseen world." This "magic" is a kind of *camera obscura*, the forerunner of film. It projects a romantic image with which each couple differently identifies, whether from a regretted past or a desired future. But as this invention operates independent of its nebbish inventor, it is more like magic than like science or art. It refutes Leopold's assurance that "There's nothing magical about our existence." The philosophy that Leopold draws from Thomas Hobbes is undermined by Andrew Hobbs' mysterious invention.

The film's antimaterialism is supported by the characters' irrational emotions. When the weekend begins each man has an appropriate mate. The inventor has a tolerant wife, the professor a beautiful intellectual, and the randy doctor a randier nurse. Because there is more to the universe than meets the senses, and more to love than logic, each well-matched man craves a different woman. Only the midsummer lunacy can sort them out.

The period setting modifies Allen's usual satire of contemporary libertinism. As the setting represents turning point in our social history, Adrian marvels at how "depraved" it must be for Ariel to sleep with Leopold before their wedding, yet accepts the variety of Maxwell's bedmates. All three women are precocious in their lived feminism. Doctor Maxwell Jordan is more serious minded and passionate than the usual layabout roles Allen has written for Tony Roberts. Moreover, the free-loving Maxwell and Ariel convert to a deeply felt monogamy.

The key conversion is that of the professor. Leopold initially epitomizes the cultured man, his knowledge spanning the political, philosophical, and musical. But only when he uncovers his primitivism does he act with true ardor and honesty. After drawing blood he asks "Who am I?" His singing ascends from the (prophetic) medieval cuckoo song, to the irrelevant Schubert *lieder*, to the Lord's Prayer (that chills Adrian's attempt to make love to Andrew), to the savage roar. Through his primitivism he transcends his physicality, becoming "at long last pure essence." After he dies, Leopold reports that the woods are haunted with the spirits of people who died making love. In his last appearance, as a firefly in the night, he transcends his function as academic illuminator. His death saves Ariel from the honeymoon visit to Carlyle's grave and a life as "the final jewel" in the pedant's "crown." The "pathetic delusions" that Leopold believed "we frightened humans cling to" are the insensitivities of insipid civilization, not mysticism.

Allen validates the unseen with one framing strategy, often holding on a vacated space, into or from which characters move (in conversations that conceal more than they disclose). Alternatively, the action proceeds out of frame: Andrew's off-camera disasters, for example, whether in flying or in love making, and the characters' mutual betrayals. The animism is confirmed by lyrical interludes, in which the Mendelssohn score enhances the natural beauty. Gordon Willis's resplendent photography attests to the vitality of the natural world, in contrast to the harsh black and white of *Stardust*

Memories and the denatured beiges of Allen's dramas—and Leopold's classroom.

In A *Midsummer Night's Sex Comedy* Allen conceives a sumptuous nature with magic, an afterlife, and blissfully compatible human spirits. But it takes an imagined Eden to find it! In its very fantasy the film coheres with Allen's bleaker vision.

20

Zelig (1983)

During the Roaring Twenties, Leonard Zelig (Woody Allen) becomes a popular culture phenomenon for changing into whomever he's with. He is treated by psychiatrist Eudora Fletcher (Mia Farrow), who attributes his transformations to his need to conform. After Zelig's half-sister exploits him as a sideshow freak, Eudora cures him through reverse psychology and they fall in love. Before they can wed, Zelig is sued by victims of his other personalities. The national hero, turned national scapegoat, flees. Eudora finds him onstage with Hitler at a Nazi rally. They escape together, Zelig flying their plane across the Atlantic upside down to another hero's welcome in America. Allen's mock documentary ends with home-movie footage of Zelig's marriage to Eudora. They kiss and walk away from the camera, to the promising strains of "I'll Get By." Zelig dies regretting—his first shame—that he couldn't finish *Moby-Dick*.

Zelig is Allen's fullest statement about magic. Ashamed he forgot to wear green on St. Patrick's Day, Zelig magically turned Irish to transform his failure. He blends into any company—Chinese, Greek, fat people, black musicians, scar-faced gangsters, a Scot, a rabbi, and a psychiatrist in his interviews with Dr. Fletcher. Zelig lives a recurring Allen gag: his one regret in life is that he is not someone else.[1] More to the point, Zelig's changes surpass the magic of Sandy Bates, Paul Pollack, and Andrew Hobbs, who fail to transcend their limitations. But he shares their common weakness in needing magic. Indeed his power to change proves to be a worse flaw, his lack of a solid self.

237

On another level, the film is Allen's own ultimate magic act. Through brilliant process work he projects himself into a variety of historical artifacts, such as Ken Murray's film of William Randolph Hearst's social life at San Simeon, photos of Babe Ruth, Eugene O'Neill, Jack Dempsey, Calvin Coolidge, and Herbert Hoover, the lyrics of Fanny Brice, Cole Porter and Eddie Cantor songs. He disrupts the platform parties, first of Pope Pius XI (who swats him with a sacred text), then of Hitler.[2] Where previously Allen presented fiction as an alternative to imperfect life, here he rewrites historical records.

Zelig is Allen's ultimate parody in that it builds parody out of parodies. While its outer form parodies the documentary, *Zelig* contains versions of home movies, newsreel footage and stagings, and a homage to the Warner Brothers "biography." In Allen's 1935 *The Changing Man* he contrasts formula biopic scenes to his "real" chronicle, compounding the film's self-referentiality. Allen even parodies himself as filmmaker in that his early film career was based on parody. He scores the self-denial inherent in assuming someone else's values, voice, or film form. As Zelig revives Allen's early nebbish persona, the film is also an exercise in Allen's self-reduction. Paradoxically, the technology behind this "magic" diminishes Allen's presence, whether as persona or as writer or performer. In injecting himself into historical materials, Allen deemphasizes his own performance.[3]

As this convincing mock documentary challenges the integrity of any film or photograph, Allen's creation becomes an act of nihilism. For Andrew Sarris, "What ties *Zelig* together is Allen's abiding attraction for that very stylized past that masquerades as 'reality' in period newspapers." But as Peter Hogue and Marion Bronson point out, "What the images convey also provokes skepticism."[4] However fascinating documentary images of Hitler remain, once we have seen Woody Allen's Hitler platform party, can we ever completely believe a Hitler photo again? Similarly, Allen exposes 'objective' film recording when Dr. Fletcher's cousin, Paul Deghuee (John Rothman), secretly films the therapy sessions, then recreates that filming process for a newsreel record. Of course, when Zelig senses he is being filmed, he plays to the camera.

Like Zelig, the film may seem a pastiche, given its tissue of allusions and cross-reference. It recalls Orson Welles's classic, *Citizen Kane*, with its similar quest into a representative American hero and its interplay of newsreel and "life." But where Welles pursued the (unsolvable) mystery of a powerful man, Allen's subject is a *schlemiel* who is distinctive only for his ability to become indistinguishable. As the meaning of Rosebud is finally illuminated in a thick, obscuring smoke, Allen prevents our confident interpretation of anything in this film. Allen also parodies Warren Beatty's *Reds* when contemporary cultural icons interpret the Zelig phenomenon, and when the heroine (Mia Farrow paralleling *Reds's* Diane Keaton) travels to Europe to find her lost lover. With Allen's ex, Keaton, then living with Beatty, the film becomes most personal at its most playfully parodic.

More humorously than in *Stardust Memories*, *Zelig* incorporates its own analysis. To Irving Howe, Zelig represents the social/psychological dilemma of the Jewish immigrant's pressure "to assimilate like crazy." Bruno Bettelheim finds him the "ultimate conformist." Saul Bellow finds Zelig craving immersion in mass anonymity, yet "His sickness was also at the root of his salvation. . . . It was his very disorder that made a hero of him." Susan Sontag considers Zelig's cure a triumph not of psychotherapy but of "aesthetic instincts." To historian John Morton Blum is attributed an apocryphal text, *Interpreting Zelig*, further confounding fiction and history. Paradoxically, the interest of this prominent Jewish-American intellectual class invalidates Zelig's need to repress his Jewishness. Further, "Among fanatics he was a handy symbol of iniquity"; the French intellectuals "see in him a symbol of everything." As Zelig reflects his viewer, a doctor who predicts Zelig will die of a brain tumor within two weeks himself dies of a brain tumor within two weeks. "See Zelig turn into you," promises the sideshow ad.

In addition to its philosophical stance, the film bristles with topical satire. This being America, Zelig is merchandised mercilessly: "We smoke Camels," he testifies in an ad. In clubs or on street corners dancers do the Chameleon. As composers cash in with "You May Be Six People But I Love You" and "Chameleon Days," Zelig is exploited by the zeitgeist as much as by his half-sister's lover, Martin Geist. The film may also reflect on Allen's having become a cultural icon, given Allen lookalikes, quiz books and even one psychiatrist's collection of patients' dreams about Woody Allen.[5] Allen satirizes medical authority when the doctors argue over Zelig's case. One "cure" has him walking up the wall; another has his lower body turned backwards. Even Eudora Fletcher's motives were originally self-serving: "Here was this unique case that I could make my reputation on." But for her as for Zelig, salvation lies in a committed love.

From the feminist perspective, Zelig's recovery is problematic. The conformist male "recovers" his normalcy only when the competent, professional woman stops being assertive. When Eudora drops her authority as psychiatrist, Zelig accepts his identity as her patient. When she asks him for advice, he admits his true self: "I'm nobody. I'm nothing." Later, when Eudora succumbs to "fear of flying" (an allusion to Erica Jong's feminist novel), Zelig assumes her knowledge and flies them home. Even in submitting, Zelig embodies the aggressive male ego.

Zelig also exposes a bigoted America. The Ku Klux Klan considers him a triple threat because he is a Jew who can turn into an Indian or a black. A spokesperson for a Christian women's group declares that because "America is a moral country . . . a God-fearing country . . . in keeping with our pure society, I say 'Lynch the little Hebe.'" Not for Allen the comfort of Hollywood's ethnic films and their assumption of a melting-pot America. The son of a Yiddish actor who played Puck in the Orthodox *Midsummer Night's Dream*, Leonard was bullied by anti-Semites; his parents sided with the bullies. That, too, is assimilation.

Allen's comedy leads into an anatomy of fascism. He reveals a continuum from American conformity to Hitler's brownshirts. As Allen told one interviewer, "I thought that desire not to make waves, carried to an extreme, could have traumatic consequences. It could lead to a conformist mentality and, ultimately, fascism."[6] In Allen's bittersweet ending, Zelig finds happiness in a normal, centrist life, retiring his genius/compulsion in preference for a very ordinary marriage. But whether he changes himself or he disappears into normalcy, Zelig avoids making waves, i.e., he adopts yet another form of the conformism that nourishes tyranny. As *Zelig* portrays the Nazi lunacy on the level of one nebbish's need to be liked, it could be the most profound parody of our time.

21

Broadway Danny Rose (1984)

At the Carnegie Deli in New York, comedians reminisce about Danny Rose (Allen), a Catskills comic who became an agent for hapless entertainers. The film recounts Danny's managing of an Italian crooner, Lou Canova (Nick Apollo Forte). When Danny coaxes Lou's mistress, Tina (Mia Farrow), to support the singer, Danny's life is threatened by her former boyfriend's brothers. At Tina's behest (before she met Danny), Lou, like all Danny's other successes, switches to a more fashionable agent. When Tina comes to apologize, Danny spurns her friendship, then relents. Their relationship is commemorated in the deli's Danny Rose Special: cream cheese on a bagel with marinara sauce.

Both stars play sharply representative types. Farrow plays a gum-snapping virago with stiletto heels and a beehive hairdo: vulgar aspiration personified. Allen's Danny is a principled loser with an overachiever's vocabulary, in a world where one's word has lost its value. As well, Danny's name reads like a sentence concluding a Jewish parable: Danny won't rise further on earth; Broadway Danny rose. To Gilbert Adair, Danny is Allen's most Chaplinesque performance: "Danny is a born loser; and the film's premise, one of the most moving it's possible to imagine, is the ultimate triumph of a loser over his fate."[1]

Though the background teems with caricatures as pointed as those in *Stardust Memories*, here the overriding spirit is (in one of

Danny's didactic relatives' words): "Acceptance. Forgiveness. Love." Responding to the work's humane tone, Brian Henderson called it "Allen's best film, indeed his only completely satisfactory one . . . the first Allen film to thematize the character's narcissism and contempt for others, not just to exhibit them." But Pauline Kael, having complained about Allen's misanthropy in *Stardust Memories*, now regretted that in this "toothless fable" Allen "has left out the hostility that made him famous."[2]

The film is subtly eloquent. For example, when Lou tells Danny he's leaving him, Allen holds his central trio in a long shot as they stride forward until Danny is isolated in close-up to register his shock. The setup suggests the betrayal is an inevitable point to which all three characters move. As we focus on the victim, we share his test: will such continuing betrayals erode his/our faith and generosity? In the last scene Danny first fails, then passes the test Tina and Lou failed. Earlier, when Danny causes serious harm to an innocent victim, Barney Dunn, Danny is reminded that even the most moral may need to be forgiven.

The romantic conclusion is only implied. In a wordless long shot Danny stops Tina, they talk, then walk off together. Only in the mixed-marriage deli sandwich is any union confirmed. In that comedic subculture, Danny Rose is accorded a status beyond him in life. The Carnegie sandwich is his happy ending. We may prefer to deduce a romantic conclusion but Allen only provides clues: the couple's instantaneous, mutual antipathy, their obvious incompatibility in every experience, taste and value, their strange erotics when they escape from bondage by wriggling together. From that we may infer their continuing love.

One of the film's major metaphors—recalling Allen's film for Martin Ritt, *The Front*—is the false front. Danny plays "beard" to help Lou slip girlfriend past wife. In a comic key, ventriloquist Barney Dunn has a bad stutter from which his dummy is free. Barney serves as Danny's "front" to escape the hoods, who mistake Danny to be Tina's lover, i.e., Lou's "front" again. The recurring shots of the Carnegie Deli front present a mythical exterior. Behind all such fronts serious moral choices must be made: Tina strips off her showgirl glitz, stares at the waif in her mirror, then decides to leave Lou.

As the antithesis of the "front" is projecting oneself, several famous people play themselves. The deli storytellers are the real Will Jordan, Corbett Monica, Jackie Gayle, Sandy Baron, Howard Storm, Morty Gunty, and Allen's longtime producer, Jack Rollins. Milton Berle, Howard Cosell, Sammy Davis, Jr., and Big Bird also appear as themselves. As in *Zelig*, the tensions between the real and the fictional characters reflect the ethical dilemmas of being oneself. Further, when Allen (as Danny) shows Farrow (as Tina) a photo of (himself outside the frame, but supposedly with) Frank Sinatra, there is a frisson in the fact that Farrow used to be married to Sinatra—who introduced her to the world and heroine-type of this film. What she lived Allen now reshapes into a moral fable. As Nancy Pogel points out, the plot of *Broadway Danny Rose* recalls *Meet Danny Wilson* (1951), where Sinatra played a singer who betrayed his agent.[3]

As Allen's fictional folk move among the real, the couple scampers among the giant heads stored for Macy's Thanksgiving Day parade. The inflated heads may emblematize people who have more ego than conscience. Typically, Allen's moral rigor weights the comedy of caricature. Without such purpose, a person can turn into a cartoon, as the characters seem to when helium gives them cartoon voices (e.g., the gunsel's squeaky-voiced "You goddam little runt").

As Danny's clients are flawed creatures striving to transcend their limitations, they become moral emblems as well as black jokes: a one-armed juggler, a one-legged tap dancer, a woman who plays music on the rims of empty glasses, a blind xylophone player, and—a paragon of integrity—the *parrot* that sings "I Gotta be Me." In all these have-nots, "Danny — has faith." In a godless age Danny still believes in people. He spouts faithful oaths (Santayana's "fossils of piety"): "My hand to God." He assumes everyone is special, predicting Broadway success for a balloon folder and an international career for Tina in interior design.

As in Allen's earlier *shicksa-schlemiel* dialectic, Danny teaches Tina "It's important to feel guilty. Otherwise you do terrible things." For her, "You do what you gotta do. Y'know, life is short." Danny tells Lou "Sooner or later you're gonna have to square yourself with The Big Guy. You're gonna pay your dues some day." To mollify

Tina, Danny assures her that Lou has "got integrity. He cheats with one person at a time." In a parody of Danny's compulsion to take responsibility, after his fiancée ran off with a pianist, "I broke off with her."

Danny's solitary faith in human nature, despite a life of failure and betrayals, contrasts to two social communities. Both the Italian and the Jewish subcultures share exuberance, talkative hands, sentimentality, and an appetite for food and festivity. Forte's song, "My Bambina," provides a variation on Allen's theme of integrity: "Keep Italian in your heart." The equivalent is Danny's stream of Yiddish/folk wisdom. Whether as ethnics or as rising stars, the moral weaklings "like to forget their beginnings." Because Lou lacks Danny's dedication to his roots, Lou's family dinner rings false beside Danny's frozen turkey Thanksgiving.

The two communities represent different moral problems. Tina derives from the Italian world of superstition and code, its order imposed by the Mafia or from faith in the neighborhood psychic. Like the Jewish comedians, the Italians also mythologize Danny—as Danny White Roses, an evil eye who holds a mysterious power over Tina. The Jewish showmen admit to joke stealing and they abstract stories from the pain of life. They may sympathize with Barney Dunn and Danny Rose but they have no real feeling for them. Only Danny visits Barney in the hospital (with well-earned guilt) and offers to pay his hospital expenses.

As *Broadway Danny Rose* is a story told within the story, its point lies less in the story told than in the outer-frame characters' response to that story. Sandy Baron's story about Danny typifies the moral reckoning that Danny teaches Lou and that Isaac taught Yale in *Manhattan*. A man is known and judged, after he is gone, by his deeds. The comedians don't acknowledge Danny's moral weight because his life becomes their joke. But a lesson has snuck in. In the end chatter, one comedian offers to pick up the tab! So Danny's legend has had a moral effect: it has taught generosity. The Carnegie frame makes *Broadway Danny Rose* a film about the storytelling process and its moral power in transforming life into art.

22

The Purple Rose of Cairo (1985)

In Allen's second *Rose* film there is an interplay between the inner and outer stories (unlike the deli schmoozers' detachment from Danny Rose). For the inner story, Allen recreates thirties escapism in a film titled *The Purple Rose of Cairo*. In the outer story, a waitress in Depression New Jersey, Cecilia (Mia Farrow), escapes her brutish husband, Monk (Danny Aiello), into Hollywood fantasy. One matinee, a character, Tom Baxter (Jeff Daniels), steps off the screen into Cecilia's life and falls in love with her. To restore normalcy, the actor who played Tom, Gil Shepherd (Daniels again), romances Cecilia away from Tom by promising to take her to Hollywood with him. Tom gone, Cecilia is abandoned by Shepherd. She retreats for solace to the silver screen, this time the remote intimacy of Fred Astaire's "Cheek to Cheek."

Allen's metaphysical conceit mingles various realities. When Cecilia leaves, Monk yells that she will return after she learns "what it's like in the real world." As he predicts, Cecilia finds her abusive marriage a refuge from the even harsher world outside, as represented by the whore, Emma (Dianne Wiest) Cecilia passes. When she leaves for Shepherd, Monk's warning again proves correct: "It ain't the movies. It's real life." Shepherd only "acts" his integrity and love for her.

Allen intercuts the "character" and the actor in parallel scenes with women. Tom's naiveté turns the whores into stereotypical sentimentalists.[1] Meanwhile, when Shepherd sings "Alabamy Bound" to Cecilia's ukelele accompaniment, the couple live the kind of musical interlude that usually happens only in movies. Though Shepherd protests, "Look, I love you. I know that only happens in movies but I do"—ultimately it does and he doesn't. In both Shepherd's date with Cecilia and Tom's visit with the whores, a hopeful idealism is defeated by human nature. Of Cecilia's three men, only the fictional character has character: "I just met a wonderful new man. He's fictional, but you can't have everything."

The screen characters reflect the "real" characters even in their difference. Everyone craves escape from a different mundanity. The first line spoken in the inner film is "Jason, I'm bored." The socialites tour Morocco, Tangiers, and Cairo, the exotic world that Tom leaves for "a madcap Manhattan weekend." He interrupts even this "escape" scene when he addresses Cecilia in the theater. The cinema audience craves consistent exotica—whether Manhattan or Morocco—for relief from their reality: "I want what happened in the movie last week to happen this week. Otherwise what's life all about anyway?"

Whereas the film provides fantasies of freedom, the freedom of the real world attracts the fictional characters. Tom eagerly escapes his glamour—"I'm free. After two-thousand performances"—into the life of the woman who has been escaping into fantasies of his. Tom's screen role has given him both powers and compulsions: "I'm sorry. It's written into my character to do it so I do it." He would rather live our unscripted life: "I want to live. I want to be free to make my own choices." But the real characters' freedom is also illusory. Cecilia, Gil, the whores, Monk—all are "scripted" within economic, social and psychological parameters. As the Zoe Caldwell character observes of our side of the screen, "It doesn't look like they're having too much fun anyway"—perhaps because they are watching the movie instead of making a life. Tom labors under illusion even when he anticipates a romance where a kiss is not followed by a fade-out,[2] for few of us can "make love without fading out." We may be free from cinematic device or from the failings the flesh is heir to, but not from both. Of course, life is equally false in the inner film, where the "champagne" is ginger ale.

The film and real characters both dread mortality. This though the fictional relive death with each end credit: "You don't know what it's like to disappear, to be annihilated. Don't turn the projector off." The film title is an emblem of fugitive immortality. Tom Baxter has been searching "in vain for the legendary purple rose" that began as an image of art (painted by a pharaoh) but "now grows wild under the tomb." Both as an eternal growth and as an image that comes to life, the purple rose is an emblem of film. Because film provides only illusions, however, the rose is mythical. Paradoxically, Tom in his inner film lives the very myth that the plot says he futilely seeks.

Our conventions of behavior are so arbitrary that one minor character's revolt disrupts both the inner and the outer film worlds. Tom has more revolutionary effect than the inner film's ranting communist (Peter McRobbie). When the Van Johnson character declares "I want to go too. I want to be free," the film's producer, Raoul Hirsch (Alexander H. Cohen), replies "That's communist talk." But the revolution is not communist. Once "It's every man for himself," Arturo (Eugene Anthony), the maitre d' at the Copacabana, breaks into a tap solo, what he's "always wanted to do." Again, "The real ones want their lives fictional and the fictional ones want their lives real." Where many reviewers found the influence of Pirandello, Vernon Young sited the film in psychoanalysis: "an ego in rebellion against the role assigned to it."[3]

On both sides of the screen, society is defined in tensions and animosities, barely checked by fictional civilities. The inner-film actors bicker over stardom. They criticize Tom for leaving their world, then for bringing Cecilia back with him. For them, the only thing worse than having to repeat the same plot is having its repetition interrupted. Otherwise what's life all about anyway?

The fictional world offers an illusion of human perfection that reality denies. As Tom remarks, "Where I come from people don't disappoint. They're consistent. They're always reliable." Not so the brute Monk or the false Shepherd. Even Tom disappoints his plot mates when he becomes "human" and enters Cecilia's world. We should probably reject the fatalism of Shepherd's lesson to Tom: "You can't learn to be real. It's like learning to be a midget. . . . Some of us are real, some of us aren't." For Shepherd proves unreal as a lover. Conversely, as Tom has real effects on the people he meets, the fictional character assumes more substance, i.e., more reality, than his vain actor.

The modest Cecilia can teach both men. She teaches Tom Baxter about the hard realities of life, including pregnancy. Tom transforms harshness into a poetry that touches the whores: "the absolutely astonishing miracle of childbirth, with all its attendant feelings of humanity and pathos. I stand in awe at existence. . . . Do you share my wonderment at the very fabric of being?" The whores respond variously: "Do you want to tie me up?"—"Are there any other guys like you out there?" The hardened whores share the naïve waitress's yearning for the Hollywood ideal.

To the worldlier Shepherd, Cecilia offers a better image of himself to live up to. She may even have aroused his love, as we infer from his brooding on the plane homeward. Shepherd fails to learn to be "real" either from the touchingly open Cecilia or from the superior character he portrayed. When Cecilia chooses Shepherd over Tom, she resigns herself to reality: "I'm a real person. . . . I have to choose the real world." That is, she adheres to the realist plot of her life, although Kitty Haynes (Karen Akers) sings "Ours could be a different sort of love affair." In choosing the real man Cecilia is inevitably disappointed, not just because Shepherd proves a heel, but because he's only human.

Where life is a reality of pain, failure, and death, Tom Baxter doesn't get hurt or bleed. He is so faithful, he spurns the whores' freebie because "I'm hopelessly head over heels in love with Cecilia. . . . Every breath she takes makes my heart dance." Such perfect love is among "the advantages of being imaginary." More typical failures are the price of being real.

Where in A Midsummer Night's Sex Comedy Andrew Hobbs's magic solved the romantic problems by providing a glimpse into a supernature, here film provides only illusions of satisfaction. Cecilia's problems remain unaddressed. Allen's concluding close-up resonates like the last shots in City Lights and his own Manhattan—with the same resignation and pathos. As she watches Fred Astaire sweep Ginger Rogers off her feet, Cecilia turns from looking teary-eyed at Shepherd's gift ukelele, up into the screen light, then slowly begins to smile. Alas, her harsh life will reclaim her after the ninety-minutes traffic of the screen. Fred may be "in heaven," but Cecilia remains in uncompromising reality.

Allen's absence from this film coheres with the theme of an absent maker in the fictional cosmos. The inner film credits Producer Raoul Hirsch but not a director; there is no director in a world in which God is dead. Sharing credit only with his dialogue coach ("a genius . . . a louse"), Shepherd claims to have "created" Tom. But Cecilia checks him: "Didn't the man who wrote the movie do that?" The actor claims to have "made him live. I fleshed him out," but he denies responsibility when Tom claims independence. For Tom, "God" refers to the screenwriters. In his beginning was their words.

In this light, the film is a theological parable about the confusion of being in a world without a director/God. Hence Milo O'Shea's stage priest in the inner film, eager to be proved right about something! To Cecilia, a world without God would be "a world without point and no happy ending"—i.e., the world in which Allen leaves her, with only the idol worship of the silver screen for consolation. With no God behind the creatures, the only good shepherd is the culpable Gil Shepherd.

In *The Purple Rose of Cairo* Allen demonstrates with sympathy and wit how we deceive ourselves through fantasy. His subject is a fragile spirit who negotiates a self-conception between the realities of loss and a refuge in illusion. With *Zelig*, *The Purple Rose of Cairo* stands as a masterpiece in Allen's self-reflective cinema, as *Manhattan* and *Hannah and Her Sisters* are of his lyrical and *Crimes and Misdemeanors* of his ethical.

23

Hannah and Her Sisters (1986)

Amid three films of nostalgic form, Allen made a classic comedy about irrationality in love. *Hannah and Her Sisters* is Allen's most optimistic vision of love. As it celebrates renewal and life, the film centers on an extended family's three Thanksgiving dinners.

Most of the characters experience regeneration. An old theatrical couple, Evan (Lloyd Nolan) and Norma (Maureen O'Sullivan), harmonize in music but bicker over their flirtations and the mother's drinking. One daughter, Lee (Barbara Hershey), is an ex-alcoholic, living with a brooding artist, Frederick (Max von Sydow). Attracted to men who teach her culture, she has an affair with her brother-in-law, Elliot (Michael Caine), then marries her English professor. The second daughter, Holly (Dianne Wiest), is a re-formed cocaine user who fails as an actress and as a caterer, then writes plays based upon her failures in life.

Both weak women are intimidated by their apparently perfect sister, Hannah (Mia Farrow). Even in her palindrome name she seems complete. Hannah learns the others' perception of her— "disgustingly perfect . . . competent . . . giving . . . too self-suffi-cient." But even such perfection is vulnerable. In bed with her husband, she says "It seems so dark tonight. I feel so alone." "You're not alone," he assures her, immediately and sincerely—for the moment. Hannah is an efficient mother, a generous sister, a pas-sionate wife and a successful actress, moving from Ibsen's Nora to

Shakespeare's Desdemona. Her accountant husband—for no reason other than the failure of perfection on earth—has a passionate affair with Lee, then reaffirms his love for Hannah.

In the subplot, Hannah's previous husband, a hypochondriacal TV comedy writer, Mickey Sachs (Allen), fears he is dying, then finds a new appreciation of life. When Mickey marries the weakest sister, Holly, Allen locates the meaning of life in imperfect pleasures. As Holly's second play concludes: "We all go through life playing the hand we're dealt." One character's "two high pair, maybe even aces up" are topped by "three deuces." Little things mean a lot, when our very existence is so insignificant. "I know 'maybe' is a very slim reed to hang your whole life on," Mickey concludes, "but that's the best we have." Though sterile while married to Hannah, at film's end Mickey has impregnated Holly. Even this bliss is tempered by the fact that the happy couple are reflected in a mirror, at a further remove from reality.

Allen is especially sensitive to the lovers' absurdities. Courting Lee with e.e. cummings, Elliot speaks more truth than error when he tells her, "I read a poem of you and thought of his last week." For his thoughts are rooted in her, not in the poem. Allen dramatizes the gulf between rational intention and emotional compulsions when, within one monologue, Elliot moves from "What passion today with Lee. She's a volcano," to "I love my wife. Now I've betrayed her. Oh, God!"—then back again after Lee phones him.

Sometimes a voice-over dramatizes the gap between the characters' actions and their impulses or pretenses. "I've got to proceed cautiously . . . very skillfully, very diplomatically," Elliot resolves, then leaps up to kiss Lee. Mickey resolves to "Keep calm. You're gonna be okay. Don't panic"— then awakens with "I'm dying! I'm dying! I know it!" Or the voice-over denotes a falsehood: Elliot is offscreen when he denies Hannah's suspicion.

As if to impose an artificial order on the chaos of human attractions and betrayals, the film is punctuated by thirteen full-screen titles. When the title expresses a character's idea (e.g., Elliot's opening "God, she's beautiful . . . "), the opinion pretends to be an objective truth (in this case true). Elliot's plotting to visit Lee is discreetly hidden in the title that refers to his client: "Dusty just bought this huge house in Southampton." The titles validate the variety of characters' perspectives instead of any single one. Thus a title may bridge contrasting scenes. The second title, "We all had a terrific time," may refer back to Elliot's summary of the family dinner or ahead to Lee's intuiting Elliot's interest in her. "The Abyss" relates back to Lee's relishing Elliot's love and ahead to Mickey's confronting mortality. The most resonant title is the Tolstoy quote: "The only absolute knowledge attainable by man is that life is meaningless."

From Tolstoy Allen also drew the idea of interweaving two plots. In *Anna Karenina*, Tolstoy intercut the love relationships with Levin's worry about his mortality. The separate dilemmas of Hannah's husbands seem unconnected but they intersect at the impossible ideal of perfection (Hannah). Both Mickey and Elliot are rationalizers who rediscover consolation in love. For both, Hannah represents perfection lost and regained. Mickey changes religions as Elliot changes lovers, before settling into solace. Mickey's obsession with death is at once both more trivial and more profound than Elliot's wandering ardor. In *Manhattan* and *Stardust Memories* the memento mori seemed more profound than the other characters' shallow infidelities. Here, however, Hannah's sustaining warmth and the harmony of her family dinners make both men seem foolish for ignoring their bounty.

Moreover, in celebrating the Farrow family domesticity, featuring both her apartment and her children, Allen seems to add a cheery twist to his flirtation with autobiography. In some respects the film is a lyric of his happiness with Mia Farrow. On the other hand, in a 1987 BBC interview he remarked that the film was "more 'up' and optimistic than I had intended, and consequently was very popular. It's only optimistic in the sections I failed."

As usual drawing upon his persona, Allen evokes all his Jewish comedy when Mickey, converting to Catholicism, unpacks a crucifix, a New Testament, a saint picture, Wonder Bread and mayonnaise, and in his father's pragmatism: "How the hell do I know why there were Nazis? I don't know how the can opener works." Of course, Mickey's attraction to Catholicism is to the "against school prayer, proabortion, antinuclear wing." With anyone other than Allen in the role, Mickey's high-tech medical examination would have been morbid, not comical.

In a similar personal vein, in casting Mia Farrow's mother as Hannah's mother, Andrew Sarris suggests Allen "forces the galvanized viewer to confront two sets of time," directly alluding to the performers' reality.[1] When Mickey resents his ex-partner's success in Hollywood, we see the uncredited Tony Roberts smugly driving his LA convertible.[2]

Similarly, casting Max von Sydow as Lee's lover makes him a Frederick not of Hollywood but of Bergmanic brooding. A misanthrope who never leaves his studio, Frederick is introduced with an offscreen "No thank you" (re: coffee or tea, but a clue to his larger nay saying). In one of the funniest moments of the film, Frederick suffers the hip handshake of a fatuous rock star (Daniel Stern as Dusty Frye). He may ironically allude to von Sydow's playing Christ in *The Greatest Story Ever Told* (George Stevens, 1965): "If Jesus came back and saw what was going on in his name he'd never stop throwing up." If casting von Sydow evokes the Bergman ethos, by relegating him to three scenes, isolated from the family, Allen eschews Bergman for a romantic conclusion.[3]

Betrayals undermine the film's surface of love, warmth, and regeneration. At the TV studio, after Mickey complains about censorship of his program, a writer complains that Mickey clipped his PLO sketch. The betrayed betray. After betraying Frederick and Hannah with Elliot, Lee feels she is betraying Elliot with her new lover.

Against the characters' betrayals and evasions Allen's camera seems a constantly moving, exposing presence. At a restaurant lunch the camera circles the three sisters to reveal a variety of tensions: Holly's need for—and her resentment for needing—Hannah's financial help, Hannah's conflicting impulses to support yet to advise Holly, and Lee's conscience.

The film's irony undermines the lyricism in Allen's score. "You Made Me Love You" attends both the opening credits, as if the romantic compulsion were a genre given, and the unexpected romance between Mickey and Holly. "Bewitched, Bothered, and Bewildered" accompanies first Elliot's affair with Lee, then his reconciliation with Hannah, then finally Mickey's reunion with Holly. As well as harmonizing, music also divides the characters. Holly and her best friend, April (Carrie Fisher), are alienated when

David (an uncredited Sam Waterston) takes first Holly, then April, to the opera. When Mickey finds Holly buying opera records, she shows she is over both her loss of David and her uncharacteristic taste for punk music. Despite their attraction, on their first date her punk conflicted with his jazz. Now they move on to the jazz section together.

As usual, Allen's characters find in art a fulfillment denied them in life. Mickey is snapped out of his suicidal mood when he goes to a movie. "To gather my thoughts and be logical and put the world back into rational perspective," he goes to—the Marx Brothers' *Duck Soup!* For her part, Holly's successful play satisfies her resentment: she has her unfaithful architect murdered by his ex-wife. This is an improvement over her dramatization of her family. For Allen, art is ineffective if it too literally reflects life's failures. So Mickey's TV assistant, Gail (Julie Kavner), suggests "Instead of the child molestation sketch, why don't we repeat the Cardinal Spellman–Ronald Reagan homosexual dance number?" At an equivalent remove from reality, the romantic regenerations of Hannah's sisters and husbands allow us the heartening, though artificial, solace of a happy ending.

24

Radio Days (1987)

In *Radio Days* we hear Allen, as Joe, recall Brooklyn life in the late 1930s and early 1940s. What we see is little Joe (Seth Green) and the mature Joe's memories of family scenes, neighborhood mythology, and fantasies of old radio programs and their stars. Not since *Stardust Memories* has Allen so abandoned conventional plot structure. However, instead of a creative block, here the fertility of the hero's imagination makes radio in effect a secular religion. It provides an idealized existence, with gods and goddesses, moral and spiritual guidance, and an emotional bond for its nationwide congregation.[1]

The radio congregation both grieve and celebrate together. When eight-year-old Polly Phelps is brought up dead from a well, a wide range of people, across the social and economic spectra, join in thoughtful grief.[2] Polly's drama turns Joey's spanking into his father's sentimental hug. Similarly, when Cousin Ruthie (Joy Newman) snoops on the party line, the resulting disharmony contrasts to the radio harmony when she is joined by her father and uncle to mime the radio's "The South American Way."

Allen makes the imaginary radio world contiguous with the real. More realistically than in *The Purple Rose of Cairo*, his living characters have access to rarified celebrity. For example, in the opening episode, two burglars win on *Guess That Tune*. But their jackpot is delivered to their victims. The Needlemans find their home ransacked, then awaken to new wealth. In this parable, reward from the heavens (i.e., the airwaves) compensates for loss beyond human understanding. More conventionally, Allen inter-cuts the mother's (Julie Kavner's) breakfast mess with the elegant life of the radio couple, Roger Daly and Irene Draper (David Warrilow and Julie Kurnitz). These worlds merge when Joey's Aunt Bea (Diane Wiest), competing on a radio quiz show, converts the family's affliction with fish into a jackpot. That is transcendence.

In other ways than reward, Allen finds an element of faith in radio listening. Aunt Ceil's (Renee Lippin's) favorite radio show features a ventriloquist. Despite the unbeliever—"He's on radio. How do you know he's not moving his lips?"—she has faith. So too the skepticism of the gangster's mother (Gina DeAngelis) in disdain-ing Sally White (Mia Farrow) for forgetting that she can't use her dancing skills on radio. On the contrary, the film celebrates how radio addresses all the senses through the listener's imagination. The very richness of the film's period detail in costume and setting prove the power of what was merely "heard." The film's dense images are Joe's memories of what radio stamped on his imagination forty years earlier.[3]

The radio religion seems evangelical when the sports announcer (Guy Le Bow) tells of pitcher Kirby Kyle (Brian Mannain), who, deprived (in order) of a leg, an arm, his sight, and finally his life, continues to pitch, ultimately "winning eighteen games in The Big League in the Sky." When we last see him, the blind pitcher stands with his glove raised expectantly, but the ball soars beyond. The fishtale-loving Uncle Abe (Josh Mostel) laps up this pop religion with relish (or tartar sauce).

Radio is, in fact, so effective a religion that it is assailed by Rabbi Baumel (Kenneth Mars) for breeding "bad values, false dreams, and lazy habits." The rabbi takes umbrage at Joey's "You speak the truth, my faithful Indian companion." Joey also confuses his allegiances when he uses Jewish National Fund money to buy the ring of his radio god, the Masked Avenger. It is the radio, not the dark Hebrew school, to which Joe attributes his imagination. The religions of radio and Judaism again conflict when Uncle Abe, going to com-plain about the neighboring communists' loud playing of the radio on Yom Kippur, returns home converted to Marxism. His indul-gence of pork chops, clams, and chocolate pudding on the day of fasting leads to indigestion, an interdenominational retribution.

Because the real and radio worlds connect, the film's central character is not Allen's Joe, but the cigarette girl, Sally White (Farrow), who achieves the success that others imagine. Where in *Purple Rose of Cairo* the Farrow character escaped only in vicarious fantasy, here her character realizes the glamorous life, overcoming her manifold lack of talent to become a radio gossip star.

Sally's story punctuates the film's plot. She is introduced at the one-quarter mark, trysting with Roger Daly (who apparently performs as his name suggests). When both characters are reflected in a mirrored column, the doubling denotes Daly as a two-timer as a husband and as an amphibian dweller both in radioland and in reality. For the blessed Sally, even her deficiencies advance her cause: "Boy, that was fast. Probably helped I had the hiccups." At the film's halfway point, the war interrupts Sally's role in Chekhov but provides a USO appearance, where her "I Don't Want to Walk without You"—a romantic/religious vow of dependency—leads to her success. After the voice of God prescribes elocution lessons, she makes her first gossip report, at the film's three-quarter mark.

In that report, as Clark Gable's date, Lolly Hays, foreshadows the doomed Polly Phelps, Allen suggests the undiscriminating flood of names and news that the radio—like life or the free-associating memory—pours forth. Indeed the last word on the Phelps tragedy is the song that segues into the celebrities' New Years Eve party: it was "Just One of Those Things." At the party Sally shares a table with— implausibly—all the other radio stars we have seen. This is the high life that Joey imagined, not what was.

The radio religion assumes an entirely subjective universe, without moral basis, with salvation and worth only in the integrity of a relationship. Thus the final scene on the rooftop contrasts the real characters' warm community with the radio stars' solitude. On the rooftop the radio characters seem to speak to themselves as, despite their festivity, they rue their transience. In contrast, Joey's family exchanges support, as when the usually teasing father (Michael Tucker) spots Aunt Bea playing solitaire: "No date tonight? Well, it's all right. We're all together, you know."

Joey's family recalls Allen's three-sister Chekhovian families in *Interiors* and *Hannah and Her Sisters*. Where Sally compromises everything but her ambition and Bea will compromise nothing,

Joey's mother, Tess, and Aunt Ceil realistically accept mates short of their ideal. "Paper Love" recalls the only time Joey saw his parents kiss. In their fantasy appearance on the radio *Court of Human Emotions*, told they deserve each other, Martin objects to being "insulted" and Tess says, "I love him, but what did I do to deserve him?" A similar warmth silvers over the bickering of Uncle Abe and Aunt Ceil. In quiet aptness, Abe continually brings home fish for his Ceil. In contrast, the third sister seems doomed to solitary flux. Aunt Bea is constantly trying to Be — the image of fashionable woman searching for a mate. Hence her compulsive modishness in clothing, dance steps, magazines, smoking, dating, and plotting for dates. The media may shape her but radio also liberates her when Orson Welles's *The War of the Worlds* exposes a dubious date. Bea is a salutary contrast to the less scrupulous Sally White, but misses the compromise of her sisters' unions.

In *Radio Days* Allen extends the optimism of *Hannah and Her Sisters*. The imaginary world of *Radio Days* signifies a plenitude in life, with its outpouring of dream and disaster, illumination and delusion. Indeed radio—like life—is something like the grandmother's unharnessable mammaries: "A woman in her seventies and her bosom is still growing." Our cups too runneth over.

But this cheer is not bought cheaply. True to form, Allen looks back in dread. The film's wartime setting includes the shadow of Hitler. The big Nazi experience in this film is Joey's vision of a phantom submarine, no less chilling an experience for being based more on his radio serials than on his perception. And sometimes the radio tells the truth: literally as well as metaphorically, wartime radio provides saber rattling. Radio brings the frightening news from the front, as well as encouraging fictions about the "Axis rats." In one shot the camera seems to follow the radio news as it wafts up the stairs to Joey in bed. His parents question the wisdom of bringing a child into their threatened world, a concern especially serious for a Jewish family in 1943. Yet even through the terror of an air-raid drill, the mother marvels at the beauty of a skylit snowfall and rues malevolence. The local madness—Mrs. Silverman (Belle Barger) paralyzed at seeing the Communists' daughter kissing a black man, Mr. Zipsky (Joel Eidelsberg) running amok in his underwear—Allen dismisses with a chuckle. But the global danger darkly shadows the film's comfort. Allen's comedy is not oblivious to dangers but a resolve maintained in their face.

Accordingly, against the threat of the Holocaust Allen posits the small but compelling satisfactions of a warm family life and the cigarette girl's access to the American Dream. In *Radio Days* the imagination and memory are a bolster against the larger movements of time, death, and loss. In a world without God, the dream factories provide Allen's characters with a pattern for their lives, guidance, and the promise (or delusion) of a brighter life beyond their own. Over "September Song" the mature Joe rues the fading of those memories and voices, his loss of that sense of an other world. In Joe's memories, a community of diversion overrides man's bloody divisions.

25

September (1987)

As in *A Midsummer Night's Sex Comedy*, in *September* Allen traces the loves of three (sort of) couples at a country retreat. But this time there is no wistful nostalgia or magic, no historical distance, no romantic resolution, nor—in a film of unrelieved interiors—any sustaining nature. On the contrary, a storm brings home the annihilating force of nature, when it floods a neighbor's house and leaves our characters "powerless," lit only by (romantic?) candles for the middle third of the film. In *September* the characters' betrayals have tragic consequences, without a leavening Woody subplot. Not only is the film devoid of comedy, it is concerned with the limits of the comic form.

Most of the loves here go unrequited. The French teacher, Howard (Denholm Elliott), loves the fragile Lane (Mia Farrow). She loves her summer tenant, an advertising man (read: compromised writer), Peter (Sam Waterston). He courts Lane's best friend, Stephanie (Dianne Wiest), who responds but returns to her marriage. Across this high-strung quartet booms Lane's ex-actress mother, Diane (Elaine Stritch), with her current husband, Lloyd (Jack Warden). Lane feels betrayed by Stephanie and Peter, as she was by her mother. At fourteen, Lane bore the guilt when her mother murdered her criminal lover. Now Lane airs that buried scandal.

Lloyd describes his profession of physics in familiar Allen terms: the universe is "all random, radiating aimlessly out of nothing and eventually vanishing forever. The universe, all space, all time, it's just a temporary convulsion. And I get paid to prove it." Against this "haphazard, morally neutral and unimaginably violent" universe, Lloyd clings to Diane: "She's warm and vital and holds me while I sleep. That's why I don't have to dream of photons and quarks." Like other forms of illusion in Allen's works, Diane provides Lloyd with refuge from what he knows.

At Lloyd's words, Allen shows Howard quietly rise and leave, pausing at the door to look out into the darkness before he steps into it. The physicist has defined in cosmic terms Howard's isolation. Peter's response is more trivial: "Don't say that. I have to sleep alone tonight." Turning to Stephanie, he uses Lloyd's nihilism to justify his amorality.

Stephanie evades her domestic versions of these cosmic threats. When the lights go out she plays the piano ("What'll I Do?"). Out of impatience with her husband, she flirts with Peter but finally prefers her friendship with Lane. For Lane she prescribes a life of small consolations, a domestic version of Diane's frivolousness: "Tomorrow will come and you'll find distractions . . . a million petty things to keep you going." Of course, none will deal with Lane's rending grief. Stephanie's "million petty things" rhymes with her warning that it takes "about a million" Valiums to suicide and the last line of the film, "There'll be a million things to keep you busy. It's going to be okay." The anodyne is astronomical.

In denying his characters the happy endings of *Hannah and Her Sisters* and *A Midsummer Night's Sex Comedy* Allen questions the very nature of comedy. Comedy axiomatically ends in romantic resolution because the genre celebrates the individual's inclusion in a fertile, harmonized community. In the springtime season of classical comedy, the lovers move from chaos and opposition into a socially sanctioned union. Or, as Chaplin observed, comedy is long shot and tragedy is close-up. Comedy deals with the individual in the social landscape, while tragedy isolates the individual against his destiny. Hence the tragic pathos in the last shots both in Chaplin's *City Lights* and in Allen's *Manhattan* and *The Purple Rose of Cairo*. (And the wag's observation that a comedy ends in a wedding and a tragedy starts with one.)

Allen usually avoids the marital resolution in his comedy. Of his sixteen features through *September*, only four—*Bananas, Sleeper*,

Zelig, and *Hannah and Her Sisters*—ended with romantic closure. More common is an open-ended resignation to loss or the bittersweet of lovers having grown apart. The failures in *September* not only acknowledge the complexities of modern love and anxiety, but imply that classic comedy no longer fits contemporary life. As well as being a realistic human drama, *September* can be viewed as a meditation on the comic form, consistent with Allen's films about fantasy and story telling.

Elaine Stritch's character can be taken to personify the comic mode. "Diane" associates her with classical verdure, which she confirms by blithely plucking flowers and strewing them about untended. She wears bright flowery clothing ("I look like I'm going to a luau"), but ultimately leaves in a suit of defoliated white ("one of the hundred neediest cases"), calm of mind, all fertility spent. The exuberant Diane seems more a force of nature, not bound by time, than a person. "Time passes and she's still here," her daughter complains. As Lloyd describes their meeting in a taxi: "By the time the meter hit three dollars she had her tongue in my ear."

Diane is also associated with the comic in her story telling. "She's full of funny stories," Howard remarks, in contrast to the blocked writer, Peter, and Lane, who represses her "story" of innocence. Also, Diane is the only character to control the comedy in her speech. The other characters may deliver an occasional chuckler but it is usually at their own expense or an unwitting irony. For instance, Stephanie confesses that she won't let her radiologist husband take an X ray of her because he would see things he could not understand and be "terribly hurt." This is a witty metaphor for a woman closed against her husband and guilty about her repressed desires. But only the anxiety, not the wit, is the character's. In contrast, Diane in her wit combines the strengths of the two mothers in *Interiors:* the vulgar vitality of Pearl (Maureen Stapleton) and the chilly authority of Eve (Geraldine Page).

When the film opens and closes with wordless tracks through the vacant rooms, cold, austere, autumnal, the objects we pick out speak of Diane's presiding spirit: her brass, snapshots, flowers. Even absent, she has a numbing effect on Lane. Diane's fictioning proves irresponsible when she forces Lane and Peter together, then misrepresents them to each other. Worse, Diane continues to evade responsibility for Lane's involvement in her murder: "I'm a tough cookie. I can file and forget."

The comic vision is fatally limited by its inability to deal with mortality. Thus Diane is sobered when she checks her makeup: "You study your face in the mirror and you know something is missing and then you realize it's your future." Later she considers trying to merge her liver spots into a tan. "When it comes to practical matters I'm a dodo"—not just dim, that is, but extinct. When she summons her murdered lover and Lane's father via ouija board, Diana mobilizes the comic's faith that death can be transcended. But she gets no answer. Like comedy, Diane has only partial vision.

Willfully ignoring the tragic dimension, the comic is self-absorbed. Diane only notices Lane's suffering when Lane no longer laughs at her jokes. She does not hear Lane's plan to sell her house and calls Lane's previous lover Jeff instead of Jack, imposing memories of her own dates with Jeff Chandler. As Lane justly charges, "Don't you ever listen when I talk?"

Diane lives a fullfilled life by leaving for others its tragedies. "Life is too short to dwell on our tragedies," she declares, but she has burdened Lane. Diane attracts Peter to what Lane calls "a frivolous existence" because he sees Diane as "a survivor," when others (especially Lane) are "annihilated by life's tragedies." Because of its blithe narrowness, the comic muse holds none of the solace for Allen that Diane has for Lloyd.

In contrast to Diane's raunchy frivolity, Allen offers humorous compassion for his characters. His close-ups of the shifting relationships between Stephanie, Lane, and Peter are both moving and witty. Without—or despite their—words, the characters express their timorous yearnings and fears. Allen's dramatic ironies make the characters seem caught and defined beyond their awareness. In Allen's typically witty score the classic tunes speak wordlessly for the characters. Stephanie concludes her piano medley with "I'm Confessing (That I Love You)" just after Howard has finally expressed his love to Lane and Lloyd has told Peter about his love for Diane. This song lets Stephanie express her love for (if not to) Peter.

Of all the songs, "Slow Boat to China" dominates; it supersedes the lover's usual desire for romantic isolation with the feeling that in that isolation lies insecurity. As Stephanie explains to Lane, "We're all up here, isolated from the world. Unpredictable things happen." What happens is the collision of emotional needs, the lovers' version of the Big Bang, dread source of our random existence. Stephanie does not have to play the Kurt Weill classic we expect because Allen's film *is* his "September Song." It affirms the failure of the spring vision of comedy to confront our mortality.[1]

26

Another Woman (1988)

In *Another Woman* Allen is more affirmative than in *September* by providing for regeneration. A fifty-year-old philosophy professor, avid for art but remote in her relationships, revives her emotional life. Wanting to be "shut off from everything" to write another book, Marion Post (Gena Rowlands) rents an apartment in which to work. But through the vent she overhears the psychoanalysis of another woman, Hope (Mia Farrow). This gives vent to both women's repressed emotions. Marion begins to perceive what others think of her and to reevaluate her own self. Intending to escape "construction noises," Marion deconstructs herself.

Marion's parents represent her polar influences of art and academic abstraction. Marion's mother wept at (and read) Rilke. Marion's father (John Houseman; played as a younger man by David Ogden Stiers) was proud of his "immunity" to love. Though he encouraged Marion's education (at his son's expense), he disparaged her "daydreaming in the woods with her watercolors."

As a Heideggerian philosopher, Marion represents self-deluding rationalization.[1] This is confirmed by two intrusions by women. In one, Marion and husband Ken (Ian Holm) are confronted by his ex-wife Kathy (Betty Buckley): "What would Emily Post say about adultery with a philosophy professor at a Holiday Inn while your wife is in hospital having her ovaries removed?" The echoing surnames make the Marion Post story something of a tragedy of manners. Later, when a former student thanks Marion for her life changing lecture on "Ethics and Moral Responsibility," Marion seems properly embarrassed.

Against academic philosophy Allen affirms the emotional illumination from art, represented specifically by a Gustav Klimt painting and two Rilke poems. In Rilke's "Archaic Torso of Apollo,"[2] a whole radiant being is inferred from a remnant torso. No warmth or radiance emanates from the part-men in Marion's life, her emotionless father and husband. But we sense such intensity in the men she has rejected—her first husband and mentor, Sam (Philip Bosco), and the passionate novelist, Larry Lewis (Gene Hackman). As the poem concludes, the work of art exposes one's hollow existence, "for there's no place therein / that does not see you. You must change your life." This line, at which her mother wept, anticipates the psychoanalyst's advice in Marion's dream: "Don't worry about humanity. Get your own life in order."

Klimt's *Hope* is an inanimate parallel to the pregnant woman, Hope, with whose analysis Marion identifies. When Marion finds her weeping at a reproduction of the painting, Hope does not see the optimism that Marion reads in Klimt's *Hope*. Hope is living the tensions and experience that are only abstracted as symbolism for Klimt and Marion. Hope's function as the living alternative to inorganic art is emphasized by the fact that Farrow was carrying Allen's child during the filming. As well, Hope represents the self that Marion has deliberately repressed: the emotional and the fecund. Her response to the picture is accordingly more emotional than the ascetic Marion's.

In her office, Marion usually falls asleep before she hears Hope's analysis from "down below." Hope is Marion's shadow self, which emerges only when she, near sleep, drops her guard. Otherwise she does not "choose to delve" beyond shallow satisfactions. The first statement Marion hears from Hope—"It was as if a curtain had parted and I could see myself clearly, and I was afraid of what I saw and what I had to look forward to"—parts Marion's "curtain" too. When Allen gives us Farrow's voice over the close-up of Rowlands, Hope speaks to their common experience. So, too, we see Marion's memory though the dialogue prepares us for Hope's.

There is kinship as well as difference in the title phrase. While Hope is "another" (i.e., different) woman to Marion, she also speaks to the feminine condition. As well, Marion is "the Other

Woman" to Kathy and to Marion's jealous friend, Claire (Sandy Dennis). Being a forceful rival also contributes to Marion's tense relationship with her sister-in-law, Lynn (Frances Conroy). However, in her exemplary manner with her stepdaughter, Laura (Martha Plimpton), Marion shows both her mothering potential and her sensitivity to the pitfalls of becoming "another mother" to Laura.

Another Woman is rooted in women's experience. In Kathy's scene Allen sympathizes both with the betrayed wife's rage and with her husband's embarrassed civility. Similarly, he reveals the patriarchal egotism in Sam's (albeit understandable) anger at young Marion's abortion, for placing her career over their personal needs. In this collision of self-interests, Sam criticizes Marion for the very quality—her professional brilliance—for which he first loved her. Marion is condemned for having internalized the values both Sam and her father had championed in her.

Marion is the most intellectual of the Allen characters who, after Alvy Singer, "sift the pieces" of a broken relationship, through memories and fantasies, for self-understanding. Hence her concluding epiphany: "I wondered if a memory is something you have or something you lost." To free herself, both as a human and as a blocked writer, Marion confronts memories she formerly chose to lose, such as her brother's failure, her abortion, Sam's suicide, and her potentially greater romance. "What can I say to change your heart?" Larry asks her. But in choosing the priggish cardiologist, Ken, instead, Marion restricts her "heart" to the clinical. At the end she can finally write freely because her intellectual activities—reading and writing—no longer deny desire but liberate it.

Allen composes Marion's bloodless world in beige and gray, with rare flushes: Laura's rich browns, red cherries on a birthday cake, the stained glass in the antique store, the false brightness of Marion's idealized childhood, the pale green and brown worn by Claire (outside Marion's sphere of influence), the brighter green worn by the young Marion before she froze her vitality. Marion's beige apartment corridor, void of life in the first shot, conceals a dark-red closet, colored as Bergman's soul (in *Cries and Whispers*). Red boarding seals the windows Marion passes in her dream.

The colorlessness of Marion's real world relates to Ken's hollow "good taste." For Allen, cultural pretensions are a debilitating insulation against our emotions. In Marion's dream her father admits he wasted his life on "stupid studies of historical figures." Ken's opera collection and Marion's claim that she "used to be a devoted Brechtian"—alienation beyond the call of philosophy—confirm Allen's critique of a culture of the cultured. After having aborted (according to Sam) to serve her "life of the mind," now Marion regards with envy and remorse the swollen belly of Hope. So, too, the equation as well as the opposition in Lydia's (Blythe Danner's) "He's not thinking, he's drinking." The two states seem the same; Allen's intelligentsia are incapacitated by their intellects.

As in *Annie Hall*, the "present" flow of the film is punctuated with strategic insets, in this case the four times Marion listens to Hope's analysis and Marion's eight "visions." These four "hearings" correspond to reading; the eight visions are a form of expression, like writing. In the other woman's experience Marion "reads" a text in life, not art. This new "reading" and "writing" free her to resume her writing proper.

At first, Hope's disclosures trigger Marion's similar memories. But by Hope's last session Marion looks to her for an image of herself. Conversely, Hope takes Marion and her "cold, cerebral life" as a warning of what she might herself become. This may be why Hope withdraws from psychoanalysis. On the level of plot, Hope leaves because seeing Marion has empowered Hope to continue her intuitive life in peace. She has (like Marion) confronted her denied self in the other woman. On the level of rhetoric, Hope disappears from the film once she has served her function: to catalyze Marion's self-discovery. To Allen's credit, the rhetorical functions nowhere override the psychological integrity of the characters.

As Marion hears Hope she "sees" the repressed aspects of herself. Her eight "visions" form a pattern of outward apprehension, a centripetal counterforce to her repression. They move from pure memory, to bolstered memory, to fantasy, to dream, then on to memories focused by the energy freed by her dream.

Marion's new "reading" especially charges her literary allusions. After Rilke's pacing panther, she envisions a white mask, the young Marion's gift to Sam (from a production of *La Giaconda*). In context the mask is also another Rilke allusion—

Masks! Masks! O let us blind Eros
For who could bear his radiant face?

—to one's use of a mask to repress one's passion or identity. When
Marion kisses Sam through the mask, she at once gives herself and
keeps herself from him, as a mask reveals but conceals. Rilke's
panther is a caged but indomitable power:

Just now and then the pupil's noiseless shutter
is lifted. — Then an image will indart,
down through the limbs' intensive stillness flutter,
and end its being in the heart.[3]

The flickering vision of the panther's misted eyes passing the cage
bars, the noiseless shutter, the indarting power, all cohere with
Hope's and Marion's parted curtain. In a school essay Marion
argued that what the panther saw was death. But the indarting
image of life might equally be the panther's impact on the viewer. In
the last shot Marion, freed and open, wears a sweater and skirt in
the solid black of the panther.

This literary vision leads to Marion's breakthrough dream. With
increasing intimacy, it frees ideas she has repressed, such as her
desire for Larry and her awareness that Sam killed himself. Though
her dream ends when she refuses to go further into her memory of
Sam, it releases such an energy that Marion confronts Ken with
their alienation and then deliberately recalls sensitive scenes with
Sam. When she recalls their abortion quarrel, though the scene
starts and ends with the image of young Marion, the mature
Marion bears both her explanation and his rebuttal.

The last "reading" and "writing" summarize Marion's freeing. So
mediated and repressed are Marion's emotions that we learn from
Hope, not Marion, that Marion has found Ken unfaithful. After
the women's lunch Marion seems unaffected; she breaks down only
after she hears Hope report Marion's seeing Ken with another
(another) woman. The last vision establishes Marion's new peace of
mind. From Larry's novel Marion reads his memoir of their first
intimacy and her kiss of checked passion. Larry's novel reminds
Marion of her emotional capacity. She reclaims a memory she

chose to lose. Marion's embrace of Larry's memory—too late for them but not for her—is a microcosm of Woody Allen's reach for self-knowledge. That includes trying to understand not just another woman but the other: woman. As so often, it is the power of a story—Hope's analysis, Larry's novel—that unlocks understanding of the self and frees the repressed spirit.[4]

27

"Oedipus Wrecks" (1989)

Allen's contribution to *New York Stories*, a trilogy of short stories with Martin Scorsese and Francis Ford Coppola, revives the themes of a dead God and magic from the early 1980s. Cast in a Jewish-American version of the classical Oedipus, though, the regal Rex is reduced here to the nebbish's "wrecks."

A successful fifty-year-old lawyer, Sheldon Mills (Allen), complains to his analyst (Martin Chatinover) about being constantly badgered and embarrassed by his mother, Mrs. Millstein (Mae Questel, erstwhile voice of Betty Boop and Olive Oyl): "I love her but I wish she would disappear." His wish comes true when a magician's Chinese Box act goes awry. At first panicked, then relaxed, Sheldon revels in his motherless life and experiences his best ever sex with his fiancée, Lisa (Mia Farrow). But Sheldon's freedom is short-lived. Mrs. Millstein reappears as a giant face in the sky, confiding in the city at large about her sensitive son's history of bed-wetting and his foolish desire to marry a blonde *koorva* with three children. A Jewish psychic, Treva (Julie Kavner), fails to solve his problem through shamanism, but Sheldon falls for Treva's boiled chicken and maternal nagging. Mrs. Millstein returns to earth, satisfied that her son is now in good hands (i.e., like hers).

In this modest fable, the magic of the showbiz magician and of Sheldon's phenomenal mother give way to Treva's unorthodox spirituality. Admitting her incompetence as a psychic, Treva explains "I always think there's more to the world than meets the eye. It never works. . . . You're right. I'm nothing. It beats being a waitress."But this time it does work. As Treva remarks, people flock to psychics "because their lives are so empty." In response, she performs rituals drawn loosely from a range of religious traditions (these include ordering a pizza from behind a witch doctor's mask). Treva's "faith" is a homey version of Jewish tradition. The dual aspects that provide meaning and center to the unmatured fifty-year-old's life are traditional Judaism (albeit a kitchen-pot version) and traditional family ties. In Treva's rites Allen spoofs religion, but in the efficacy of her Jewish-mother ways he validates a traditional moral identity that works through responsible human relations. Colloquialism and cuisine convey the fading heritage of moral integrity and human commitment that Allen more fully articulates through Professor Levy in *Crimes and Misdemeanors*.

As a performer in costume and mask, Treva is also another of Allen's artist figures. Sheldon, stuffed with her deflavored chicken, calls her "a terrific storyteller." She is also a figure of constancy, true to a code of conduct however savaged by post-Portnoy satire, and in contrast to Lisa's fickleness: "It's funny. You wake up one morning and suddenly you're out of love." The old-fashioned woman, "just like Mom," proves smotheringly more reliable.

Sheldon's "mother complex" is not Oedipal but constellated feelings of contrary desires: to remain a son yet to become a man; to assimilate into a socially preferable alien yet to cling to cultural roots. His charged feelings of desire and insecurity are translated into the autonomous projection (Mother in the Sky—with a guilt trip). Sheldon finds assurance and security in the familiar pain because it is familiar. In choosing Treva he chooses a self-identity of which he can be sure, instead of the disconcerting difference his mother finds in Lisa: "Where do you come to a blonde with three children? What are you, an astronaut?" In embracing Treva's motherly ministrations, Sheldon affirms the self he had been trying to abandon.

In a nonanalytic context, Mrs. Millstein's pervasive nagging calls the assimilated Jew back to his cultural as well as familial roots. After all, the conservative boss before whom she humiliates Sheldon is only "Bates, the one with the mistress." Mrs. Millstein also corrects Sheldon's desire (like that of the moral weaklings in *Broadway Danny Rose* and the Cybill Shepherd character in *Alice*) to forget his beginnings. In fact, Mrs. Millstein's apparition over the Chrysler Building embodies the guilt of the assimilated.

Although cast as a joke—with the Oedipus title accompanied by "I want a girl just like the girl that married dear old dad"—it becomes a moral parable. Mrs. Millstein's appearance in the skies is like an Old Testament proof of Jehovah's power and pertinence in an alien society. But in taking the place of a god, Mrs. Millstein fills the moral (as well as the psychological and emotional) vacuum left in our atheistic age. Sheldon's cancelation of his private eye's search for her—"Don't find her. Uh, don't look for her anymore"—evokes his who-killed-God? plot of "Mr. Big." With God dead, the Jewish mother rules the man too insecure either to detach himself from his past or to acknowledge it. But she is also a distorted version of the archetypal mother, the Great Mother godhead in her own right.

Mrs. Millstein's moral effect goes beyond Sheldon. A traffic jam of people relish the chance to show off their children's pictures and to prove their brother's keeper (if not meddler). Mayor Koch appears on television to endorse Mrs. Millstein's civil rights and to approve her intervention in the city's crime. As Allen replays the Jewish mother joke as an Orwellian Big Mother, the immature hero's mother complex is projected upon a city. You don't have to be Jewish to need such humiliating moral guidance from the heavens—or one's mother—but it helps.

28

Crimes and Misdemeanors (1989)

In *Crimes and Misdemeanors* a murderer and a corrupt hack are rewarded while a virtuous artist loses his job, marriage, and love, and a life-affirming philosopher kills himself. It's a comedy of tragedies. Combining two stories originally planned as separate films, Allen shows the sweeping failure of moral responsibility in our Godless age, both in petty misdemeanors and major crimes.[1]

In the comic story, Clifford Stern (Allen) hopes to improve the world through his recherché documentary films. Cliff is frustrated in his marriage and hates his wife's brother Lester (Alan Alda), a successful TV producer. Commissioned to film a PBS homage to Lester, Cliff falls in love with a bright PBS producer, Halley Reed (Mia Farrow). When he cuts the material into an exposé of Lester's corruption, Cliff is fired. Meanwhile he works on his documentary about a life-affirming philosopher, Professor Louis Levy (Martin Bergmann), whose idealism survived the concentration camps. Cliff is shocked when Levy commits suicide, then again when the Reed he has been clinging to agrees to marry Lester.

The somber story centers on an esteemed eye surgeon, Dr. Judah Rosenthal (Martin Landau). When his mistress, Dolores Paley (Anjelica Huston), threatens to expose their affair and his use of charity funds, he has his shady brother Jack (Jerry Orbach) hire a hit man to kill Dolores. Initially shaken with guilt, Judah recovers his composure and resumes his normal life.

Allen joins the stories through two sets of brothers and the related theme of familial unity and communal responsibility. Judah is his brother's keeper both figuratively (he deflects credit for the new ophthalmology wing to the other peoples' "spirit of community, generosity, and mutual caring and answered prayers") and literally (the murder repays Judah's financial support for Jack). In the comic story, Cliff's wife, Wendy (Joanna Gleason), has two successful brothers, the shallow Lester and a wise rabbi, Ben (Sam Waterston), who goes blind during the course of the film.

Ben links the stories, as he is treated by Dr. Rosenthal and advises him on his dilemma. Each treats the other's (real or metaphoric) blindness. According to Ben, Judah sees the world "as harsh and empty of values and pitiless," but Ben believes in "a moral structure with real meaning and forgiveness and some kind of higher power. Otherwise there's no basis to know how to live." The stories converge in the last scene, the lavish wedding (which Lester paid for) of Ben's daughter.

Crimes and Misdemeanors raises the ante on Allen's familiar themes. The triviality that Tony Roberts commonly portrays in Allen's films is divided here into separate characters. His Amoral Success is vested in Lester, a "national phenomenon" who is corrupt and insensitive. In Judah, Allen amplifies into Villain the casual infidelities of the characters Allen earlier fashioned with Roberts, Michael Caine, Sam Waterston, and Ian Holm. A misdemeanor swells into a crime. As Ben puts it, "We went from a small infidelity to the meaning of existence."

To Ben, wisdom is finally realizing "the difference between what's real and deep and lasting versus the superficial payoff of the moment." Judah's "payoff" is far more serious than Lester's. The continuity from misdemeanor into massive crime is paralleled in Lester's formulae for comedy: "If it bends it's funny, if it breaks it's not funny." That is, a slight excess may make for a qualitative (and destructive) difference. Or, "Comedy is tragedy plus time": something profoundly serious can be laughed away in time—for someone of Lester's or Judah's pragmatism. To calm Judah, Jack dismisses the murder as "a small burglary, nothing more," assuming the police perspective instead of the moral one.

Allen's "gag" (since *Annie Hall*) of an adult revisiting a childhood scene here becomes an act of conscience. At a seder young Judah's family debate God's function as a moral source and the murder for which Judah is responsible. For Aunt May (Anna Berger) the Holocaust proves that there is no absolute moral structure in the universe: "Might makes right. . . . For those who want morality there's morality. Nothing's handed down in stone." She anticipates Judah's salved conscience: "If he can do it and get away with it and he chooses not to be bothered by the ethics, then he's home free. Remember. History is written by the winners." In contrast, Judah's Orthodox father, Sol (David S. Howard), is confident that even if his faith were to prove unfounded, "Then I still have a better life than all of those who doubt. . . . If necessary I will always choose God over truth."

In the last scene, Allen gives his familiar play on the tensions between film and life a moral bite. As the two men in tuxedoes sit apart from the party, Judah claims they are the same: "Off by yourself, huh? Just like me." But there is a difference: one personifies evil rewarded, the other virtue punished. Where Cliff was playfully plotting to murder the successful Lester, Judah has lived out his "great murder story." Judah describes his character's triumph over guilt: "Mysteriously the crisis is lifted. . . . His life is completely back to normal, back to his protected world of wealth and privilege. . . . Once in a while he has a bad moment. But it passes."

Cliff sees through the happy ending in this supposed fiction: the character's peace rests on the fact that "His worst beliefs are realized," the universe is morally neutral. For Judah, "People carry awful deeds around with them. What do you expect him to do, turn himself in? I mean, this is reality. In reality we rationalize, we deny, or we couldn't go on living." Indeed, the stern Cliff proposes that to give the story tragic proportions the hero should turn himself in, in the absence of God assuming responsibility himself. "But that's fiction," Judah replies, "That's movies. . . . If you want a happy ending you should go see a Hollywood movie." This is history written by the winner.

By converting his history into a story, Judah manages an easy "confession," without the costs of confessing the adultery to his wife or (later) the murder to the police. Allen shows how much easier it is to make moral stories than to live a moral life. Yet Judah has a compulsion—like the Ancient Mariner—to unburden himself of his story.

The film's main metaphor is eyes. In an archetypal paradox, spiritual vision is vested in the sightless Rabbi Ben, while the eye specialist is morally blind. Though Judah speaks of himself as a man of science, a religious skeptic, he remembers his father's teaching "that the eyes of God are always on us" and thinking God's eyes are "unimaginably penetrating." Significantly, Judah's father is named Sol, not spelled Saul but as an abbreviation of the wise Solomon or as the pagan sun, the revealing force of light. In becoming an ophthalmologist Judah chose the order of nature over the order of grace, affirming the physical vision over the spiritual.

In one flashback, Dolores asks if Judah agrees that the eyes are the windows of the soul. "I believe they're windows," he replies, "but I'm not sure it's the soul I see"—as he kisses her. Dolores later wears sunglasses (even in a car at night in the rain). When Judah visits the murdered Dolores's apartment to recover his mementos, his part in the murder is imaged when he snuffs his headlight. A continuous line of perception and responsibility is suggested in the camera's pan from Judah's eyes down his natty suit along the empty, pale floor to his dead lover's wide open eyes. "There was nothing behind her eyes," he recalls, "All you saw was a black void."

Where Ben holds out for "The Law, Judah. Without the law it's all darkness," Halley is the new pragmatic, a bright hope (comet-like?) fallen. She is a law graduate who opted for the idealism of Public Broadcasting but is edging into Lester's corrupt world. Whether Lester won her by roses and caviar, quoting Emily Dickinson or advancing her career, her choice signifies the daily ways in which corruption is chosen over virtue.

So does Dolores—"the sad one." Anjelica Huston's performance holds our sympathy even as it makes Judah's impatience understandable. At first Dolores, a beautiful, nurturing stewardess, served Judah's vanity in return for stability and hope. But when Judah withholds the commitment that he implied, she loses her "faith" in him. As another creature of the secular order, a flyer of the skies not the heavens, Dolores despairs to the point that she would destroy his reputation in order to win him. In her ardor and need, she is a sympathetic variation on the theme of self-serving rationalization. Like Judah, she grasps for peace of mind at whatever cost to others. But only he can afford to buy it. Judah justifies the murder by putting his own rights and interests ahead of others: "What good is the law if it prevents me from receiving justice?"[2]

Despite the moral resignation inherent in the plot, Allen holds out two forms of hope. One is individual integrity. As Allen told Roger Ebert, "You'll never get rid of all the terrible social evils that plague people until it [integrity] emanates from inside each individual himself."[3] The other is preparing our children to become better adults than we are. Cliff educates his niece, Jenny (Jenny Nichols), with film matinees and good advice: "Never listen to your teachers. Just see what they look like." He gives her a book of photographs of the lost, Edenic New York.

The movie clips parallel the main plot lines, from the tensions of an annulled marriage in Hitchcock's *Mr. and Mrs. Smith* (1941), through Betty Hutton's brassy "Murder, He Says," from *Happy Go Lucky* (1943). Just as the first clip quotes Hitchcock's only foray into Allen territory, romantic comedy, *Crimes and Misdemeanors* is Allen's first foray into the Hitchcock genre, the moral thriller, in which a smug hero takes one wrong step into a moral abyss. When Cliff assures Jenny that a B-film murder contract "only happens in the movies," he is wrong in context but right morally: Judah errs in doing the horrid things we see in films. This explains Cliff's charge that Lester promotes values "that deaden the sensibilities of a great democracy."

Where the matinees provide ironic reflections of the characters' lives, Professor Levy's philosophy illuminates them. Levy's point— "It is only we, with our capacity to love, that give meaning to the indifferent universe"—dignifies the characters' concerns over their sexual relationships. The characters' sexual liberties are an index to their moral awareness, which indicates their responsibility to a moral order in the universe. When Cliff's sister sympathizes over his chilled marriage, "Once the sex goes, it all goes," he replies with a telling metaphor: "The last time I was inside a woman is when I visited the Statue of Liberty." The film condemns the ethos of Judah's sexual liberty as the misdemeanor that led to his crime. When Levy kills himself, he has nothing more to say, so his note is curt and factual: "I've gone out the window." His more ambitious words proved as ineffectual as Sol's lessons to Judah.

In *Crimes and Misdemeanors* Allen has made a Happy Ending film that denies the happy ending. In the ambivalent last scene, the blind rabbi dances with his just-married daughter. In the light of our discussion of *September*, the wedding signifies a comedic resolution for the Ben-Lester story, but it excludes from its grace both the comic loser Cliff and the false "winner" Judah. The officiating rabbi's confidence of being "in the presence of God, the guardian of our homes," is overridden by Levy's last statement. Over a montage of scenes from the film we hear Levy say we define ourselves by the "agonizing decisions, moral choices" we make, mostly on small matters of daily life. "Events unfold so unpredictably, so unfairly, human happiness does not seem to have been included in the design of creation."

Allen wields Levy's words against the moral darkness. As Cliff teaches Jenny, Allen seconds Levy's hopes by including at the wedding little children, innocent in pink, discreetly playing—and stealing icing from the cake! The music to which the proud, blind father waltzes is "I'll Be Seeing You," as recorded by the icon of glitz, Liberace. The film concludes with an uneasy tension between hope and self-deception, faith and skepticism, evasion and con- frontation. The social pillar gets away with murder because he has status and a self-rationalizing conscience. That civilized monster is us.

29

Alice (1990)

In *Alice* Allen studies Another Woman who is prompted to self-discovery. Alice is an affluent broker's bored and pampered wife who lives in a wonderland of hired help, beauty appointments and chauffeured shopping expeditions. Bringing this upscale woman down to self-realization reverses Cecilia's rise to glamorous fantasy in *The Purple Rose of Cairo*.

A Chinese sage, Dr. Yang (Keye Luke), diagnoses Alice's chronic back pain as a problem of the head and heart. He gives her herbs that enable her, in order, to be erotically aggressive, to be invisible, to conjure the ghost of her first love, Eddie (Alec Baldwin), and to be irresistible to men. Able "to observe without being observed" (the familiar condition of the film viewer), Alice witnesses her husband's (William Hurt's) infidelity. She then has a tentative but ardent affair with a tenor saxaphonist, Joe (Joe Mantegna). Concurrently, her reawakened writing ambition is assisted by a world-wise muse (Bernadette Peters), who encourages her to write about the people and experiences that shaped Alice's life. Through her self-reflection, Alice discovers the shallowness of her current friendships and life-style and reconciles with her more grounded attorney-sister, Dorothy (Blythe Danner). Finally, Alice abandons her wealth and comfort and goes to Calcutta to work with Mother Teresa. When she returns to New York it is to do volunteer work in the ghettos and to raise her two children in a materially simple but emotionally rich environment. Our last view is of a newly blissful Alice playing with her children on the swings of a public park.

The setting in the opening shot, the penguin house of the Central Park Zoo, is emblematic of the layered—conscious and unconscious—mind; the penguins' world comprises barren surface and dark water. As their "tuxedo" look seems to parody the New York high life, their mating for life contrasts to the humans' formal appearance of fidelity. Beneath the elegant surface of Alice's society, she sees intrigue, infidelity, and deception. Paralleling the two-layered setting, Alice's TV-writing professor (James Toback) speaks of "the two aspects of the consciousness of words," the internal, meditative use in the novel, and the external, expressive use in theater and film.

Gradually, Alice learns to cultivate her inner self instead of shallow externals. From accepting the counsel of an affected interior designer (Julie Kavner), who offers ("a steal at $900") a wicker eel trap for a lamp base or flower holder, she moves to the unpretentious and emancipating Dr. Yang. Like *Interiors*, the film contrasts the external concerns of "interior design" with the more important concerns for the inner being.

The film's dominant verbal theme is the insides of women. "It's just not in me" to have an affair, Alice initially believes. A friend's vaginal tumors are in remission. Wanting the ghost to assure her of her writing promise, Alice asks, "Do you think I have it in me?" The Muse redefines the professor's deep interest in Alice's writing: "Very deep is exactly where he wants to put it." As her self-discovery progresses, Alice tells Doug that "I've done things I didn't know I had in me." Ultimately, she discovers that what she has in her are properties of capability, function, and worth that she had neglected for her spoiled life. In contrast to her psychological changes, her friends gossip about their rivals' physical operations, face-lifts, and liposuctions.

Alice's life diverged from her sister's when Alice followed the advice of her alcoholic ex-actress mother (Gwen Verdon) and married for security instead of love. Her mother's self-esteem was exclusively rooted in her beauty, so she relied upon her husband for support against its inevitable loss. Alice's self-denigration led to a similarly debilitating marriage. As Marion Post rejects Larry Lewis for the chilly cardiologist, Alice rejects the reckless and passionate painter, Eddie, and marries the ultrawealthy Doug (Hurt).

Alice is led to confront her repression by an alternative form of psychoanalysis, Dr. Yang's treatment. He questions Alice about her past and encourages her to confront her desires. Likewise, the Muse's advice for her writing is equivalent to analysis. When Alice shares the invisibility herb with Joe, his witnessing his ex-wife's analysis reveals her love and prompts him to recommence their relationship.

With this implicit faith in analysis, Allen here varies his usual flashback form. Alice's projections into the past are often mental rather than physical. With only a lighting change, no props beyond a neon sign, no change in physical situation, Dr. Yang has Alice relive her first date with her husband. Their words alone suggest that the site of their first meeting, an amusement park, has replaced the herbalist's office in Alice's awareness. Later, Eddie's ghost appears spectrally, then materializes to take her on an out-of-body flight over New York, then back to an old haunt now burned down. In a more physical flashback, under a dose of opium, she revisits the family home with Dorothy and takes one last confession.

Also, although Dr. Yang is a significant reversal of Allen's scientific skeptics (Professor Sturgis in *Midsummer Night's Sex Comedy*, the physicist of *September*, the cardiologist of *Another Woman*, and the ophthalmogist of *Crimes and Misdemeanors*), like them he is presented as an alternative to the traditional Western religious guide. In fact, in Alice's last visit, the isolating framing and an intervening wall suggest a conversation between a priest and a confessor. As an oriental acupuncturist and herbalist, Dr. Yang operates outside the Western traditions (playfully confirmed in the Oriental additions to the Dixieland score). He works by intuition and with faith in traditional Eastern values and means (hence his departure to study newly discovered ancient scrolls in Tibet). In this light he is less the scientist than its antithesis, Allen's Magician figure. Indeed, by Yang's magic Alice has supernatural experiences that lead her to a more balanced life. In Allen's usual pessimistic optimism, we need some magic to see our way through to wisdom.

Or does it? When Alice declines to use the last of her aphrodisiac to reactivate the lover of her choice, she (like Cecilia in *The Purple Rose of Cairo*) opts for a realistic solution over a magical one. But unlike Cecilia, Alice asserts the will to remake her life, free of consoling illusions. Still, unable to provide an untempered happy ending, Allen skips over the details that would have made the conclusion convincing, such as Alice's experiences in India and the difficult process by which she presumably rebuilt her character. Allen's movie is not about such hard realities, but about the discovery of the falseness in a pampered life, with the stock footage of the flight suggesting a "magical" transformation at the end.

With this pat ending Allen affirms his faith in analysis. Another unexamined life is freed once the repressed inner self is discovered. In this respect, self-analysis, whether prompted by a therapist or by a probing film such as this, provides a realistic alternative to magic both for self-discovery and to handle the "much suffering" that inevitably derives from the irrationality of love. As Dr. Yang further observes, "freedom is frightening." So it is easier to live the superficial life, as the voice-over gossips do when they equate Alice's transformation with mere cosmetic surgery.

Allen's emphasis on Alice's Catholicism addresses a wider cultural dilemma than the Jewish-American. Indeed in this film Mia Farrow more than ever before plays the familiar Allen nebbish. Alice's dedication to Mother Teresa helps Alice/Farrow replace Allen's Jewish conscience with a Catholic one. It also adds to Dr. Yang's magic the ethical concern of Allen's late-eighties films, with his rising indignation at the moral legacy of the Reagan era.

Wrap-up 2:
Beyond Persona

In the beginning was the parody. Woody Allen found his film voice by playfully "trying out" a series of film and literary forms, culminating in *Love and Death* (1975). In *Zelig* and *The Purple Rose of Cairo* he returned to the genre only to transcend it. So *Zelig* seems an encyclopedic apotheosis of parody and the inner-film of *The Purple Rose of Cairo*, like the clips of Sandy Bates's films in *Stardust Memories*, an encapsulation, as if Allen were playing with the form. In the eighties Allen abandoned parody to extend his personal vision from *Annie Hall* and *Manhattan*.

As his personal voice firmed, Allen stepped away from his persona as well as from parody. If the negative inflection of his image made *Stardust Memories* too abrasive for his audience, Allen recovered its useful charm in his later appearances as Andrew Hobbs, Zelig, Broadway Danny Rose, and Cliff Stern (in *Crimes and Misdemeanors*). So iconic has Allen's image become that in Paul Mazursky's *Scenes from a Mall* (1991) there is a comic charge when the Allen character defends Los Angeles against a New Yorker's charge that it is a cultural wasteland, when he is revealed to be a successful philanderer and a former Public Defender now making sponsorship deals for young athletes—and when he drives a car! At the same time, Allen cedes to Mia Farrow (in *Alice*) the function of moral exemplar that he formerly assumed for himself in his *shicksa-schlemiel* comedies. In Alice's rediscovery of service to others Allen posits a Catholic equivalent to the Jewish tradition in which he found his own moral base (as in *Broadway Danny Rose* he developed parallel social satire of the Italian and Jewish subcultures).

In the eighties Allen's moral imperative edged out his comedy. The pivotal tension between confronting reality and escaping into comic diversion continues from *Stardust Memories* through *Broadway Danny Rose, The Purple Rose of Cairo, Hannah and Her Sisters, September,* and *Crimes and Misdemeanors.* When Alice outgrows her bored affluence for service and humanity, Allen reflects back upon the self-seeking that characterized Ronald Reagan's America. *Alice* focused the cultural critique implicit in both the murderous ophthalmogist and the corrupt TV magnate in *Crimes and Misdemeanors.* If Marion Post dreams her psychiatrist's instruction—"Don't worry about humanity. Get your own life in order"— the examples of Judah (negative) and Alice (positive) remind us that properly to order one's life is to confront the lot of humanity and our individual responsibility to improve it however we can. Anything else is to rationalize our indulgence. Thus Allen's eighties' films abound with self-serving betrayals: *Stardust Memories, Midsummer Night's Sex Comedy, Broadway Danny Rose, Purple Rose of Cairo, Hannah and Her Sisters, September, Another Woman.* Whims and pecadilloes culminate in the murder of *Crimes and Misdemeanors.*

As a moral counterpoise to self-indulgence, Allen proffers the potential of art. At first he is fascinated by the interplay between life and its illusionist transformation, whether Sandy Bates's filmmaking, Paul Pollack's magic, or the myth that Broadway Danny Rose lives for the deli gossips. For the fact that we live on through our deeds and their report should prompt us to live by creed not self-indulgence.

In this transforming effect Allen finds in art something of the potential of magic. Although it is an essentially sterile, isolating activity, magic and art can provide a glimpse into a superior reality and a model of being to which to aspire. Sometimes the magic works: the child's in *Stardust Memories, Midsummer Night's Sex Comedy, Zelig, Alice.* Sometimes it doesn't: the adult's in *Stardust Memories, The Floating Light Bulb, Crimes and Misdemeanors.* Where it does work, the magic is not a matter of supernature but of characters confronting the reality of their lives, whether physical, spiritual or emotional. So Allen's ultimate magician is Dr. Yang, who brings from a remote and ancient culture a meld of magic, therapeutic analysis and the storyteller's captivating web.

Though Allen's early parodies proved him fascinated with film-making, in the eighties he moves on to the larger compulsions and magic of story telling. Thus the lesson absorbed in the telling of the Broadway Danny Rose story at the Carnegie Deli. Hence, too, the fertile outpouring of the wholly narrated *Radio Days*. At the opposite extreme lie the stories told in *Crimes and Misdemeanors*, futilely by Professor Levy and Cliff Stern, of briefly salving but limited relief in Judah's fictionalized confession. Diane's comic stories in *September* may briefly enliven her days and soothe her husband's nights but they fail to confront the reality of her life; they leave her responsible for burdening others.

Committed to the moral function of story telling, Allen has experimented with different kinds of narrative. His subjective delivery of *Annie Hall* is varied in the reminiscence of *Radio Days*. The straightforward cautionary model of *Manhattan* is replayed to more somber effect in *Another Woman* and *September*. But *September* is also a variation upon the multicouple tangle of *Midsummer Night's Sex Comedy*. These crowded-center dramas contrast to the fragmented narrative of *Radio Days* and *Hannah and Her Sisters*. In *Zelig* the central romance is shattered by the proliferation of formal parody that subordinates the love story to the public phenomenon—and diagnosis. *Zelig*, *Broadway Danny Rose*, and *The Purple Rose of Cairo* all use frame structures, setting their story off within the film proper. In *Another Woman* and in *Alice* the inset stories are stages in the heroine's self-discovery. In *Crimes and Misdemeanors* the narrative is at once more linear and more rounded, as it alternately interweaves and separates the worlds of Cliff Stern and Judah.

In short, Allen has refused to stand still. In art as in his moral position, he continues to question himself and to challenge the spirit of his time. He still makes films that are immensely humorous. But the laughter of his congregation in the dark is only to bolster us against our common moral fallibility and our mortality. If that's not a laughing matter, what is?

Notes

Introduction

1. See listing in discography.
2. Alfred Bester, "Conversation with Woody Allen," *Holiday*, May, 1969, p. 84.
3. Eric Lax, *On Being Funny: Woody Allen and Comedy*, Charterhouse Press (New York, 1975), p. 72.
4. Leo Lerman, "Woody the Great," *Vogue*, December, 1972, p. 144.
5. Charles Marowitz, "Everything you always wanted to know about Woody Allen," *The Listener*, July 7, 1977, p. 9.
6. Penelope Gilliatt, "Guilty With an Explanation," *The New Yorker*, February 4, 1974, p. 42.

Part One: The Public Face of Woody Allen

1. Larry Wilde, *The Great Comedians*, Citadel Press (Secaucus, N.J., 1973), p. 29.
2. Woody Allen, "The Girls of *Casino Royale*," *Playboy*, February, 1967, pp. 109–11.
3. *The New Yorker*, February 28, 1970.
4. Wilde, p. 31.
5. Sarah McMurphy, "The Life and Two Loves of Woody Allen," *Toronto Sunday Star*, October 30, 1977, Section C, p. 1.

1: The Monologues

1. Joanne Stang, " 'Verbal Cartoons'," *New York Times Magazine*, November 3, 1963, p. 120.
2. *Time*, February 15, 1963, p. 78.
3. William K. Zinsser, "Bright New Comic Clowns toward success," *Saturday Evening Post*, September 21, 1963, p. 26.
4. Leo Lerman, "Woody the Great," p. 144.
5. Richard Schickel, "The basic Woody Allen joke," *New York Times Magazine*, January 7, 1973, p. 33.
6. Vivian Gornick, "Face it, Woody Allen, You're Not a Schlep Anymore," *The Village Voice*, January 5, 1976, p. 10.
7. Edwin Miller, "The Tallest Dwarf in the World," *Seventeen*, May, 1966, p. 204.
8. Woody Allen, *Without Feathers*, Warner Books paperback (New York, 1976), p. 214.
9. Gornick, p. 9.
10. Schickel, p. 33.

2: The Actor as Hired Image

1. Adelaide Comerford, "What's New, Pussycat?" Films in Review, August-September, 1965, pp. 446–47.
2. Andrew Sarris, "What's New, Pussycat?" The Village Voice, August 5, 1965, p. 14. (Sarris's first review of the film appeared in the July 8, 1965, Voice, p. 13.)
3. Raymond Durgnat, The Crazy Mirror, Faber and Faber (London, 1969), pp. 243–44.
4. Clive Donner, Quoi de Neuf, Pussycat? L'Avant-Scène, Numéro 59: Le Nouveau Cinéma Anglais (Paris, 1966).
5. Woody Allen, "What's Nude, Pussycat?" Playboy, August, 1965, p. 100.
6. Sarris, p. 14.
7. Eric Lax, On Being Funny, p. 59.
8. Edwin Miller, "The Tallest Dwarf in the World," p. 212.
9. Loc. cit.
10. Marvin H. Albert, What's New, Pussycat? Mayflower-Dell paperback (London, 1965), p. 85.
11. Albert, p. 109.
12. Woody Allen: An American Comedy, a film produced and directed by Harold Mantell.
13. Edwin Miller, "The Tallest Dwarf in the World," p. 210.
14. Woody Allen, "The Girls of Casino Royale," p. 111.
15. Guy Flatley, "Woody Allen: 'I Have No Yen To Play Hamlet'," New York Times, October 3, 1976, Arts and Leisure section, pp. 15, 22.
16. Rex Reed, Valentines and Vitriol, Dell Publishing (New York, 1977), p. 106.
17. George W. S. Trow, "A Film About a Very Funny Man," Film Comment, May-June, 1977, pp. 32–33.

Part Two: Woody in the Theater

1. David Wallechinsky, Irving Wallace, and Amy Wallace, eds., A Book of Lists, William Morrow, 1977, Bantam edition, 1978, p. 188.

3: Don't Drink the Water

1. Quotations are from the Samuel French edition of the play (New York, 1967).
2. Salcia Landmann, quoted in Sig Altman, The Comic Image of the Jew, Fairleigh Dickinson University Press (Cranbury, N.J., 1971), p. 165.
3. Woody Allen: An American Comedy, a film by Harold Mantell.
4. Eric Lax, On Being Funny, p. 207.

4: Play It Again, Sam

1. Quotations are from the Samuel French edition of the play (New York, 1969).
2. Stanley Price, "Play it Again Sam," Plays and Players, November, 1969, p. 24.
3. Woody Allen, "How Bogart Made Me the Superb Lover I Am Today," Life, March 21, 1969, pp. 64–67.
4. Harry Wasserman, "Woody Allen: Stumbling through the Looking Glass," The Velvet Light Trap Review of Cinema, No. 7 (Winter, 1972–73), pp. 37–40.

5. Alfred Bester, "Conversation with Woody Allen," *Holiday*, May, 1969, p. 71.
6. Woody Allen, *Play It Again, Sam* (film edition), edited by Richard Anobile, Grossett and Dunlop (New York, 1977), p. 7.

5: *The One-Act Plays*

1. "Death Knocks" is in *Getting Even*, Random House (New York, 1971), pp. 41–53.
2. "Death" is in *Without Feathers*, Warner Books (New York, 1976), pp. 43–106.
3. Eric Lax, *On Being Funny*, p. 227.
4. "God" is in *Without Feathers*, pp. 129–90.
5. "The Query," *The New Republic*, September 18, 1976, pp. 11–13. Allen may have taken the Lincoln anecdote from David Reuben, *Everything you always wanted to know about sex but were afraid to ask*, Bantam edition, 1970, p. 6.

Part Three: *Woody the Writer*
6: *The Pose behind the Prose*

1. "No Kaddish for Weinstein," *Without Feathers*, pp. 205–210.
2. "Lovborg's Women Considered," *Without Feathers*, pp. 29–34.
3. "My Philosophy," *Getting Even*, pp. 27–33.
4. "Conversations with Helmholtz," *Getting Even*, pp. 113–21.
5. "Selections from the Allen Notebooks," *Without Feathers*, pp. 7–10.
6. "A Guide to Some of the Lesser Ballets," *Without Feathers*, pp. 18–23.
7. "Slang Origins," *Without Feathers*, pp. 217–21.
8. "Count Dracula," *Getting Even*, pp. 95–101.
9. "Reminiscences: Places and People," *The New Yorker*, December 29, 1975, pp. 20–21.
10. "Confessions of a Burglar," *The New Yorker*, October 18, 1976, pp. 35–37.
11. "Spring Bulletin," *Getting Even*, pp. 55–61.
12. "But Soft . . . Real Soft," *Without Feathers*, pp. 196–98.
13. "The Condemned," *The New Yorker*, November 21, 1977, pp. 57–59.
14. "A Twenties Memory," *Getting Even*, pp. 89–93.
15. "A Little Louder, Please," *Getting Even*, pp. 103–11.
16. "Fabrizio's: Criticism and Response," *The New Yorker*, February 5, 1979, pp. 31–32.
17. "The Metterling Lists," *Getting Even*, pp. 3–11.
18. "The UFO Menace," *The New Yorker*, June 13, 1977, pp. 31–33.
19. "The Scrolls," *Without Feathers*, pp. 24–28.
20. "The Schmeed Memoirs," *Getting Even*, pp. 19–26.
21. "Remembering Needleman: At the Cremation," *The New Republic*, July 24, 1976, pp. 4–6.
22. "By Destiny Denied," *The New Yorker*, February 23, 1976, pp. 33–35.
23. "Examining Psychic Phenomena," *Without Feathers*, pp. 11–17.
24. "Fabulous Tales and Mythical Beasts," *Without Feathers*, pp. 191–95.
25. "Notes from the Overfed," *Getting Even*, pp. 81–87.
26. "If the Impressionists Had Been Dentists," *Without Feathers*, pp. 199–204.
27. *Getting Even*, p. 104.
28. "Viva Vargas," *Getting Even*, pp. 123–33.
29. "Yes, But Can the Steam Engine Do This?" *Getting Even*, pp. 35–40.

7: Woody's Wide, Wild World

1. William K. Zinsser, "Bright New Comic Clowns toward success," p. 27.
2. *Time*, February 15, 1963, p. 78.
3. "Nefarious Times We Live In," *The New Republic*, November 22, 1975, pp. 7–8.
4. Edwin Miller, "Lines from the Face of a Funny Man," *Seventeen*, May, 1972, p. 204.
5. *Without Feathers*, p. 10.
6. "Mr. Big," *Getting Even*, pp. 139–51.
7. "A Look at Organized Crime," *Getting Even*, pp. 13–18.
8. "Hassidic Tales," *Getting Even*, pp. 63–69.
9. *Getting Even*, p. 10.
10. "The Kugelmass Episode," *The New Yorker*, May 2, 1977, pp. 34–39.
11. *Getting Even*, p. 120.
12. "Attention!" *Esquire*, February 1966, pp. 67–91.
13. "The Gossage-Vardebedian Papers," *Getting Even*, pp. 71–80.
14. "The Irish Genius," *Without Feathers*, pp. 122–27.
15. "The Lunatic's Tale," *The New Republic*, April 23, 1977, pp. 17–19.
16. "The Whore of Mensa," *Without Feathers*, pp. 35–41.

Part Four: Woody's Films

1. Eric Lax, *On Being Funny*, pp. 188–97.
2. Cf. "Swedish Movie" on recording *Woody Allen, Volume 2*.
3. Lax, pp. 206–7.
4. Lax, p. 198.

9: Take the Money and Run

1. Mark Rosin, "Woody Allen: The Power of an Imperfectionist," *Harper's Bazaar*, December 19, 1971, pp. 62–63.

10: Bananas

1. Mel Gussow in *Making Films in New York*, August, 1971, p. 40.
2. Robert Mundy and Stephen Mamber, "Woody Allen: An Interview," *Cinema* (Los Angeles), Winter, 1972–73, p. 16.

11: Everything You Always Wanted To Know About Sex

1. Mark Rosin, "Woody Allen: The Power of an Imperfectionist," p. 63.
2. Penelope Gilliatt, *Unholy Fools*, Secker and Warburg (London, 1973), p. 39.
3. David Reuben, *Everything you always wanted to know about sex but were afraid to ask*, David McKay Publishing, 1969; Bantam paperback, 1970, pp. 8–9.
4. Gilliatt, *Unholy Fools*, p. 39.
5. Leonard Maltin, "Take Woody Allen—Please!" *Film Comment*, March-April, 1974, p. 43.
6. Harry Wasserman, "Woody Allen: Stumbling through the Looking Glass," p. 39.
7. Rosin, p. 63.
8. Charles Marowitz, "Everything you always wanted to know about Woody Allen," *The Listener*, July 7, 1977, p. 9.

9. Eric Lax, *On Being Funny*, p. 74.
10. Reuben, p. 227.
11. Lax, pp. 151–64.
12. Reuben, p. 214. Compare the television show, *What's My Disease?* in Terry Southern's novel, *Flash and Filigree*, and *Beat the Reaper* on *Monty Python's Flying Circus*.
13. Burt Reynolds's image as a superstud was so well established in such films as *Shark, Fuzz*, and *100 Rifles* that John Boorman could play against it in *Deliverance* (1972), released the same year as his Allen film and his famous nude fold-out in *Cosmopolitan*.
14. "Everything You've Always Wanted to Know About Sex You'll Find in My New Movie," *Playboy*, September, 1972, pp. 115–19.

12: Sleeper

1. Eric Lax, *On Being Funny*, p. 67.
2. In the French print, *Woody et Les Robots*, there is an intervening scene that I have not noticed in any English print. At dinner with Luna, Miles eats quickly, in time to the music. Then he does his Suave Lover act, which concludes with him eating the candle and napkin. He then does several magic tricks that charm Luna out of her earlier dislike for him.
3. Lax, p. 71.
4. Barry Gross, "O Shikse! O Shaygetz! O Jew! I Must Have You! The Jewish-Gentile Attraction," an unpublished paper.

13: Love and Death

1. Eric Lax, *On Being Funny*, p. 174.
2. Gabriel Miller, "A Laugh Gains the Upper Hand: Woody Allen's *Love and Death*," *Bright Lights*, No. 7, pp. 29–31.
3. Lax, pp. 231, 232.
4. Woody Allen, "On *Love and Death*," *Esquire*, July 19, 1975, pp. 79–83.

14: Annie Hall

1. Iain Johnstone, "Anhedonia and *Annie Hall*," *The Listener*, May 11, 1978, pp. 603–4.
2. Frank Rich, "Woody Allen Wipes the Smile off his Face," *Esquire*, May, 1977, p. 76.
3. Ernest Becker, *The Denial of Death*, The Free Press, 1973; paperback edition, 1975; pp. 32, 45, 42.
4. Becker, pp. 109, 32.
5. Becker, p. 167.

15: Interiors

1. *Interiors* may well be the best modern American film never to win an Oscar. However, it did have five nominations: Geraldine Page for best actress, Maureen Stapleton for best supporting actress, art direction, and Woody Allen for best director and for best original screenplay. It fared better in England, where *Films and Filming* named it the best film of 1978, and Geraldine Page best actress. The British Academy of Film and Television Arts named Geraldine Page best supporting actress.

2. Ira Halberstadt, "Scenes from a Mind," *Take One*, November, 1978, p. 17.
3. Yvonne Baby, "Dealing with Death," *The Guardian*, January 14, 1979, p. 14.
4. Ernest Becker, *The Denial of Death*, The Free Press, 1973; paperback edition, 1975, p. 167.
5. Becker, pp. 151–52.
6. Baby, p. 14.
7. Halberstadt, p. 17.
8. Becker, pp. xi, 186.
9. Halberstadt, p. 16.
10. Halberstadt, p. 16.
11. Baby, p. 14.
12. Halberstadt, p. 17.
13. Andrew Sarris, "Frowns of a Summer Night," *The Village Voice*, August 7, 1978, p. 30.
14. Becker, p. 220.

16: Manhattan

1. The box-office success of *Manhattan* proves Allen's enlarged following after *Annie Hall*. The May 16 and May 23 issues of *Variety* declared *Manhattan* the top-grossing film in the United States for those weeks, well ahead of such other successes as *The Exorcist* (re-issue), *Dawn of the Dead*, *Love at First Bite* and *The Deer Hunter*. A separate news report declared the film was playing well in proverbial Peoria, where word-of-mouth and a rave review were helping it to a one-month run that outgrossed *Coming Home* and *Not the Size That Counts* (!).
2. The film was sensitively reviewed by Penelope Gilliatt, "The Black-and-White Apple," *The New Yorker*, April 30, 1979, pp. 110–13, and Andrew Sarris, " 'S Wonderful," *The Village Voice*, April 30, 1979, pp. 51, 54. Rather belated recognition of Allen's maturity came from Natalie Gittelson, "The Maturing of Woody Allen," *The New York Times Magazine*, April 22, 1979, pp. 30–32, 102–7, and Richard Schickel, "Woody Allen Comes of Age," *Time*, April 30, 1979, pp. 62–65.

Wrap-up 1: Jester and Outsider

1. Ernst Becker, *The Denial of Death*, p. 7.
2. Yvonne Baby, "Dealing with Death," p. 14.
3. Vivian Gornick, "Face it, Woody Allen, You're Not A Schlep Anymore," p. 10.
4. Frank Rich, "Woody Allen Wipes the Smile off his Face," p. 75.
5. Philip Roth, *Portnoy's Complaint*, Bantam paperback, 1970; p. 236.
6. Becker, p. 96.
7. Ernest Kolowrat, "A Loser on Top," *Senior Scholastic*, November 22, 1963, p. 23.
8. Alfred Bester, "Conversation with Woody Allen," *Holiday*, May, 1969, p. 71.
9. Becker, p. 164.
10. Becker, p. 91.

Part Five: Through the Eighties

1. Allen to Michiko Kakutani, "How Woody Allen's *Zelig* Was Born in Anxiety and Grew into Comedy," *New York Times*, July 18, 1983, p. 13.

17: *Stardust Memories*

1. As the monologue that opens *Annie Hall* seemed to show Allen, slipping into the character of Alvy Singer.

2. In a similar scene in *Manhattan*, Isaac (Allen) concludes a list of life's blessings with "Tracy's face." This secular salvation may recall the Knight (Max von Sydow) treasuring the picnic of wild strawberries and cream in Bergman's *The Seventh Seal* (1957), but this validation does not hold up for Bergman as it does for the nostalgic Fellini.

3. Richard Combs surveys the attacks on the film in "Chameleon Days," *Monthly Film Bulletin*, November, 1983, pp. 295–96. Typical of the film's harsh reception are Pauline Kael, *Taking It All In*, Holt, Rinehart and Winston (New York: 1984), pp. 86–92; Andrew Sarris, "Woody Doesn't Rhyme with Federico," *The Voice*, October 1, 1980, pp. 49, 121; John Simon, "Sandy Stardust," in *Reverse Angle*, Clarkson N. Potter (New York: 1982), pp. 417–19. More sympathetic approaches can be found in Vincent Canby, "The Humor, Hostility and Mystery of Woody Allen," *New York Times*, September 28, 1980, Section D, pp. 21, 33; Karen Jaehne, "Stardust Memories," *Film Quarterly*, Winter, 1980–81, pp. 40–44; John Pym, "Stardust Memories," *Sight and Sound*, Winter, 1980–81, p. 66; Mark Siegel, "Ozymandias Melancholia: The Nature of Parody in Woody Allen's *Stardust Memories*," *Literature/Film Quarterly*, 13, ii (1985), pp. 76–84; David Goodwin, "Woody Allen," *Stills*, I, ii (Spring, 1981), pp. 29–31; Tony Schwartz, "The Conflicting Life and Art of Woody Allen," *New York Times*, October 20, 1980, pp. 1, 28.

4. Tom Shales, "Woody: The First Fifty Years," *Esquire*, April, 1987, pp. 88–95. The filming was reported on by Penelope Gilliatt is "Woody Allen in the Driving Seat," *The Sunday Times*, April 13, 1980, p. 39, and in a movie by André Delvaux, *To Woody Allen from Europe with Love*.

5. The "celebrity trilogy" also included *Zelig* and *The Purple Rose of Cairo*, according to Krin Gabbard and Glen O. Gabbard, in *Psychiatry and the Cinema*, University of Chicago (Chicago: 1987), but Broadway Danny Rose is also deployed as a celebrity among real-life celebrities.

6. Father Drobney in *Don't Drink the Water* was also an amateur magician.

7. Robert Munk is the young brother of Jonathan Munk, who played Alvy Singer as a child. See Diane Solway, "Portrait of the Artist As a Young Woody Allen," *New York Times*, November 8, 1987, pp. 25, 30.

18: *The Floating Light Bulb*

1. John Lahr dramatized eighteen stories and routines as *The Bluebird of Unhappiness: A Woody Allen Review*, which was presented at the Royal Exchange in Manchester.

2. Quoted in John Corry, "Woody Allen's New Broadway Play Might Just Be about Woody Allen," *New York Times*, April 26, 1981, pp. 1, 6. In *The Voice* Jan Hoffman dismissed the "not-quite play" as a "bloodless little tussle between drama and comedy" (April 29, 1981, p. 85). Stephen Koss called it "more a dirge than a

play" ("Only forty watts," *Times Literary Supplement*, May 29, 1981, p. 602). For Walter Kerr, "Woody Allen Makes a Brave Try" (*New York Times*, May 10, 1981, D-3, 7).

3. Unless otherwise noted quotations are from Woody Allen, *The Floating Light Bulb*, Random House (New York, 1982).

19: A Midsummer Night's Sex Comedy

1. John Pym outlines the Bergman parallels in "'Well moused, Lion': A *Midsummer Night's Sex Comedy*," *Sight and Sound*, Autumn, 1982, p. 300. See Janet Maslin, "Woody Allen: Shunning Mastery?" *New York Times*, July 25, 1982, pp. 13, 16; Andrew Sarris, "Woody's Walpurgisnacht," *The Voice*, July 20, 1982, p. 41; and Pauline Kael, *Taking It All In*, pp. 365–68.

2. Professor Sturgis is a comic version of the stolid rationalist Gunnar Bjornstrand used to play for Bergman.

20: Zelig

1. The gag was quoted on the dust jackets of both *Getting Even* and *Side Effects*.

2. On the technology behind the film see Michelle Bogre, "Gordon Willis, ASC, and *Zelig*," *American Cinematographer*, April, 1984, pp. 43–48; Leonard Quart, "*Zelig*," *Cineaste*, XIII, iii (1984), pp. 42–43; and Evelyn Roth, "Photo Fictions: Brilliantly Faked Pictures of Woody Allen's *Zelig* Invent a Nonexistent Past," *American Photographer*, May, 1984, pp. 68–73.

3. Richard Combs finds the film a response to Pauline Kael's complaint that at the end of *Annie Hall* "Alvy and the story had disappeared; there was nothing left but Woody Allen's sadness" (Richard Combs, "Chameleon Days," *Monthly Film Bulletin*, November, 1983, pp. 295–96).

4. Peter Hogue and Marion Bronson, "*Zelig*," *Film Quarterly*, Fall, 1984, pp. 28–31; Andrew Sarris, "Woody Allen at the Peak of Parody," *The Voice*, July 19, 1983, p. 39. See too Peter Biskind, "Chameleon Man," *Vanity Fair*, December, 1983, p.96 ff; Richard Roud, "Is the Wizardry Worth It?" *The Guardian*, August 14, 1983, p. 19; Marshall Delaney (Robert Fulford), "The Kafka of Comedy," *Saturday Night*, November, 1983, pp. 83–84; Pauline Kael, *State of the Art*, pp. 23–25; John Pym, "Duke Ellington's brother: *Zelig*," *Sight and Sound*, Autumn, 1983, p. 283. For fuller analyses see Richard Feldstein, "The Dissolution of the Self in *Zelig*," *Literature/Film Quarterly*, 13, iii (1985), pp. 155–60; Ruth Perlmutter, "*Zelig* According to Bakhtin," *Quarterly Review of Film and Video*, 12, i–ii (1990), pp. 37–47; and Douglas Rathgeb, "Faces in the Newsreel: Illuminating *Citizen Kane* through Woody Allen's *Zelig*," *Post Script*, Spring/Summer, 1987, pp. 31–44.

5. Dee Burton, *I Dream of Woody*, William Morrow and Co. (New York, 1984).

6. Michiko Kakutani, "How Woody Allen's *Zelig* Was Born in Anxiety and Grew into Comedy," *New York Times*, July 18, 1983, p. 13.

21: Broadway Danny Rose

1. Gilbert Adair, "*Broadway Danny Rose*," *Monthly Film Bulletin*, September, 1984, p. 273.

2. Brian Henderson, "*Broadway Danny Rose*," *Film Quarterly*, Spring, 1986,

pp. 46–50; Pauline Kael, *State of the Art*, pp. 122–25. Cf. Mike Wilmington, "Orchids for Danny Rose," *LA Weekly*, February 17, 1984, pp. 27–28; Vincent Canby, " 'Danny Rose': Runyonesque But Pure Woody Allen," *New York Times*, January 29, 1984, p. 13; Michiko Kakutani, "Mia Farrow and Her Director on Their Film Collaboration," *New York Times*, January 22, 1984, pp. 1, 17; J. Hoberman, "Hecksapoppin," *The Voice*, March 12, 1986, p. 46; John Pym, "Sharing the Limelight: *Broadway Danny Rose*," *Sight and Sound*, Autumn, 1986, p. 300; Crystal Downing, "*Broadway Danny Rose*: Woody Allen's Romantic Inheritance," *Literature/Film Quarterly*, 17, i (1989), pp. 13–17.
   3. Nancy Pogel, *Woody Allen*, Twayne (New York, 1987), p. 193, 223.

22: *The Purple Rose of Cairo*

   1. Jeff Daniels has an open face and general image that suited the double role better than the too-contemporary Michael Keaton, whom he replaced two weeks into filming.
   2. This is one of the film's many echoes of Buster Keaton's *Sherlock Jr.* (1924). Allen's plot also recalls Fellini's *The White Sheik* (1951) and his closing close-up, with the heroine's recollecting resolve and optimism, the last shot of *Nights of Cabiria* (1956).
   3. Vernon Young, "Movie within a Movie," *The Film Criticism of Vernon Young*, edited by Bert Cardullo, University Press of America (Lanham, N.Y., 1990), pp. 388–93. Cf. Tim Pulleine, "Off-screen romance," *The Guardian*, July 25, 1985, p. 21; Vincent Canby, "Woody Allen Journeys from Page to Screen," *New York Times*, March 17, 1985, pp. 19, 26; J. Hoberman, "Hecksapoppin," *The Voice*, March 12, 1985, p. 46; Terrence Rafferty, "Slide!: *The Purple Rose of Cairo*," *Sight and Sound*, Summer, 1985, pp. 219–20. Pauline Kael found this Allen's "most purely charming film" (*State of the Art*, pp. 335–40). For fuller studies see Arnold Preussner, "Woody Allen's *The Purple Rose of Cairo* and The Genres of Comedy," *Literature/Film Quarterly*, 16, i (1988), pp. 39–43; Michael Dunne, "*Stardust Memories*, *The Purple Rose of Cairo*, and the Tradition of Metafiction," *Film Criticism*, Fall, 1987, pp. 19–27. Allen is interviewed in Eric Lax, "Woody Allen—Not Only a Comic," *New York Times*, February 24, 1985, p. 24; Henry Behar, *T.O.*, March/April, 1985, pp. 30–52. The film won the "best foreign film" award in France and the London film critics' award as best English-language film of the year, but Roland Joffe was the latter's Best Director for *The Killing Fields*.

23: *Hannah and Her Sisters*

   1. Andrew Sarris, "Woody Allen: You're the Top," *The Voice*, February 11, 1986, pp. 53–62. Sarris called *Hannah* "the great American film of the '80s." See Vincent Canby, "Woody Allen Tops Himself—Again," *New York Times*, February 9, 1986, pp. 23, 40; Anna Crystal, "*Hannah and Her Sisters*," *Films and Filming*, June, 1986, pp. 24–25; Caryn James, "Auteur! Auteur!" The Creative Mind of Woody Allen," *New York Times Magazine*, January 19, 1986; Pauline Kael, *Hooked*, E.P. Dutton (New York, 1989), pp. 113–16; Joe Klein, "Woody on the Town," *Gentleman's Quarterly*, February, 1986, pp. 170–75, 242–43. A detailed study is provided by Paul Salmon and Helen Bragg, "Woody Allen's Economy of Means: An Introduction to *Hannah and Her Sisters*," *Literature/Film Quarterly*, 16, i (1988), pp. 44–48. For a dissenting negative response see Richard Zoglin,

"Manhattan's Methuselah," *Film Comment*, June, 1986, pp. 16–20. Richard Combs objected to its "compendious . . . rambling, digressive" indulgence of Allen's familiar materials (in *"Hannah and Her Sisters," Monthly Film Bulletin*, July, 1986, pp. 196–98). On Allen's women's ensemble see Georgia A. Brown, "Much Ado about Mia," *American Film*, March, 1987, pp. 24–28; Maureen Dowd, "The Five Women of 'Hannah and Her Sisters,'" *New York Times*, February 2, 1986, pp. 1,33; and Ron Rosenbaum, "The Fall and Rise of Barbara Hershey," *American Film*, May, 1986, pp. 21–25. The film won Oscars for Allen's screenplay and for the supporting performances of Wiest and Caine.

2. In an even in-ner joke, the physician informing Mickey of his low sperm count, Dr. Smith, is played by Yale University President Benno C. Schmidt Jr.

3. Paradoxically, even in this position Allen finds himself evoking the Bergman of *Fanny and Alexander* (1982). The parallel emphasizes the epic scope of *Hannah and Her Sisters*—at 105 minutes Allen's longest film to date.

24: *Radio Days*

1. This discussion is adapted from the author's "The Religion of *Radio Days*," *Journal of Popular Film and Television*, Summer, 1988, pp. 80–87. On the making of *Radio Days* see Thierry de Navacelle, *Woody Allen on Location*, William Morrow (New York, 1987). For representative reviews see David Edelstein, "Easy Listening," *The Voice*, February 3, 1987. pp. 53, 60; Janet Maslin, "Woody Allen Savors the Details," *New York Times*, February 1, 1987, pp. 21, 28; Andrew Sarris, "Is Woody Strictly Kosher?" *The Voice*, February 10, 1987, p. 47; Armond White, "Class Clowns," *Film Comment*, April, 1987, pp. 11–14. Pauline Kael dismissed the film as "a museum piece" of reductive nostalgia (*Hooked*, pp. 274–78). Pearl K. Bell attacked the film for continuing Allen's "Jewish self-contempt . . . a witless misalliance of nostalgia and revulsion" (in "Woody Allen, Cultural Phenomenon," *Encounter*, June, 1988, pp. 72–75). David Lawrence interviewed Allen in "The fears of a clown," *The Independent*, June 22, 1987, p. 11.

2. This sentiment contrasts to the more common sensationalism, as in *Ace in the Hole* (a.k.a. *The Big Carnival*; Billy Wilder, 1951).

3. At fifteen million dollars, this was Allen's most expensive film.

25: *September*

1. This discussion is based on the author's review of *September* published in *Film Quarterly*, Fall, 1988, pp. 46–49. Pauline Kael dismissed the film as "all pallid and pristine" (*Hooked*, pp. 425–27). In an interview Allen called *September* "a small, intimate kind of film, principally dramatic but hopefully with some laughs in it" (William E. Geist, "The *Rolling Stone* Interview: Woody Allen," *Rolling Stone*, April 9, 1987, pp. 39 ff).

26: *Another Woman*

1. In "Remembering Needleman" Allen parodied Heidegger as a scandalously self-serving rationalizer. Woody Allen, *Side Effects* (New York: Random House, 1980), pp. 3–8.

2. Rainer Maria Rilke, *New Poems* (London: The Hogarth Press, 1964), translated by J. B. Leishman, p. 165.

3. Rilke, "The Panther," in *New Poems*, p. 89.

4. Tim Pulleine called the film "arguably the most substantial achievement" of Allen's career, in "*Another Woman*," *Monthly Film Bulletin*, August, 1989, pp. 232–33. Cf. Pauline Kael, "What's Wrong with This Picture?" *New Yorker*, October 31, 1988, pp. 81–83; Richard Combs, "Making His Day: Woody Allen," *Sight and Sound*, Summer, 1989, pp. 209–10.

28: Crimes and Misdemeanors

1. The film's apparent seriousness prompted the *New York Times* to invite analyses by a Lutheran professor, a rabbi, and an English professor (October, 15, 1989, pp. 15–16). Cf. Richard Allen, "*Crimes and Misdemeanors*," *Cineaste*, XVII, iv (1990), pp. 44–46; Richard Combs, "Woody's Wars," *Sight and Sound*, Summer, 1990, pp. 207–8; Janet Maslin, "Lately the Lens Frames Moral Issues," *New York Times*, October 22, 1989, pp. 15, 25. On the film's relation to *Hannah and Her Sisters* see Marcia Polly, "'Crimes' Story," *Film Comment*, November–December, 1989, pp. 11–15.

2. Pauline Kael objected that "If Woody Allen were interested in drama (rather than pieties), he wouldn't make us reject the emotional plight of the doctor's mistress" ("Floating," *The New Yorker*, October 30, 1989, pp. 76–78). She dismisses the film as "tony . . . fundamentalism."

3. *Roger Ebert's Movie Home Companion*, pp. 629–31.

Filmography

What's New, Pussycat? (1965). Director: Clive Donner. Producer: Charles K. Feldman. Screenplay: Woody Allen. Photography: Jean Badal (Technicolor, Scope). Music: Burt Bacharach. Editor: Fergus McDonell. Sound: William-Robert Sivel. Art Director: Jacques Saulnier. Assistant Director: Enrico Isacco. Special Effects: Bob MacDonald. A Famous Artists Production. 120 minutes.

Peter Sellers (Fritz Fassbender). Peter O'Toole (Michael James). Romy Schneider (Carol Werner). Capucine (Renée Lefebvre). Paula Prentiss (Liz Bien). Woody Allen (Victor Shakapopolis). Ursula Andress (Rita). Edra Gale (Anna Fassbender). Catherine Schaake (Jacqueline). Jess Hahn (Perry Werner). Eleanor Hirt (Sylvia Werner). Nicole Karen (Tempest O'Brien). Jean Paredes (Marcel). Michel Subor (Philippe). Jacqueline Fogt (Charlotte). Robert Rollis (Car Renter). Daniel Emilfork (Gas Station Attendant). Louis Falavigna (Jean, his friend). Jacques Balutin (Etienne). Annette Poivre (Emma). Sabine Sun (Nurse). Jean Yves Autrey, Pascal Wolf, Nadine Papin (Fassbender children). Tanya Lopert (Miss Lewis). Colin Drake (Durell), Norbert Terry (Kelly). F. Medard (Nash). Gordon Felio (Fat Man). Louise Lasser (The Nutcracker). Richard Saint-Bris (Mayor). Françoise Hardy (Mayor's secretary). Douking (Renée's concierge).

What's Up, Tiger Lily? (1966). Original version: *Kagi No Kagi (Key of Keys)*, (Japan, 1964). Director: Senkichi Taniguchi. Script: Hideo Ando. Photography: Kazuo Yamada (Eastmancolor, Scope). Produced by Tomoyuki Tanaka for Toho. 94 minutes.

Re-release Director: Woody Allen. Production Conception: Ben Shapiro. Editor: Richard Krown. Script and Dubbing: Woody Allen, Frank Buxton, Len Maxwell, Louise Lasser, Mickey Rose, Julie Bennett, Bryna Wilson. Music: The Lovin' Spoonful. 79 minutes.

Tatsuya Mihashi (Phil Moskowitz). Mie Hana (Terry Yaki). Akiko Wakayabayashi (Suki Yaki). Tadao Nakamaru (Shepherd Wong). Susumu Kurobe (Wing Fat).

Casino Royale (1967). Directors: John Huston, Kenneth Hughes, Val Guest, Robert Parrish, Joseph McGrath. Producers: Charles K. Feldman and Jerry Bresler. Screenplay: Wolf Mankowitz, John Law, Michael Sayers, suggested by the novel by Ian Fleming. Photography: Jack Hildyard (Panavision, Technicolor). Editor: Bill Lenny. Production Designer: Michael Ayringer. Special Effects: Cliff Richardson, Roy Whybrow. Music: Burt Bacharach. Titles, Montage: Richard Williams. A Famous Artists Production, released by Columbia Pictures. 131 minutes.

Peter Sellers (Evelyn Tremble). Ursula Andress (Vesper Lynd). David Nivin (Sir James Bond). Orson Welles (Le Chiffre). Joanna Pettet (Mata Bond). Deborah Kerr (Widow McTarry). Daliah Lavi (The Detainer). Woody Allen (Jimmy Bond). William Holden (Ransome). Charles Boyer (Le Grand). John Huston (M). Kurt Kaznar (Smernov). George Raft (Himself). Jean-Paul Belmondo (French Legionnaire). Terence Cooper (Cooper). Barbara Bouchet (Moneypenny). Angela Scoular (Buttercup). Gabriella Licudi (Eliza). Tracey Crisp (Heather). Jacky Bisset (Miss Goodthings). Anna Quayle (Frau Hoffner). Derek Nimmo (Hadley). Ronnie Corbett (Polo). Colin Gordon (Casino Director). Bernard Cribbens (Taxi Driver). Tracy Reed (Fang Leader). Duncan Macrae (Inspector Mathis). Graham Stark (Cashier). Richard Wattis (British Army Officer). Percy Herbert (First Piper).

Don't Drink the Water. (1969). Director: Howard Morris. Producer: Charles Joffe. Screenplay: R. S. Allen and Harvey Bullock, based upon the stageplay by Woody Allen. Photography: Harvey Genkins (Movielab, color). Music: Pat Williams. Art Director: Robert Gundlach. Editor: Ralph Rosenblum. Assistant Director: Louis Stroller. 98 minutes.

Jackie Gleason (Walter Hollander). Estelle Parsons (Marion Hollander). Ted Bessell (Axel Magee). Joan Delaney (Susan Hollander). Richard Libertini (Drobney). Michael Costantine (Krojack). Avery Schreiber (Sultan). Also: Howard St. John, Danny Mehan, Pierre Olaf, Phil Leeds, Mark Gordon, Dwayne Early, Joan Murphy, Martin Danzig, Rene Constantineau, Howard Morris.

Take the Money and Run (1969). Director: Woody Allen. Script: Woody Allen and Mickey Rose. Photography: Lester Shorr (Technicolor). Editing: Paul Jordan, Ron Kalish. Music: Marvin Hamlisch. Art Director:

Fred Harpman. Special Effects: A. D. Flowers. Assistant Directors: Louis Stroller, Walter Hill. Produced by Charles H. Joffe for Palomar Pictures. 85 minutes.

Woody Allen (Virgil Starkwell). Janet Margolin (Louise). Marcel Hillaire (Fritz). Jacqueline Hyde (Miss Blair). Lonnie Chapman (Jake). Jan Merlin (Al). James Anderson (Chain gang warden). Howard Storm (Red). Mark Gordon (Vince). Micil Murphy (Frank). Minnow Moskowitz (Joe Agneta). Nate Jacobson (Judge). Grace Bauer (Farm-house lady). Ethel Sokolow (Mother Starkwell). Henry Leff (Father Starkwell). Don Frazier (Psychiatrist). Mike O'Dowd (Michael Sullivan). Jackson Beck (Narrator). Louise Lasser (Kay Lewis).

Bananas (1971). Director: Woody Allen. Script: Woody Allen and Mickey Rose. Photography: Andrew M. Costikyan (Deluxe Color). Production Designer: Ed Wittstein. Music: Marvin Hamlisch. Editor: Ron Kalish. Associate Producer: Ralph Rosenblum. Assistant Director: Fred T. Gallo. Special Effects: Don B. Courtney. Produced by Jack Grossberg for Rollins and Joffe Productions. 81 minutes.

Woody Allen (Fielding Mellish). Louise Lasser (Nancy). Carlos Montalban (General Vargas). Natividad Abascal (Yolanda). Jacobo Morales (Esposito). Miguel Suarez (Luis). David Ortiz (Sanchez). Rene Enriquez (Diaz). Jack Axelrod (Arroyo). Howard Cosell (Himself). Roger Grimsby (Himself). Don Dunphy (Himself). Charlotte Rae (Mrs. Mellish). Stanley Ackerman (Dr. Mellish). Dan Frazer (Priest). Martha Greenhouse (Dr. Feigen). Axel Anderson (man tortured). Tigre Perez (Perez). Baron de Beer (British ambassador). Arthur Hughes (Judge). John Braden (Prosecutor). Ted Chapman (Policeman). Dorthi Fox (J. Edgar Hoover). Dagne Crane (Sharon). Ed Barth (Paul). Nicholas Saunders (Douglas). Conrad Bain (Semple). Eulogio Peraza (Interpreter). Norman Evans (Senator). Robert O'Connel and Robert Dudley (FBI). Marilyn Hengst (Norma). Ed Crowley and Beeson Carroll (FBI Security). Allen Garfield (Man on cross). Princess Fatosh (Snakebite lady). Dick Callinan (Ad man). Hy Anzel (Patient).

Play It Again, Sam (1972). Director: Herbert Ross. Production Supervisor: Roger M. Rothstein. Screenplay: Woody Allen, based on his stageplay. Photography: Owen Roizman (Technicolor). Music: Billy Goldenberg. Editor: Marion Rothman. Assistant Director: William Gerrity. An Arthur P. Jacobs Production for Paramount Pictures. 84 minutes.

Woody Allen (Allan Felix). Diane Keaton (Linda). Tony Roberts

(Dick). Jerry Lacy (Bogart). Susan Anspach (Nancy). Jennifer Salt (Sharon). Joy Bang (Julie). Viva (Jennifer). Suzanne Zenor (Discotheque girl). Diana Davila (Museum girl). Mari Fletcher (Fantasy Sharon). Michael Green and Ted Markland (Hoods).

Everything You Always Wanted To Know About Sex* (*but were afraid to ask) (1972). Director: Woody Allen. Script: Woody Allen, from the book by David Reuben. Photography: David M. Walsh (DeLuxe Color). Assistant Directors: Fred T. Gallo, Terry M. Carr. Editor: Eric Albertson. Music: Mundell Lowe. Production Design: Dale Hennesy. Produced by Charles H. Joffe for United Artists. 87 minutes.

Woody Allen (Fool, Fabrizio, Victor, Sperm). John Carradine (Dr. Bernardo). Lou Jacobi (Sam). Louise Lasser (Gina)'. Anthony Quayle (King). Tony Randall (Operator). Lynne Redgrave (Queen). Burt Reynolds (Switchboard). Gene Wilder (Dr. Ross). Jack Barry (Himself). Erin Fleming (The Girl). Elaine Giftos (Mrs. Ross). Toni Holt (Herself). Robert Q. Lewis (Himself). Heather Macrae (Helen). Pamela Mason (Herself). Sidney Miller (George). Regis Philbin (Himself). Titos Vandis (Milos). Stanley Adams (Stomach operator). Oscar Beregi (Brain control). Alan Caillou (Fool's father). Dort Clark (Sheriff). Geoffrey Holder (Sorcerer). Jay Robinson (Priest). Ref Sanchez (Igor). Don Chuy and Tom Mack (football players). Baruch Lumet (Rabbi Baumel). Robert Walden (Sperm). H. E. West (Bernard Jaffe).

Sleeper (1973). Director: Woody Allen. Script: Woody Allen, Marshall Brickman. Photography: David M. Walsh (DeLuxe Color). Editor: Ralph Rosenblum. Production Designer: Dale Hennesy. Assistant Directors: Fred T. Gallo, Henry J. Lange, Jr. Special Effects: A. D. Flowers. Music by Woody Allen with the Preservation Hall Jazz Band and the New Orleans Funeral Ragtime Orchestra. Dr. Melik's house designed by Charles Deaton, architect. Produced by Jack Grossberg for Jack Rollins and Charles Joffe Productions. 88 minutes.

Woody Allen (Miles Monroe). Diane Keaton (Luna Schlosser). John Beck (Erno Windt). Mary Gregory (Dr. Melik). Don Keefer (Dr. Tryon). John McLiam (Dr. Agon). Bartlett Robinson (Dr. Orva). Chris Forbes (Rainer Krebs). Marya Small (Dr. Nero). Peter Hobbs (Dr. Dean). Susan Miller (Ellen Pogrebin). Lou Picetti (Master of Ceremonies). Jessica Rains (Woman in the mirror). Brian Avery (Herald Cohen). Spencer Milligan (Jeb Hrmthmg) [sic]. Stanley Ross (Sears Swiggles).

Love and Death (1975). Director: Woody Allen. Photography: Ghislain Cloquet (DeLuxe Color). Script: Woody Allen. Editing: Ralph Rosenblum, Ron Kalish. Assistant Directors: Paul Feyder, Bernard Cohn. Special Effects: Kit West. Music: S. Prokofiev. Art Director: Willy Holt. Costume Designer: Gladys De Segonzac. Produced by Charles H. Joffe for Jack Rollins and Charles H. Joffe Productions. 85 minutes.

Woody Allen (Boris). Diane Keaton (Sonia). Georges Adet (Old Nehamken). Frank Adu (Drill sergeant). Edmond Ardisson (Priest). Feodor Atkine (Mikhail). Albert Augier (Waiter). Yves Barsaco (Rimsky). Lloyd Battista (Don Francisco). Jack Berard (General Lecoq). Eva Bertrand (Woman in hygiene lesson). George Birt (Doctor). Yves Brainville (Andre). Gerard Buhr (Servant). Brian Coburn (Dmitri). Henri Coutet (Minskov). Patricia Crown (Cheerleader). Henry Czarniak (Ivan). Despo Diamantidou (Mother). Sandor Eles (Soldier). Luce Fabiole (Grandmother). Florian (Uncle Nikolai). Jacqueline Fogt (Ludmilla). Sol L. Frieder (Voskovec). Olga Georges-Picot (Countess Alexandrovna). Harold Gould (Count Anton). Harry Hankin (Uncle Sasha). Jessica Harper (Natasha). Tony Jan (Vladimir Maximovitch). Tutte Lemkow (Pierre). Jack Lenoir (Krapotkin). Leib Lensky (Father Andre). Ann Lonnberg (Olga). Roger Lumont (Baker). Alfred Lutter III (Young Boris). Ed Marcus (Raskov). Jacques Maury (Second). Narcissa McKinley (Cheerleader). Aubrey Morris (Soldier). Denise Peron (Spanish Countess). Beth Porter (Anna). Alan Rossett (Guard). Shimen Ruskin (Borslov). Persival Russel (Berdykov). Chris Sanders (Joseph). Zvee Scooler (Father). C. A. R. Smith (Father Nikolai). Fred Smith (Soldier). Bernard Taylor (Soldier). Clement-Thierry (Jacques). Alan Tilvern (Sergeant). James Tolkan (Napoleon). Helene Vallier (Madame Wolfe). Howard Vernon (General Leveque). Glenn Williams (Soldier). Jacob Witkin (Sushkin).

The Front (1976). Produced and Directed by Martin Ritt. Script: Walter Bernstein, Music: Dave Grusin. Photography: Michael Chapman (Panavision color). Art Director: Charles Bailey. Editor: Sidney Levin. Assistant Directors: Peter Scoppa, Ralph Singleton. A Martin Ritt-Jack Rollins-Charles H. Joffe Production, distributed by Columbia Pictures. 94 minutes.

Woody Allen (Howard Prince). Zero Mostel (Hecky Brown). Herschel Bernardi (Phil Sussman). Michael Murphy (Alfred Miller). Andrea Marcovicci (Florence Barrett). Remak Ramsay (Hennessey). Marvin Lichterman (Myer Prince). Lloyd Gough (Delaney). David Margulies

(Phelps). Joshua Shelley (Sam). Norman Rose (Howard's Attorney). Charles Kimbrough (Committee Counselor). M. Josef Sommer (Committee Chairman). Danny Aiello (Danny La Gattuta). Georgann Johnson (TV interviewer). Scott McKay (Hampton). David Clarke (Hubert Jackson). J. W. Klein (Bank teller). John Bentley (Bartender). Julie Garfield (Margo). Murray Moston (Boss). McIntyre Dixon (Harry Stone). Rudolph Wilrich (Tailman). Burt Britton (Bookseller). Albert M. Ottenheimer (School principal). William Bogert (Parks). Joey Faye (Waiter). Marilyn Sokol (Sandy). John J. Slater (TV director). Renee Paris (Girl in hotel lobby). Joan Porter (Stage-hand). Andrew and Jacob Bernstein (Alfred's children). Matthew Tobin (Man at party). Marilyn Persky (His date). Sam McMurray (Young man at party). Joe Jamrog and Michael Miller (FBI men). Jack Davidson and Donald Symington (Congressmen). Patrick McNamara (Federal Marshal).

Woody Allen: An American Comedy (1977). Produced and Directed by Harold Mantell, for Films for the Humanities, Inc. (P.O. Box 2053, Princeton, N.J., 08540). Narrated by Woody Allen. 30 minutes.

Annie Hall (1977). Director: Woody Allen. Script: Woody Allen and Marshall Brickman. Photography: Gordon Willis (Panavision DeLuxe). Editor: Ralph Rosenblum. Art Director: Mel Bourne. Animated Sequences: Chris Ishii. Assistant Directors: Fred T. Gallo, Fred Blankfein. Costume Designer: Ruth Morley. Produced by Charles H. Joffe for Jack Rollins and Charles H. Joffe Productions. Distributed by United Artists. 93 minutes.

Woody Allen (Alvy Singer). Diane Keaton (Annie Hall). Tony Roberts (Rob). Carol Kane (Allison). Paul Simon (Tony Lacy). Shelley Duvall (Pam). Janet Margolin (Robin). Colleen Dewhurst (Mom Hall). Christopher Walken (Duane). Donald Symington (Dad Hall). Helen Ludlam (Granny Hall). Mordecai Lawner (Alvy's father). Joan Newman (Alvy's mother). Jonathan Munk (Alvy, aged 9). Ruth Volner (Alvy's aunt). Martin Rosenblatt (Alvy's uncle). Hy Ansel (Joey Nichols). Rashel Novikoff (Aunt Tessie). Russell Horton (Man in theater line). Marshall McLuhan (Himself). Christine Jones (Dorrie). Mary Boylan (Miss Reed). Wendy Girard (Janet). John Doumanian (Coke fiend). Bob Maroff and Rick Petrucelli (Men outside theater). Lee Callahan (Ticket-seller at theater). Chris Gampel (Doctor). Dick Cavett (Himself). Mark Leonard (Navy Officer). Dan Ruskin (Comedian at rally). John Glover (Actor boyfriend). Bernie Styles (Comic's agent). Johnny

Haymer (Comic). Ved Bandhu (Maharishi). John Dennis Johnston (Los Angeles Policeman). Lauri Bird (Tony Lacy's girlfriend). Jim McKrell, Jeff Goldblum, William Callaway, Roger Newman, Alan Landers, Jean Sarah Frost (Lacy's party guests). Vince O'Brien (Hotel Doctor). Humphrey Davis (Alvy's psychiatrist). Veronica Radburn (Annie's psychiatrist). Robin Mary Paris (Actress in rehearsal). Charles Levin (Actor in rehearsal). Wayne Carson (Rehearsal stage manager). Michael Karm (Rehearsal director). Petronia Johnson, Shaun Casey (Tony's dates at nightclub). Ricardo Bertoni, Michael Aronin (Waiters at nightclub). Lou Picetti, Loretta Tupper, James Burge, Shelly Hack, Albert Ottenheimer, Paula Trueman (Street strangers). Beverly D'Angelo, Tracey Walter (Stars in Rob's TV show). David Wier, Keith Dentice, Susan Mellinger, Hamit Perezic, James Balter, Eric Gould, Amy Levitan (Alvy's classmates). Gary Allen, Frank Vohs, Sybil Bowan, Margaretta Warwick (Teachers). Lucy Lee Flippen (Health Food waitress). Gary Muledeer (Man at restaurant). Sigourney Weaver (Alvy's date outside theater). Walter Bernstein (Annie's date outside theater). Artie Butler (Annie's accompanist).

Interiors (1978). Written and Directed by Woody Allen. Photography: Gordon Willis. Editor: Ralph Rosenblum. Production Designer: Mel Bourne. Assistant Director: Martin Berman. Costume Designer: Joel Schumacher. Produced by Charles H. Joffe for Jack Rollins-Charles H. Joffe Productions. Distributed by United Artists. 93 minutes.

Kristen Griffith (Flyn). Mary Beth Hurt (Joey). Richard Jordan (Frederick). Diane Keaton (Renata). E. G. Marshall (Arthur). Geraldine Page (Eve). Maureen Stapleton (Pearl). Sam Waterston (Mike).

Manhattan (1979). Director: Woody Allen. Script: Woody Allen and Marshall Brickman. Photography: Gordon Willis (black and white). Editor: Susan E. Morse. Production Designer: Mel Bourne. Costumes: Albert Wolsky. Music by George Gershwin, adapted and arranged by Tom Pierson; performed by the New York Philharmonic, conducted by Zubin Mehta, and the Buffalo Philharmonic, conducted by Michael Tilson Thomas. Assistant Directors: Fredric B. Blankfein, Joan Spiegel Feinstein. Executive Producer: Robert Greenhut. Produced by Charles H. Joffe for Rollins-Joffe Productions. Distributed by United Artists. 96 minutes.

Woody Allen (Isaac Davis). Diane Keaton (Mary Wilke). Michael Murphy (Yale). Mariel Hemingway (Tracy). Meryl Streep (Jill). Anne

Byrne (Emily). Karen Ludwig (Connie). Michael O'Donoghue (Dennis). Victor Truro, Tisa Farrow, Helen Hanft (party guests). Bella Abzug (guest of honor). Gary Weis, Kenny Vance (TV producers). Charles Levin, Karen Allen, David Rasche (TV actors). Damion Sheller (Willie). Wallace Shawn (Jeremiah). Mark Linn Baker, Frances Conroy (Shakespearean actors). Bill Anthony, John Doumanian (Porsche owners). Ray Serra (pizzeria waiter). "Waffles" trained by Dawn Animal Agency.

Stardust Memories (1980). Director: Woody Allen. Script: Woody Allen. Photography: Gordon Willis. Editor: Susan Morse. Production Designer: Mel Bourne. Costume Designer: Santo Loquasto. Produced by Robert Greenhut for Jack Rollins and Charles Joffe Productions. 89 minutes.

Woody Allen (Sandy Bates). Charlotte Rampling (Dorrie). Jessica Harper (Daisy). Marie-Christine Barrault (Isobel). Tony Roberts (Tony). Daniel Stern (actor). Amy Wright (Shelley). Helen Hanft (Vivian Orkin). John Rothman (Jack Abel). Anne De Salvo (Sandy's sister). Joan Neuman (Sandy's mother). Ken Chapin (Sandy's father). Leonardo Cimino (Sandy's analyst). Eli Mintz (old man). Bob Maroff (Jerry Abraham). Gabrielle Strasun (Charlotte Ames). David Lipman (Sandy's chauffeur). Robert Munk (boy Sandy). Jaqui Safra (Sam). Sharon Stone (beauty on train). Andy Albeck, Robert Friedman, Douglas Ireland, Jack Rollins (studio executives). Howard Kissel (Sandy's manager). Max Leavitt (Sandy's doctor). Renee Lippin (Sandy's press agent). Sol Lomita (Sandy's accountant). Irving Metzman (Sandy's lawyer). Dorothy Leon (Sandy's cook). Roy Brocksmith (Dick Lobel). Simon Newey (Mr. Payson). Victoria Zussin (Mrs. Payson). Frances Pole (Libby). Judith Roberts (singer: "Three Little Words"). Barry Weiss (dancer: "Three Little Words"). Noel Behn (Doug Orkin). Candy Loving (Tony's girl friend). Benjamin Rayson (Dr. Paul Pearlstein). Mary Mims (Claire Schaeffer). Charles Lowe (vaudeville singer). Marie Lane (singer: "Brazil"). Joseph Summo (Hostility). Victor Truro (Hostility psychoanalyst). E. Brian Dean (police sergeant). Marvin Peisner (Ed Rich). Philip Lenkowsky (assassin). Vanina Holasek (Isoberl's daughter). Michel Touchard (Isobel's son). Wade Barnes (astrologer). Alice Spivak (nurse). John Doumanian (Armenian fan). Jack Hollander (police arresting Sandy). Jazz Heaven Orchestra Featuring Joe Wilder, Hank Jones, Richie Pratt, Arvell Shaw, Earl Shendell. Piano music arranged and performed by Dick Hyman.

A Midsummer Night's Sex Comedy (1982). Director: Woody Allen. Script: Woody Allen. Photography: Gordon Willis. Color: Technicolor. Editor:

Susan Morse. Production Designer: Mel Bourne. Costume Designer: Santo Loquasto. Animation effects: Kurtz & Friends, Zander's Animation Parlour. Inventions: Eoin Sprott Studio. Produced by Robert Greenhut for Jack Rollins and Charles H. Joffe Productions. 88 minutes.

Woody Allen (Andrew Hobbs). Mia Farrow (Ariel Weymouth). Jose Ferrer (Professor Leopold Sturgis). Julie Hagerty (Dulcy Ford). Tony Roberts (Dr. Maxwell Jordan). Mary Steenburgen (Adrian Hobbs). Adam Redfield (student Foxx). Moishe Rosenfeld (Mr. Hayes). Timothy Kenkins (Mr. Thomson). Michael Higgins (Reynolds). Sol Frieder (Carstairs). Boris Zoubok (Purvis). Thomas Barbour (Blint). Kate McGregor-Stewart (Mrs. Baker).

Zelig (1983). Director: Woody Allen. Script: Woody Allen. Photography: Gordon Willis. Production Designer: Mel Bourne. Costume Designer: Santo Loquasto. Editor: Susan Morse. Music: Dick Hyman. Produced by Robert Greenhut for Jack Rollins and Charles Joffe Productions. 79 minutes.

Woody Allen (Zelig). Mia Farrow (Dr. Eudora Fletcher). John Buckwalter (Dr. Sindell). Marvin Chatinover (Glandular Diagnosis Doctor). Stanley Swerdlow (Mexican Food Doctor). Paul Nevens (Dr. Birsky). Howard Erskine (Hypodermic Doctor). George Hamlin (Experimental Drugs Doctor). Ralph Bell, Richard Whiting, Will Hussong (Other Doctors). Robert Iglesia (Man in barber chair). Sol Lomita (Martin Geist). Mary Louise Wilson (Sister Ruth). Marianne Tatum (Actress Fletcher). Charles Denny (Actor Doctor). Michael Kell (Actor Koslow). Garrett Brown (Actor Zelig). Sharon Ferroll (Miss Baker). Richard Litt (Charles Koslow). John Rothman (Paul Deghuee). Stephanie Farrow (Sister Meryl). Jean Trowbridge (Eudora's Mother). Deborah Rush (Lita Fox). Stanley Simmonds (Zelig's lawyer). Susan Sontag, Irving Howe, Saul Bellow, Bricktop, Bruno Bettelheim, John Morton Blum (Contemporary Interviews), Ellen Garrison (Older Dr. Fletcher). Sherman Loud (Older Paul Deghuee). Elizabeth Rothschild (Older Sister Meryl). Patrick Horgan (Narrator). Ed Herlihy, Dwight West, Gordon Gould, Windy Craig, Jurgen Kuehn (Announcers).

Broadway Danny Rose (1984). Director: Woody Allen. Script: Woody Allen. Photography: Gordon Willis. Editor: Susan Morse. Production Designer: Mel Bourne. Costume Designer: Jeffrey Kurland. Music: Dick Hyman. "Agita" and "My Bambina" by and performed by Nick Apollo Forte. Produced by Robert Greenhut for Jack Rollins and Charles Joffe Productions. 84 minutes.

Woody Allen (Danny Rose). Mia Farrow (Tina Vitale). Nick Apollo Forte (Lou Canova). Sandy Baron, Corbett Monica, Jackie Gayle, Morty Gunty, Will Jordan, Howard Storm, Jack Rollins, Milton Berle, Joe Franklin, Howard Cosell (Themselves). Craig Vandenburgh (Ray Webb). Herb Reynolds (Barney Dunn). Paul Greco (Vito Rispoli). Frank Renzulli (Joe Rispoli). Edwin Bordo (Johnny Rispoli). Gina DeAngelis (Johnny's mother). Peter Castellotti (Warehouse hood). Sandy Richman (Teresa). Gerald Schoenfeld (Sid Bacharach). Olga Barbato (Angelina). David Kissell (Phil Chomsky). Gloria Parker (Waterglass virtuoso). Bob Rollins and Etta Rollins (Balloon act). Bob Weil (Herbie Jayson). David Kieserman (Ralph). Mark Hardwick (Blind xylophonist). Alba Ballard (Bird lady). Maurice Shrog (Hypnotist). Belle Berger (Lady in trance). Herschel Rosen (Husband). Maggie Ranone (Lou's daughter). Charles D'Amodio (Lou's son). Joie Gallo (Angelina's assistant). Carl Pistilli (Tommy's brother). Lucy Iacono (Tommy's mother). Tony Turca (Rocco). Gilda Torterello (Annie). Ronald Maccone (Vincent). Dom Matteo (Carmine). John Doumanian (Waldorf manager). Leo Steiner (Deli owner).

The Purple Rose of Cairo (1985). Director: Woody Allen. Script: Woody Allen. Photography: Gordon Willis. Editor: Susan Morse. Production Designer: Stuart Wurtzel. Costume Designer: Jeffrey Kurland. Music: Dick Hyman. Produced by Robert Greenhut for Jack Rollins and Charles Joffe Productions. 82 minutes.

Mia Farrow (Cecilia). Jeff Daniels (Tom Baxter, Gil Shepherd). Danny Aiello (Monk). Irving Metzman (Theater manager). Stephanie Farrow (Cecilia's sister). David Kieserman (Diner boss). Tom Degidon (Ticket taker). Mary Hedahl (Popcorn seller). Ed Herrmann (Henry). John Wood (Jason). Deborah Rush (Rita). Van Johnson (Larry). Zoe Caldwell (The Countess). Eugene Anthony (Arturo). Ebb Miller (Bandleader). Karen Akers (Kitty Haynes). Annie Joe Edwards (Delilah). Milo O'Shea (Father Donnelly). Peter McRobbie (Communist). Camille Saviola (Olga). Juliana Donald (Usherette). Dianne Wiest (Emma). Alexander Cohen (Raoul Hirsh). John Rothman (Mr. Hirsh's lawyer). Michael Tucker (Gil's agent). Glenne Headley, Willie Tjan, Lela Ivey, Drinda LaLumia (Hookers). Loretta Tupper (Music store owner).

Hannah and Her Sisters (1986). Director: Woody Allen. Script: Woody Allen. Photography: Carlo DiPalma. Color: Technicolor. Editor: Susan Morse. Production Designer: Stuart Wurtzel. Costume Designer: Jeffrey Kurland. Produced by Robert Greenhut for Jack Rollins and Charles Joffe Productions. 107 minutes.

Woody Allen (Mickey Sachs). Michael Caine (Elliot). Mia Farrow
(Hannah). Carrie Fisher (April). Barbara Hershey (Lee). Lloyd Nolan
(Evan). Maureen O'Sullivan (Norma). Daniel Stern (Dusty). Max von
Sydow (Frederick). Dianne Wiest (Holly). Sam Waterston (David). Tony
Roberts (Mickey's ex-partner). Lewis Black (Paul). Julia Louis-Dreyfus
(Mary). Christian Clemenson (Larry). Julie Kavner (Gail). J. T. Walsh (Ed
Smythe). John Turturro (Writer). Rusty Magee (Ron). Allen DeCheser and
Artie DeCheser (Hannah's twins). Ira Wheeler (Dr. Abel). Richard Jenkins
(Dr. Wilkes). Tracy Kennedy (Brunch guest). Fred Melamed (Dr. Grey).
Benno Schmidt (Dr. Smith). Joanna Gleason (Carol). Maria Chiara
(Manon Lescaut). Stephen deFluiter (Dr. Brooks). The 39 Steps (Rock
band). Bobby Short (Himself). Rob Scott (Drummer). Beverly Peer (Bass
player). Daisy Previn and Moses Farrow (Hannah's children). Paul Bates
(Theater manager). Carotte Pappas and Mary Pappas (Theater executives).
Bernie Leighton (Audition pianist). Ken Costigan (Father Flynn). Helen
Miller (Mickey's mother). Leo Postrel (Mickey's father). Susan Gordon-
Clark (Hostess). William Sturgis (Elliot's analyst). Daniel Haber (Krishna).
Verna Hobson (Mavis). Ivan Kronenfeld (Lee's husband). Woody Allen
(Narrator).

Radio Days (1987). Director: Woody Allen. Script: Woody Allen. Pho-
tography: Carlo DiPalma. Color: DuArt. Editor: Susan Morse. Production
Designer: Santo Loquasto. Costume Designer: Jeffrey Kurland. Music:
Dick Hyman. Produced by Robert Greenhut for Jack Rollins and Charles
Joffe Productions. 88 minutes.

Seth Green (Little Joe). Julie Kavner (Mother). Michael Tucker (Father).
Dianne Wiest (Aunt Bea). Josh Mostel (Uncle Abe). Renee Lippin (Aunt
Ceil). William Magerman (Grandpa). Leah Carrey (Grandma). Joy New-
man (Ruthie). Mia Farrow (Sally White). Julie Kurnitz (Irene). David
Warrilow (Roger Daly). Wallace Shawn (Masked Avenger). Kenneth Mars
(Rabbi Baumel). Jeff Daniels (Biff Baxter). Danny Aiello (Rocco). Gina
DeAngelis (Rocco's mother). Tony Roberts ("Silver Dollar" Emcee). Diane
Keaton (New Year's singer). Guy LeBow (Bill Kern). Marc Colner (Whiz
Kid). Richard Portnow (Sy). Roger Hammer (Richard). Mike Starr and
Paul Herman (Burglars). Don Pardo ("Guess That Tune" host). Martin
Rosenblatt (Mr. Needleman). Helen Miller (Mrs. Needleman). Danielle
Ferland (Child star). William Flanagan (Avenger Announcer). Hy Anzell
(Mr. Waldbaum). Judith Malina (Mrs. Waldbaum). Fletcher Farrow Pre-
vin (Andrew). Mindy Morgenstern ("Show and Tell" Teacher). Andrew
Clark (Sidney Manulis). Tito Puente (Latin bandleader). Denise Dumm-
ont (Communist's daughter). Belle Berger (Mrs. Silverman). Brian Man-

nain (Kirby Kyle). Stan Burns (Ventriloquist). Todd Field (Crooner). Peter Lombard (Abercrombie host). Martin Sherman (Mr. Abercrombie). Roberta Bennett (Teacher with carrot). J. R. Horne (Biff announcer). Sydney Blake (Miss Gordon). Kitty Carlisle Hart (Radio singer). Ivan Kronenfeld (On-the-spot newsman). Frank O'Brien (Fireman). Yolanda Childress (Polly's mother). Greg Almquist, Jackson Beck, Wendell Craig, W. H. Macy, Ken Roberts, Norman Rose, Kenneth Welsh (Radio voices).

September (1987). Director: Woody Allen. Script: Woody Allen. Photography: Carlo DiPalma. Color: DuArt. Editor: Susan Morse. Production Designer: Santo Loquasto. Costume Designer: Jeffrey Kurland. Produced by Robert Greenhut for Jack Rollins and Charles Joffe Productions. 83 minutes.

Denholm Elliott (Howard). Dianne Wiest (Stephanie). Mia Farrow (Lane). Elaine Stritch (Diane). Sam Waterston (Peter). Jack Warden (Lloyd). Ira Wheeler (Mr. Raines). Jane Cecil (Mrs. Raines). Rosemary Murphy (Mrs. Mason).

Another Woman (1988). Director: Woody Allen. Script: Woody Allen. Photography: Sven Nykvist. Color: DuArt. Editor: Susan Morse. Production Designer: Santo Loquasto. Costume Designer: Jeffrey Kurland. Produced by Robert Greenhut for Jack Rollins and Charles Joffe Productions. 81 minutes.

Gena Rowlands (Marion Post). Mia Farrow (Hope). Ian Holm (Ken). Blythe Danner (Lydia). Gene Hackman (Larry Lewis). Betty Buckley (Kathy). Martha Plimpton (Laura). John Houseman (Marion's father). Sandy Dennis (Claire). David Ogden Stiers (Young Marion's father). Philip Bosco (Sam). Harris Yulin (Paul). Frances Conroy (Lynn). Fred Melamed (Patient's voice). Kenneth Welsh (Donald). Bruce Jay Friedman (Mark). Bernie Leighton (Piano player). Jack Gelber, Paul Sills, John Schenck (Birthday party guests). Noel Behn, Gretchen Dahm, Janet Frank, Dana Ivey, Fred Melamed, Alice Spivak (Engagement party guests). Mary Laslo (Clara). Carol Schultz (Young Clara). Dax Munna (Little Paul). Heather Sullivan (Little Marion). Margaret Marx (Young Marion). Jennifer Lynn McComb (Young Claire). Caroline McGee (Marion's mother). Stephen Mailer (Young Paul). Jacques Levy (Jack). Dee Dee Friedman (Waitress). Josh Hamilton (Laura's boyfriend). Kathryn Grody (Cynthia). John Madden Towey (Waiter). Michael Kirby (Psychiatrist). Fred Sweda (Tom Banks). Jill Whitaker (Eleanor Banks).

New York Stories (1989). "Oedipus Wrecks." Director: Woody Allen. Script: Woody Allen. Photography: Sven Nykvist. Color: Technicolor.

Editor: Susan Morse. Production Designer: Santo Loquasto. Costume Designer: Jeffrey Kurland. Produced by Robert Greenhut for Jack Rollins and Charles Joffe Productions.

Woody Allen (Sheldon Mills). Marvin Chatinover (Psychiatrist). Mae Questel (Sadie Millstein). Mia Farrow (Lisa). Molly Regan (Sheldon's secretary). Ira Wheeler (Mr. Bates). Joan Bud (Board member). Jessie Keosian (Aunt Ceil). Michael Rizzo (Waiter). George Schindler (Shandu the Magician). Bridgit Ryan (Rita). Larry David (Theater manager). Paul Herman (Detective Flynn). Herschel Rosen (Store clerk). Lola Andre, Martin Rosenblatt, Helen Hanft, Annie-Joe, Ernst Muller, Adele French, Selma Hirsch, Briz, Lou Riggiero, Elena Cooper (Citizens). Andrew MacMillan (Newscaster). Jodi Long, Nancy Giles (TV Interviewers). Mayor Edward Koch (Himself). Mike Starr, Richard Grund (Hardhats). Julie Kavner (Treva).

Crimes and Misdemeanors (1989). Director: Woody Allen. Script: Woody Allen. Photography: Sven Nykvist. Color: DuArt. Editor: Susan Morse. Production Designer: Santo Loquasto. Costume Designer: Jeffrey Kurland. Produced by Robert Greenhut for Jack Rollins and Charles Joffe Productions. 104 minutes.

Caroline Aaron (Barbara). Alan Alda (Lester). Woody Allen (Clifford Stern). Claire Bloom (Miriam Rosenthal). Mia Farrow (Halley Reed). Joanna Gleason (Wendy Stern). Anjelica Huston (Dolores Paley). Martin Landau (Judah Rosenthal). Jenny Nichols (Jenny). Jerry Orbach (Jack Rosenthal). Bill Bernstein (Testimonial speaker). Stephanie Roth (Sharon Rosenthal). Gregg Edelman (Chris). George Manos (Photographer). Sam Waterston (Ben). Zina Jasper (Carol). Dolores Sutton (Judah's secretary). Joel S. Fogel, Donna Castelanno, Thomas P. Crow (TV Producers). Martin Bergmann (Professor Louis Levy). Kenny Vance (Murray). Jerry Zakes (Man on campus). Barry Finkel, Steve Maidment (TV writers). Nadia Sanford (Alva). Chester Malinowski (Hit man). Stanley Garrett Simowitz (Young Judah). Frances Conroy (House owner). Anna Berger (Aunt May). Victor Argo (Detective). Grace Zimmerman (Bride). Randy Aaron Fink (Groom). Rabbi Joel Zion (Rabbi). Major Halley Jr., Walter Levinsky, George Masso, Charles Miles, Derek Smith, Warren Vache (Jazz band). Pete Antell, Anthony Gorrusso, Gary Allen Meyers, Lee Musiker, Tony Sotos, Tony Tedeasco (Wedding band).

Alice (1990). Director: Woody Allen. Script: Woody Allen. Photography: Carlo DiPalma. Editor: Susan Morse. Production Designer: Santo Loquasto. Costume Designer: Jeffrey Kurland. Produced by Robert Greenhut for Jack Rollins and Charles H. Joffe Productions.

Joe Mantegna (Joe). Mia Farrow (Alice). William Hurt (Doug). June Squibb (Hilda). Marceline Hugot (Monica). Dylan O'Sullivan Farrow (Kate). Matt Williamson (Dennis). Julie Kavner (decorator). Billy Taylor (trainer). Holland Taylor (Helen). Michael-Vaughn Sullivan (Hair stylist). Robin Bartlett (Nina). Linda Wallem (Penny). Gina Gallagher (Joe's daughter). Patience Moore (School teacher). Diane Cheng (Dr. Yang's assistant). Kim Chan (Dr. Yang's patient). Keye Luke (Dr. Yang). Lynda Bridges (Saleslady). Anthony Cortino (dog groomer). Judy Davis (Vicki). Cybill Shepherd (Nancy Brill). Alec Baldwin (Eddie). Katja Schumann (circus equestrienne). Vanessa Thomas (aerialist). Blythe Danner (Dorothy). Gwen Verdon (Alice's mother). Patrick O'Neal (Alice's father). Kristy Graves (Alice at eighteen). Laurie Nayber (young Dorothy). Rachel Miner (Alice at twelve). Amy Louise Barrett (Mrs. Keyes). Caroline Aaron (Sue). Alexi Henry (Kimberley). James Toback (Professor). Bernadette Peters (Muse). Elle Macpherson (model). Ira Wheeler, Lisa Marie (office party guests). Diane Salinger (Carol). Alfred Cherry (Vicki's analyst). David Spielberg (Ken). Bob Balaban (Sid Moscowitz). Peggy Miley (Dorothy's maid).

Discography

Woody Allen: Colpix CP 488, 1964.
Woody Allen, Vol. 2: Colpix CP 518, 1965.
The Third Woody Allen Album: Capitol ST 2986, n.d.
Woody Allen: The Night-Club Years, 1964–1968: United Artists UA 9968, 1976.
Woody Allen: Standup Comic, 1964–1968: United Artists UA-LA 849-J2, 1978.

Bibliography

Works by Woody Allen

Annie Hall, *L'Avant-Scène*, Paris, December 15, 1977.

"Attention! See Europe with the King of the International Set (me)." *Esquire*, February, 1966, pp. 67–91.

"By Destiny Denied," *The New Yorker*, February 23, 1976, pp. 33–35.

"The Condemned," *The New Yorker*, November 21, 1977, pp. 57–59.

"Confessions of a Burglar," *The New Yorker*, October 18, 1976, pp. 35–37.

Death, Samuel French, Inc., 1975.

Don't Drink the Water, Samuel French, Inc., 1967.

"Everything You've Always Wanted To Know About Sex You'll Find In My New Movie," *Playboy*, September, 1972, pp. 115–19.

"Fabrizio's: Criticism and Response," *The New Yorker*, February 5, 1979, pp. 31–32.

Getting Even, Random House, 1971.

"The Girls of *Casino Royale*," *Playboy*, February, 1967, pp. 109–11.

God, Samuel French, Inc., 1975.

"How Bogart Made Me the Superb Lover I Am Today," *Life*, March 21, 1969, pp. 64–67.

"The Kugelmass Episode," *The New Yorker*, May 2, 1977, pp. 34–39.

"The Lunatic's Tale," *The New Republic*, April 23, 1977, pp 17–19.

"Nefarious Times We Live In," *The New Republic*, November 22, 1975, pp. 7–8.

Non-Being and Somethingness, Random House, 1978.

"On *Love and Death*," *Esquire*, July 19, 1975, pp. 79–83.

Play It Again, Sam (play), Samuel French, Inc., 1969.

314

Play It Again, Sam (film), edited by Richard Anobile, Grossett and Dunlop, 1977.
"The Query," *The New Republic*, September 18, 1976, pp. 11–13.
Quoi de Neuf, Pussycat?, *L'Avant-Scène*, Paris, Numéro 59, 1966.
"Remembering Needleman: At the Cremation," *The New Republic*, July 24, 1976, pp. 4–6.
"Reminiscences: Places and People," *The New Yorker*, December 29, 1975, pp. 20–21.
"The UFO Menace," *The New Yorker*, June 13, 1977, pp. 31–33.
"What's Nude Pussycat?" *Playboy*, August, 1965, pp. 99–107.
Without Feathers, Random House, 1975; Warner Books paperback, 1976.
"Woody, The Would-Be Critic," *The New York Times*, Sunday, May 2, 1971, Arts and Leisure section, p. 11.

Secondary Sources

Adler, Bill, and Jeffrey Feinman, *Woody Allen: Clown Prince of American Humor*, Pinnacle Books, 1975.
Albert, Marvin H., *What's New, Pussycat?* (novelization of screenplay), Mayflower-Dell paperback, London, 1965.
Alley, Robert, *The Front* (novelization of screenplay), Pocket Books, 1976.
Altman, Sig, *The Comic Image of the Jew*, Fairleigh Dickinson University Press, Cranbury, N. J., 1971.
Baby, Yvonne, "Dealing with Death," *The Guardian*, January 14, 1979, p. 14.
Becker, Ernest, *The Denial of Death*, The Free Press, 1973; paperback edition, 1975.
Bester, Alfred, "Conversation with Woody Allen," *Holiday*, May, 1969, pp. 70–71, 83–84.
Comerford, Adelaide, "*What's New, Pussycat?*" *Films in Review*, August-September, 1965, pp. 446–47.
Corliss, Richard, " 'A Little Faith in People,' " *Film Comment*, May-June, 1979, pp. 16–17.
Dempsey, Michael, "The Autobiography of Woody Allen," *Film Comment*, May-June, 1979, pp. 9–16.
Drew, Bernard, "Woody Allen Is Feeling Better," *American Film*, May, 1977, pp. 10–15.
Durgnat, Raymond, *The Crazy Mirror*, Faber and Faber, London, 1969.
Flatley, Guy, "Woody Allen: 'I Have No Yen To Play Hamlet'," *The New York Times*, October 3, 1976, Arts and Leisure section, pp. 15, 22.

Gilliatt, Penelope, *Unholy Fools*, Secker and Warburg, London, 1973.

———, "Guilty, with an Explanation," *The New Yorker*, February 4, 1974, pp. 39–44.

———, "Woody Reverberant," *The New Yorker*, August 7, 1978, pp. 76–78.

———, "The Black-and-White Apple," *The New Yorker*, April 30, 1979, pp. 110–13.

Gittelson, Natalie, "The Maturing of Woody Allen," *The New York Times Magazine*, April 22, 1979, pp. 30–32, 102–7.

Gornick, Vivian, "Face it, Woody Allen, You're Not A Schlep Anymore," *The Village Voice*, January 5, 1976, pp. 9–11.

Greenfield, Robert, "Seven Interviews with Woody Allen," *Rolling Stone*, September 30, 1971, p. 16.

Gross, Barry, "O Shikse! O Shaygetz! O Jew! I Must Have You! The Jewish-Gentile Attraction." Unpublished paper by Barry Gross, Department of English, Michigan State University, East Lansing, Michigan.

Guthrie, Lee, *Woody Allen: A Biography*, Drake Publishers, 1978.

Halberstadt, Ira, "Scenes from a Mind," *Take One*, November, 1978, pp. 16–20.

Johnstone, Iain, "Anhedonia and *Annie Hall*," *The Listener*, May 11, 1978, pp. 603–4.

Kolowrat, Ernest, "A Loser on Top," *Senior Scholastic*, November 22, 1963, p. 23.

Lax, Eric, *On Being Funny: Woody Allen and Comedy*, Charterhouse Press, 1975.

Lerman, Leo, "Woody the Great," *Vogue*, December, 1972, pp. 144–51.

Maltin, Leonard, "Take Woody Allen—Please!"*Film Comment*, March-April, 1974, pp. 42–45.

Mamber, Stephen, "Woody Allen," *Cinema* (Los Angeles), Winter, 1972–73, pp. 10–12.

Marowitz, Charles, "Everything you always wanted to know about Woody Allen," *The Listener*, July 7, 1977, pp. 8–10.

Maslin, Janet, "*Interiors*—The Dark Side of *Annie Hall*," *The New York Times*, Sunday, November 12, 1978, Arts and Leisure section, p. 23.

McMurphy, Sarah, "The Life and Two Loves of Woody Allen," *Toronto Sunday Star*, October 30, 1977, Section C, p. 1.

Mee, Charles L., Jr., "On Stage: Woody Allen," *Horizon*, May, 1963, pp. 46–47.

Miller, Edwin, "The Tallest Dwarf in the World," *Seventeen*, May, 1966, pp. 159, 204, 210–12.

————, "Lines from the Face of a Funny Man," *Seventeen*, May, 1972, pp. 144, 203–4.

Miller, Gabriel, "A Laugh Gains the Upper Hand: Woody Allen's *Love and Death*," *Bright Lights*, No. 7, pp. 29–31.

Mundy, Robert, "Woody Allen," *Cinema* (Los Angeles), Winter, 1972–73, pp. 6–8.

————, and Mamber, Stephen, "Woody Allen: An Interview," *Cinema* (Los Angeles), Winter, 1972–73, pp. 14–21.

Perez, Gilberto, "The Interior of the Decorator," *New York Arts Journal*, November, 1978, pp. 10–11.

Price, Stanley, "*Play It Again, Sam*," *Plays and Players*, November, 1969, pp. 24–25.

Probst, Leonard, *Off Camera*, Stein and Day, 1975.

Reed, Rex, *Valentines and Vitriol*, Dell, 1977.

Reuben, David, *Everything you always wanted to know about sex*, David McKay, 1969; Bantam edition, 1970.

Rich, Frank, "Woody Allen Wipes the Smile Off His Face," *Esquire*, May, 1977, pp. 72–76, 148–49.

————, "An Interview with Woody," *Time*, April 30, 1979, pp. 68–69.

Rosin, Mark, "Woody Allen: The Power of an Imperfectionist," *Harper's Bazaar*, December 19, 1971, pp. 62–63.

Roth, Philip, *Portnoy's Complaint*, Random House, 1969; Bantam edition, 1970.

Saban, Stephen, "Through a Lens, Darkly," *The Soho Weekly News*, August 3, 1978, pp. 35–36.

Sarris, Andrew, "*What's New, Pussycat?*" *The Village Voice*, July 8, 1965, p. 13; August 5, 1965, p. 14.

————, "*Take the Money and Run*," *The Village Voice*, August 21, 1969, p. 37.

————, "Frowns of a Summer Night," *The Village Voice*, August 7, 1978, pp. 1, 30–31.

————, " 'S Wonderful," *The Village Voice*, April 30, 1979, pp. 51, 54.

Schickel, Richard, "The basic Woody Allen joke," *The New York Times Magazine*, January 7, 1973, pp. 10, 33–37.

————, "Woody Allen Comes of Age, *Time*, April 30, 1979, pp. 62–65.

Spoto, Donald, *Camerado: Hollywood and the American Man*, New American Library, 1978.

Stang, Joanne, " 'Verbal Cartoons'," *The New York Times Magazine*, November 3, 1963, pp. 120, 128.

Trow, George W. S., "A Film about a Very Funny Man," *Film Comment*, May–June, 1977, pp. 32–33.

Wallechinsky, David, Irving Wallace, and Amy Wallace, eds., *A Book of Lists*, William Morrow, 1977; Bantam edition, 1978.

Wasserman, Harry, "Woody Allen: Stumbling through the Looking Glass," *The Velvet Light Trap Review of Cinema*, No. 7 (Winter, 1972–73), pp. 37–40.

Wetzsteon, Ross, "Woody Allen: Schlemiel as Sex Maniac," *Ms.*, November, 1977, pp. 14–15.

Wilde, Larry, *The Great Comedians*, Citadel Press, Secaucus, N. J., 1973.

Zinsser, William K., "Bright New Comic Clowns toward Success," *Saturday Evening Post*, September 21, 1963, pp. 26–27.

Additional Bibliography

Works by Woody Allen

The Floating Light Bulb, Random House, 1982.
Four Films of Woody Allen, Random House, 1982.
Hannah and Her Sisters, Vintage, 1987.
Three Films of Woody Allen, Random House, 1987.

Secondary Sources

Bell, Pearl K., "Woody Allen, Cultural Phenomenon," *Encounter*, June, 1988, pp. 72-75.

Benayoun, Robert, *The Films of Woody Allen*, Harmony Books, 1986. Translated from French, *Au-Dela du Language*, Editions Herscher, 1985.

Bendazzi, G., *The Films of Woody Allen*, Ravette, 1987.

Bogre, Michelle, "Gordon Willis, ASC, and *Zelig*," *American Cinematographer*, April, 1984, pp. 43-48.

Brode, Douglas, *Woody Allen: His Films and Career*, Citadel Press, 1985.

Burton, Dee, *I Dream of Woody*, William Morrow & Co., 1984.

Canby, Vincent, "Notes on Woody Allen and American Comedy," *New York Times*, May 13, 1979, p. 1.

Cebe, Gilles, *Woody Allen*, Henri Veyrier, 1981.

Didion, Joan, "Review of *Annie Hall, Interiors*, and *Manhattan*," *New York Review of Books*, August, 1979, p. 18.

Downing, Crystal, "*Broadway Danny Rose*: Woody Allen's Romantic Inheritance," *Literature/Film Quarterly*, 17, i (1989), pp. 13-17.

Dunne, Michael, "*Stardust Memories, The Purple Rose of Cairo*, and the Tradition of Metafiction," *Film Criticism*, Fall, 1987, pp. 19-27.

Dureau, C., *Woody Allen*, PAC, 1985.

Feldstein, Richard, "The Dissolution of Self in *Zelig*," *Literature/Film Quarterly*, 13, iii (1985), pp. 155-60.

Friedman, Lester, *Hollywood's Image of the Jew*, Frederick Ungar, 1982.

Fuchs, W.J., *Die vielen Gesichter des Woody Allen*, Taschen, 1986.

Gabbard, Krin and Glen O. Gabbard, *Psychiatry and the Cinema*, University of Chicago, 1987.

Geist, William E., "The Rolling Stone Interview: Woody Allen," *Rolling Stone*, April 9, 1987, pp. 39 ff.

Gittelson, N., "The Maturing of Woody Allen," *New York Times Magazine*, April 22, 1979, pp. 30-32 et passim.

Hirsch, Foster, *Love, Sex, Death, and the Meaning of Life*, McGraw-Hill, 1981.

Jacobs, Diane, . . . *but we need the eggs: The Magic of Woody Allen*, St. Martin's Press, 1982.

James, Caryn, "Auteur! Auteur! The Creative Mind of Woody Allen," *New York Times Magazine*, January 19, 1986, pp. 18-30.

Kakutani, Michiko, "How Woody Allen's *Zelig* Was Born in Anxiety and Grew into Comedy," *New York Times*, July 18, 1983, p. 13.

Klein, Joe, "Woody on the Town," *Gentleman's Quarterly*, February, 1986, pp. 170-75, 242-43.

Lasch, Christopher, *The Culture of Narcissism: American Life in an Age of Diminishing Expectations*, W. W. Norton, 1978.

Lax, Eric, "Woody Allen — Not Only a Comic," *New York Times*, February 24, 1985, p. 24.

———, *Woody Allen: A Biography*, Knopf, 1991.

Lebrun, M., *Woody Allen*, PAC, 1979.

Liebman, Robert, "Rabbis or Rakes, Schlemiels or Supermen? Jewish Identity in Charles Chaplin, Jerry Lewis, and Woody Allen," *Literature/Film Quarterly*, January, 1984, pp. 195-201.

McCann, Graham, *Woody Allen: New Yorker*, Polity Press, 1990.

Moss, Robert, "Creators on Creating: Woody Allen," *Saturday Review*, November, 1980, pp. 40-44.

Navacelle, Thierry de, *Woody Allen on Location*, William Morrow and Company, 1987.

Palmer, Myles, *Woody Allen: An Illustrated Biography*, Proteus, 1980.

Perlmutter, Ruth, "*Zelig* According to Bakhtin," *Quarterly Review of Film and Video*, 12. i-ii (1990), pp. 37-47.

Pogel, Nancy, *Woody Allen*, Twayne, 1987.

Preussner, Arnold, "Woody Allen's *The Purple Rose of Cairo* and the Genres of Comedy," *Literature/Film Quarterly*, 16, i (1988), pp. 39-43.

Rathgeb, Douglas, "Faces in the Newsreel: Illuminating *Citizen Kane* through Woody Allen's *Zelig*," *Post Script*, Spring/Summer, 1987, pp. 31-44.

Roberts, Tony, "Woody Allen: The Neurotic Philosopher," in *Close-Ups*, ed. Danny Peary, Workman Publishing, 1978, pp. 50-54.

Rosenblum, Ralph, and Robert Karen, *When the Shooting Stops . . . the Cutting Begins*, Viking, 1979.

Roth, Evelyn, "Photo Fictions: Brilliantly Faked Pictures of Woody Allen's *Zelig* Invent a Nonexistent Past," *American Photographer*, May, 1984, pp. 68-73.

Salmon, Paul, and Helen Bragg, "Woody Allen's Economy of Means: An Introduction to *Hannah and Her Sisters*," *Literature/Film Quarterly*, 16, i (1988), pp. 44-48.

Schechner, Mark, "Woody Allen: The Failure of the Therapeutic," in *From Hester Street to Hollywood*, ed. Sarah Blacher Cohen, Indiana University Press, 1983, pp. 231-44.

Schwartz, Tony, "The Conflicting Life and Art of Woody Allen," *New York Times*, October 20, 1980, pp. 1, 28.

Shales, Tom, "Woody: The First Fifty Years," *Esquire*, April, 1987, pp. 88-95.

Shapiro, Barbara, "Woody Allen's Search for Self," *Journal of Popular Culture*, Spring, 1986, pp. 47-62.

Siegel, Mark, "Ozymandian Melancholia: The Nature of Parody in Woody Allen's *Stardust Memories*," *Literature/Film Quarterly*, 13, ii (1985), pp. 76-84.

Stam, Robert, *Reflexivity in Film and Literature: From Don Quixote to Jean-Luc Godard*, UMI Research Press, 1985.

White, Armond, "Class Clowns," *Film Comment*, April, 1987, pp. 11-14.

Yacowar, Maurice, "Beyond Parody: Woody Allen in the Eighties," *Post Script*, Winter, 1987, pp. 29-42.

———, "The Religion of *Radio Days*," *Journal of Popular Film and Television*, Summer, 1988, pp. 80-87.

Zoglin, Richard, "Manhattan's Methuselah," *Film Comment*, June, 1986, pp. 16-20.

(Reviews are cited in the text footnotes.)

Index

321